Facing Postmodern

This book discusses some of the major responses to postmodernity by contemporary French thinkers. Through chapters on the city, new racism, post-Holocaust debates, the crisis of culture and questions of new citizenship, it explores postmodern interconnections between culture and society. A number of major themes prominent in Western societies today are discussed here, including questions of history, representation, identity, community, ethics and rights.

France embodied in a unique way the ideological and political aspirations of modernity which are now in crisis. French thinkers and commentators are caught between the nostalgic longing for a unified republic of citizens and an awareness of the pluralism and fragmentation of contemporary processes, a condition that many people in the Western democracies are experiencing. This book is therefore aimed not only at those with an interest in France but at anyone wanting to know more about the recent debates around identity and community at the time of the millennium.

Max Silverman is senior lecturer in French at the University of Leeds.

SOCIAL FUTURES SERIES
Barry Smart

Facing Postmodernity
Contemporary French thought
on culture and society

Max Silverman

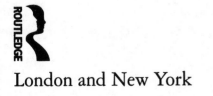

London and New York

First published 1999
by Routledge
11 New Fetter Lane, London EC4P 4EE

Simultaneously published in the USA and Canada
by Routledge
29 West 35th Street, New York, NY 10001

©1999 Max Silverman

Typeset in Garamond by Routledge
Printed and bound in Great Britain by
Creative Print and Design (Wales), Ebbw Vale

British Library Cataloguing in Publication Data
A catalogue record for this book is available from the
British Library

Library of Congress Cataloging in Publication Data
Silverman, Maxim.
Facing postmodernity: contemporary French thought on
culture and society/Max Silverman
p. cm. – (Social futures)
Includes bibliographical references and index.
1. France – Civilization – 1945– 2.
Postmodernism – France. 3. France –
Intellectual life – 20th century – Social
aspects.
I. Title. II. Series: Routledge social futures series.
DC33.7.S575 1999
944.082–dc21   98-36493
                                                            CIP

ISBN 0–415–12893–5 (hbk)
ISBN 0–415–12894–3 (pbk)

For Nina, Rosa, Sam, Anna and Joe, with love

Contents

Acknowledgements

I wish to thank Zygmunt Bauman and John Schwarzmantel for their constructive comments on a first draft of this book and for their constant support for this project. I would also like to thank Leora Auslander and other members of the Chicago Group on Modern France at the University of Chicago for their helpful suggestions on an earlier draft of Chapter 3. The Department of French at the University of Leeds has provided me with the perfect environment for exploring some of the ideas expressed here and has allowed me the time and space to complete this project. Mari Shullaw at Routledge has been the model of patience while waiting for the final manuscript. My warmest and most heartfelt thanks go to Nina Biehal who has been, as always, my closest reader.

Earlier drafts of ideas and arguments expressed here were first published as chapters in Silverman 1995a, 1995b, 1996a, 1996b, 1998a, 1998b.

All translations from the French are my own except where otherwise stated.

Introduction
The unmaking of modern France

France was the quintessential modern nation-state. Nowhere else did the star of equality, freedom and solidarity burn so bright. Yet nowhere else was that brightness deemed to be under such threat of eclipse by visions of disharmony and backwardness. France epitomized the essential Janus-face of modernity.

On the one hand, French Enlightenment philosophy provided the concepts for the pursuit of a higher form of humanity. The Revolution of 1789 was the political blueprint for transforming those concepts into 'natural' law and became the model adopted by nascent nationalisms elsewhere. The spirit of French republicanism, embodied in the slogan 'the one and indivisible Republic (*la République une et indivisible*)', symbolized the persistence of that Utopian dream of a shared humanity throughout the second half of the nineteenth century and the first half of the twentieth century. This was a dream founded on a passionate belief in the power of reason and science to usher in the new dawn. And which nation had greater faith in reason than France?

Yet, on the other hand, reason, science and a new transcendent humanity were dependent on the stigmatization of their opposites: ignorance, superstition and sub-human species. As Alain Touraine has observed:

> the dominant image of modernity is that of a world which opens up to human action guided by reason, in which the barriers of tradition, belief and privilege are transcended, a world which is unifying and in which universalist values, those of science and the law, sweep away the shadows of ignorance, superstition and arbitrary taste.
>
> (Dubet and Wieviorka 1995: 21)

Touraine's description highlights the double-headed nature of modernity: facing towards the light but for ever casting anxious glances back at the shadows which must be removed. To proclaim France as the quintessential modern nation-state is therefore to suggest that it was there that the Utopian construction of 'Man' and new visions of sub-human life – that is, the Apollonian and Dionysiac faces of modernity respectively – find their most complete expression. The space of rationality, science, history, civilization and universality, which was the cornerstone of the French Enlightenment, could only be realized against the backcloth of new concepts of madness, belief, stasis, barbarity and parochialism. The lightness of being of the French *Lumières* hence called forth its demons. Modernity was therefore not so much a *reaction against* the forces of backwardness which had to be transcended in the name of progress and history. Instead, it was the *construction* of those 'dark' forces at the same moment as the construction of civilization and humanity. The unity and autonomy of the modern 'self' was an illusory coherence underpinned irrevocably by the diversity, contradictions and ambivalence of the modern 'other'. They were two sides of the same coin, the unconscious tracking of the conscious mind, as Freud was to discover.

However, the task of Enlightenment thought, in its pursuit of a higher form of humanity, was not simply to disentangle the light from the shadows but to construct them as two separate realms, to depict the ambivalent Janus-face in terms of a dichotomy. And although this process of boundary-drawing was a fundamental feature of modernity in general, we might once again suggest that France was exemplary. For in which nation were rationality and the irrational, science and superstition, nation and race orchestrated so systematically as ideological opposites as in France? French modernity was built on the clear distinction between separate realms which organized knowledge, culture and humanity (and therefore power) into a hierarchy of terms, the creation of what we now call (after deconstructionist philosophy and feminist and post-colonial theory) binary opposites. Science, rationality, the public sphere, the nation, 'Man', the universal were all elevated to the lofty realm of transcendent humanity by displacing all elements of ideology, tradition, particularisms and backwardness on to others: the 'dangerous classes', women, colonial subjects, Jews and other marginals, the private sphere. Modernity was a perpetual struggle to control and repress, assimilate or expel the opposite terms in each binary, the inferior elements in each hierarchy, in order to fix the boundaries of humanity, progress, civilization and order.

Of all the modern industrializing nations of the nineteenth century, none pursued this Utopian dream with the same vigour as

France. The clearest manifestation of this lies in the development, in the second half of the nineteenth century, of a state-based, centralizing, unitarian and strictly non-pluralist model of the nation, with its sharp divide between the public and private spheres. The homogenizing zeal of republicanism under the Third Republic (1871–1940), born from the mission to vanquish the 'forces of reaction' and to fuse the nation into an indissoluble unity in the name of rationality and progress, did not have its direct equivalents elsewhere. The assimilation of diverse people around common goals, leading to a mad quest for uniformity in the name of equality, was not the obsessive driving force behind the institutions of the state and the intellectuals of progress in the same way as it became in France. Hence, the tensions between uniformity and difference, order and disorder, progress and reaction, science and belief, seem sharper in France. For the greater the quest for assimilation of differences and the unification of diversity, the more visible difference and diversity became. The impossible dream of a public sphere purified of all ideology and partisanship was at the expense of relegating all partisanship (or particularisms) to the private sphere, which seethed with the 'waste' which any such dream inevitably generates.

French modernity therefore epitomized the essential paradox of the drive for uniformity in the name of equality, since the pursuit of sameness was both a source of emancipation (for some) and the repression of difference. On the one hand, the ideals of reason, equality and citizenship could eventually save Alfred Dreyfus, at the turn of the century, from being condemned for treason simply by dint of being Jewish. On the other hand, those same ideals could legitimize the 'civilizing mission' of colonialism abroad and nation-building at home (again, two sides of the same coin), and thus become the ideological tools of colonial racism and intolerance towards minorities, condemning 'inferior' and 'backward' peoples to 'subject' status because of their failure to match up to the universal values of 'humanity'.

We now understand some of the paradoxes and contradictions inherent in French modernity's hierarchical system of classification. Yet these were first exposed at the time of the construction of the system itself – in the form of cultural modernism. Rationalizing modernity's classification of distinct spheres was in fact the essential motor for the counter-cultures of modernism. Modernism thrived on the transgression of boundaries – between order and disorder, between uniformity and heterogeneity, between the public and private spheres – and the confusion of distinct realms. Marginality, the transitory, diversity, imagination and desire – indeed, the whole panoply of 'dark'

forces and processes which constituted the otherness of rational order –
were central to cultural modernism's challenge to the permanence and
coherence of rationalized modern society.

Is it too much of an exaggeration, then, to suggest that here too, in
the major cultural movements of modernity, France epitomizes most
clearly modernity's fundamental ambivalence? From Baudelaire to
Surrealism and beyond, the fleeting and heterogeneous nature of
modern everyday life (especially city life) was aestheticized and
mythologized, hence removing it from the rational framework of positivist and utilitarian political and economic planning, and inserting it
within a different space, in which the boundaries between subjective
desire and external 'reality', imagination and rational design, the
psyche and the social, the unconscious and conscious, are blurred. If it
is true that Paris was the centre of modernist ferment at the end of the
last decades of the nineteenth century and the first few decades of the
twentieth century, then there is a strong case to be made in favour of
viewing France as the paradigm of the modern struggle between
culture and counter-culture.

France was arguably the quintessential modern nation-state because
the profound ambivalence and tensions at the heart of modernity were
expressed with greater clarity there than in other modern industrializing nations. The drive for uniformity was more systematically
theorized and institutionalized while, at the same time, the detritus of
that process was more heroically championed by opponents of rationalization. What, though, of today, for this book deals essentially with
the contemporary crisis of the structures of modernity?

Today is no longer the heyday of the modern nation-state or the
high point of cultural modernism. Terms like post-industrial, postmodern, post-communist, post-historical and post-ideological
illustrate the attempt to articulate profound shifts which have taken
place in modern (and mostly Western) industrialized societies. If
modernity was intricately connected with industrial society and class
conflict (Schwarzmantel 1998), the nationalizing mission of the state,
colonialism and the cultural avant-garde, then today's transformations
in the industrial fabric of society, the attack on the so-called
sovereignty of the nation-state from above and below (through globalization and localization), post-colonialism and the broadening of the
cultural sphere to encompass what were formerly designated as the
political and social spheres, all bear witness to the crisis of modernity.

In France, 'crisis' seems to be the most popular term employed to
describe this predicament (although *malaise* must run it a close second:
see, for example, Yonnet 1993; 'Malaise dans la démocratie' in *Le Débat*

1988; 'Autour du malaise français' in *Le Débat* 1993). Commentators talk of the crisis of the modern nation-state, the crisis of universalist values, the crisis of assimilation (or integration), the crisis of civilization. Pluralism challenges uniformity, relativism challenges truth, hierarchies have been flattened, assimilation has broken down, the margins are at the centre. A sense of history has given way to an undifferentiated present. Faith in the future and progress has dissolved into a multitude of anxieties about the self and the world. Science and rationality are viewed sceptically and must compete with other belief systems as ways of interpreting the world. Nobody has any all-encompassing solutions any more, for interconnections are all too *complex* today, and anyway, we are, as the philosopher Jean-François Lyotard (1979) famously remarked, at the 'end of grand narratives'. Krysztof Pomian (1990) observes that the transformation from the age of 'isms' to the age of 'posts' signifies the passage from an age of confidence and certainty to one rooted in fear and uncertainty. Alain Minc (1993: 205) wonders whether this signals the 'degree zero of ideology' and, consequently, the end of 'modern times'.

It is perhaps the breakdown of the sharp boundaries constituted by cognitive social planning and the 'contamination' of distinct realms which perhaps best characterizes this sense of crisis. The paradoxes, contradictions and ambivalence of hierarchical systems of classification explored by the cultural avant-garde at the turn of the century have now become our everyday reality. Uncertainty, indeterminacy, ambivalence and moral relativism are no longer confined to the margins but have become the general rule (cf. Bauman 1991a). The spirit of cultural modernism (offering a more profound vision of reality than rationalized Utopias) has been 'democratized' and in the process, some would argue, stripped of its radical potential and converted into a simple object of consumption among others. This breakdown in a fixed order of principles and values, and the clash between culture and counter-culture, signals the end of the high points of modernity and cultural modernism, and the moment of transition towards a different order. In other words, today the hierarchical structures of modernity are in crisis. As I will argue in the following pages, we are facing post-modernity.[1]

France, of course, is not alone in facing a crisis in the structures of modernity. Postmodernity has been a major theme for debate in numerous countries for at least two decades. Yet once again I would want to make out a case for the exemplary nature of the French situation today. I contend that the level of 'malaise' experienced in France is in direct proportion to the idealized perception of the French

Enlightenment tradition of modernity. The mythology surrounding the French republican model of the nation and culture is simply not matched elsewhere. The sense of crisis in France today therefore frequently appears sharper than in other countries because of the widely held perception in France that that model – founded on universalism, progress, the political nation, republicanism, the word, Culture – is being resolutely effaced by contemporary trends. Intellectual debates are often framed in terms of the threat that today's *democratic* processes pose to the values of the *Republic* (and, implicitly or explicitly, in terms of the 'Anglo-Saxon' threat to what Charles de Gaulle called 'a certain idea of France').

On the other hand, perhaps it is not too simplistic to suggest that the power of this archetypal Enlightenment model of the Republic (and the fixity of the binary oppositions which held it in place) is also responsible for the strength of the backlash that one finds in French anti-humanist and deconstructionist philosophy, which has had such a major effect on postmodern critical thought elsewhere. Contemporary French debates on culture and society often appear to be caught between a profound nostalgia for a golden age of culture and national unity and an extreme rejection of the hierarchies that characterized that age. It could very well be the case, then, that the quintessential modern nation-state, characterized by the culture and counter-cultures of rationality, has today evolved into the nation-state which most clearly epitomizes the crisis of modernity.

It is for this reason that the French debates around the crisis of modernity are of special interest. The rearguard action to preserve the 'purity' of the 'republican tradition' – abstract equality, citizenship, secularism (*la laïcité*), the separation between the public and private spheres – in the face of the contemporary processes of democratization, diversification and fragmentation produces a particular tension and passion to these debates which signals a specifically French purchase on them. In France, the term 'postmodernity' itself is often employed only in the context of a tragic vision of the decline of humanity. Clearly there are many overlaps here with the experiences of other Western democracies, and much of the discussion in this book is informed by the wider debates around postmodernity. But facing postmodernity presents both a common and a different challenge for individual countries (and their major theorists) and it is precisely this balance between common processes and a particular French response that this book considers.

This book therefore attempts to chart some of the most important responses in France to the wider crisis in the structures of modernity. It deals with debates and ideas rather than policy and practice. It does not claim to be a survey of recent political and cultural developments in France, although the discussion often makes reference to these developments. It is, instead, an engagement with recent trends in French intellectual history concerning culture and society. My focus is therefore not so much on France as on contemporary French thought, although the complex interweaving of ideas and practices makes this a tenuous distinction. Even here I make no claims for an exhaustive coverage of recent debates. My purpose is to consider some of the major themes that recur in these debates and some of the important contributors to them. A number of the theorists discussed are already familiar outside France, while others will be less familiar to an English-speaking audience.

If the backdrop to the following discussion is the specific nature of French modernity and my starting point the crisis in the structures of modernity, my treatment of the response to this crisis is then pursued through a consideration of five areas, which constitute the main part of the text: post-Holocaust debates, new racisms, the city, cultural debates and questions of citizenship. This choice of topics is, in a sense, arbitrary. Others might well have been included in a book on contemporary French debates. Yet the choice is dictated by two over-lapping concerns: the first is the relationship between culture and society today and the second is the relationship between the individual and the community in a transformed landscape and the vexed question of a new ethics *vis-à-vis* 'the other'. The topics I have chosen allow an exploration of these themes in different contexts and an engagement with significant aspects of the crisis of modernity in France at the time of the millennium.

I start with reflections on the Holocaust because of the important symbolic role that this event has come to play in the wider discussion around modernity and postmodernity. A specific purchase on 'Auschwitz' and 'the Jew' has been crucial to the assault by anti-humanist and anti-representationalist French philosophy on the Western Enlightenment tradition. My intention is not to survey French post-structuralist and deconstructionist thought (which has been treated extensively elsewhere) but rather to point up the prob-lematic nature of adopting 'Auschwitz' as a paradigm for the failure of Western modernity and the figure of 'the Jew' as a paradigm for 'otherness' (*altérité*).

The second chapter discusses the ways in which concepts of differ-ence and identity are at the heart of new racisms today. Following my previous work in this area (Silverman 1992), I suggest that the French response to new racisms has been largely over-determined by the powerful republican model of the nation which consigns difference to the undemocratic, exclusionary and racist traditions of the far Right. I argue that another paradigm for the understanding of difference and identity, more appropriate to the pluralism and diversity of contemporary societies, is a prerequisite for the reformulation of democracy today.

Chapters 3 and 4, on the city and culture respectively, broaden out the discussion to encompass wider social and cultural transformations. The city has become an important site for the consideration of postmodern developments and there is now an extensive literature which deals with it. My discussion makes use of some of this literature from diverse sources. However, my specific focus is on French commentators on the city whose reflections frequently express regret for the passing of the modern city as a site of meeting and memory.

Contemporary debates around the nature and function of culture overlap with many of the themes to be found in discussions of the city, especially those concerning the collapse of a sense of depth, meaning and a hierarchy of values. I consider whether this collapse of hierarchies and the rise of an 'anything goes' eclectic ethos signifies the flowering or the demise of marginal and transgressive counter-cultures. If, as Steven Connor (1989: 61) says of the work of Jean-François Lyotard, Jean Baudrillard and Fredric Jameson, 'postmodernity may be defined as those plural conditions in which the social and the cultural become indistinguishable', then a crucial question for our times is whether this blurring of boundaries and conflation of the 'separate' spheres of culture and society is in the name of a democratic pluralism or a triumphant commodity capitalism.

The final chapter pursues this question in relation to contemporary debates around citizenship: does the breakdown of the boundary between the public and private spheres signify 'the end of the social' in favour of a rampant individualism, or can citizenship, solidarity and democracy be rethought in accordance with the new times in which we live? I argue that the stumbling block in France to such a rethinking is, once again, the power of the republican concept of nation and citizenship and its stigmatization of difference. However, there are those who recognize the anachronistic nature of this model and argue for a less abstract and more pluralistic version of citizenship. The conclusion to the book suggests that, despite the new dangers inherent in negotiating difference today, the abstract vision of 'Man' at the heart of the project of French modernity must surely give way in the new millennium to a less Utopian and more pluralistic version of humanity.

It is hoped that the framework adopted for this book will shed light on some of the most important and persistent debates of recent times while drawing specific attention to the French contributions to these debates. However, the choice of topics and the recurrence of a number of themes across all chapters inevitably reflect my own concerns as much as those of the theorists discussed. I attempt to avoid either an unconditional celebration or a bitter denigration of 'postmodern times' by adopting a more nuanced stance. Whether 'the other' is any safer under postmodern conditions than under modern conditions is, I believe, an open question. The sociologist and major theorist of postmodern times, Zygmunt Bauman (1991b), has characterized postmodernity as both chance and menace (cf. Beck 1992). It is under the sign of this new Janus-face that this book has been written.

1 In the shadow of the Holocaust

The Holocaust rediscovered

In the immediate post-war years, discussion of the catastrophe that had just taken place rarely mentioned the plight of the Jews or the genocide which became known as the Holocaust. In *Le Spectateur engagé*, Raymond Aron recalls his conversation with Jean-Paul Sartre in 1945 about this silence:

> We asked ourselves the question why is there not one single article, not one that says: 'Welcome home to Jews, back once more in the French community.' The fundamental reason for this silence is that what had happened had been erased.
>
> (cited in Finkielkraut 1996: 41)

Sartre himself remarked on this silence about the Jews in his famous *Réflexions sur la question juive* (1954) written in 1946 (although this same book contains no references to the Holocaust itself), and the anti-racist organisation MRAP (Movement against Racism and for Friendship Between Peoples) was established in 1949 with the specific aim of preserving the memory of victims of anti-Semitism and guarding against its reappearance in all its forms. It is also true, as Michael Bernstein (1998) points out, that David Rousset's *L'Univers concentrationnaire* (1946), Robert Antelme's *L'Espèce humaine* (1947) and novels by Roger Ikor (*Les Fils d'Avrom: Les Eaux mêlées*) and André Schwarz-Bart (*Le Dernier des justes*) in the 1950s show that serious work about the Holocaust was being written shortly after the war in France. Yet these were isolated voices. As the film-maker and critic Claude Lanzmann has said, in an explicit reference to Sartre's work on anti-Semitism, 'the Holocaust is an event [which] no one at the time could grasp in its full scope' (cited in Kritzman 1995a: 5).

In fact, the talk in the immediate post-war years was predominantly of the victims of and resistance to *fascism*, not *anti-Semitism*. As the Belgian historian Jean-Michel Chaumont points out:

> this was the era of the almost absolute hegemony of the anti-fascist model. The survivor from Buchenwald was the emblematic witness of Nazi crimes and it was his or her version of history and experience, filtered by organizations usually under the direction of the Communist Party, which was transmitted via the media to the public. Even in 1967, at the time of the inauguration of the international monument at Birkenau, Jews were hardly mentioned in official discourse and the plaques erected at the monument were dedicated to the indistinct mass of 'victims of Nazi barbarism'.[1]
>
> (Chaumont 1994: 77)

The 'anti-fascist model' was itself bound up with the process of '*épuration* (cleansing)' after the war, whose *raison d'être* was to purge France of foreign (German) influences, to marginalize Vichy (and certainly fascism) from mainstream French republicanism, and confirm the story of a France which heroically resisted occupation (cf. Rousso 1987).[2]

At this time, it was not simply a question of the hegemony of the anti-fascist model for the revelations about the camps in the USSR provided another model for extermination of 'undesirables'.[3] Annette Wieviorka (1992: 20) refers to these two post-war debates – anti-fascist and anti-communist – which both, in their different ways, removed attention from the specificity of Nazi crimes, the Holocaust and the annihilation of the Jews. It seems astonishing today that Alain Resnais's classic film about the Holocaust, *Nuit et brouillard* (*Night and Fog*) (1955) – made to commemorate the tenth anniversary of the end of the war – makes virtually no reference to Jews. But this becomes understandable if we remember to what extent, in those post-war years, 'the perception of genocide was in France inextricably associated with that of deportation to Nazi concentration camps' (A. Wieviorka 1992: 20), a process which, of course, involved non-Jews as well as Jews.[4] As Éric Conan and Daniel Lindenberg observe, France preferred 'political and resistance deportees to so-called "racial" deportees'. The relationship between Vichy and the 'final solution' was merely of secondary importance.

> The majority of condemnations arising from the *épuration*, based on a classical body of law, invoked Article 75 of the penal code which refers to 'intelligence with the enemy'. The notion of crimes against humanity, defined in 1945 and used in 1946 at the

Nuremberg trial, was never invoked. And the question of state anti-Semitism, which was introduced spontaneously and independently by the Vichy regime, was not the object of any specific judicial debates (Conan and Lindenberg 1992: 10) (cf. Klarsfeld and Rousso 1992).

In the aftermath of the war, the attention of the newly created Fourth Republic was focused elsewhere, especially on the Cold War, the struggle against communism and colonial wars in the Far East and North Africa (Edwy Plenel, 'Le piège Touvier', *Le Monde*, 22 April 1992).

This relative silence about the Holocaust in the immediate post-war period (and 'occultation' of the genocide of the Jews) seems astonishing today in the light of the sea-change that has occurred in perceptions of that event. At the beginning of the 1970s, the death of Charles de Gaulle (1969) and the challenge to the great resistance myth that he personified – epitomized by Marcel Ophuls's documentary *Le Chagrin et la pitié* (1971) and Robert Paxton's book (1972) on Vichy France – opened the way to a reappraisal of the question of anti-Semitism and the relationship between Vichy and the 'final solution'. Since then the Holocaust – recognized as the genocide of the Jews, and frequently referred to now as the Shoah – has become the major focus for commentators on that period.[5] This 'judeocentric' approach (Chaumont 1994) has brought to the fore the experience and the memories of survivors as witnesses, the question of crimes against humanity, and the irreducible nature of the event itself. Annette Wieviorka (1992:19) lists the proliferation of debates and controversies about the Holocaust which have taken place in France over the last twenty-five years, including 'the Faurisson affair, the affair of the American soap-opera *Holocaust*, the Roques affair, the affair of the convent at Auschwitz, the Barbie trial, the indictments of Leguay, Touvier, Papon and Bousquet, the affair of Le Pen's "detail", and the Carpentras affair', to which we might add the controversies over Claude Lanzmann's film *Shoah* (1985), the Farias/Heidegger affair, and the Paul de Man affair.

This obsession with the Holocaust in recent years is as linked to the contemporary conjuncture as much as the former silence around it was a product of the post-war period. The challenge to the Gaullist and communist myths about the Second World War, and the accompanying charge of French involvement in the 'final solution', are themselves symptomatic of a new problematic around national identity and national history which was taking shape during the 1960s. New demands for 'the right to difference' for minorities (*le droit à la différence*), the challenge to the state's monolithic hold on memories of national history, and the anti- and post-colonial critique of the ethnocentrism and racism of the West in general all threatened the post-war consensus on national unity. Furthermore, there was a renewal of Jewish thought in the 1960s (especially that of Emmanuel Lévinas) which had a considerable influence on French anti-humanist philosophy and the challenge to 'the order of the ego, self-consciousness and freedom' (Rose 1993: 14) of rationalizing Western modernity.

In other words, the rediscovery of the Holocaust is symptomatic of the crisis of modern France and Western modernity as a whole. Michael Bernstein (1998) suggests that the contemporary obsession with 'the issues raised by the Nazi genocide' is not so much a question of the return of the repressed but rather 'our readiness to see those issues as simultaneously unique to the devastation of European Jewry and yet paradigmatic for Western culture as a whole'. In France this obsession epitomizes a country ill at ease not only with its own involvement in genocide but also with the very ideals of modernity which France upheld. The following discussion therefore considers not those events connected directly with the Vichy regime (about which much has been written in recent years; see, for example, Rousso 1987, *Esprit* 1992, Kedward and Wood, eds, 1995) but some of the ways in which the Holocaust, and also the figure of 'the Jew', have been mobilized in the wider contemporary polemic around the crisis of Western modernity. In terms of the philosophical debate, this polemic has pitted humanist neo-Kantians against anti-humanist Heideggerians; in terms of the cultural debate, it has pitted neo-representationalists against anti-representationalists. It could be defined as the moment at which the post-Holocaust era meets the postmodern era.

'Jews', 'Greeks' and the decline of the West

The pronouncement by the German philosopher Theodor Adorno on the impossibility of thought after Auschwitz transformed the Holocaust into a metaphor for the end of modernity. Auschwitz became the point of transition from an age of rational planning of societies – whose ultimate goal was human emancipation and freedom – to one of scepticism of all social engineering. As the political and cultural commentator and editor of the journal *Esprit*, Olivier Mongin, observes, 'Adorno's question on the possibility of thought after Auschwitz exacerbated a profound scepticism at the heart of modern society' (Mongin 1994a: 73). For some, the Holocaust has become the sign of the totalitarian nature of the West, and the point of departure for a rejection of all totalizing systems of thought. Zygmunt Bauman (1988), for example, has argued that the absence of a moral dimension which made the Holocaust possible was a direct product of the techno-logical and bureaucratic instrumentalism of modern industrial society.

Adorno's injunction is therefore the starting point for what one might term postmodern philosophy's 'appropriation' of 'Auschwitz' for the purpose of challenging Western philosophy. Jean-François Lyotard (1988a: 110) recognizes his debt to Adorno: 'Following Theodor Adorno, I have used the name "Auschwitz" to signify the inconsistency between the course of Western history and the "modern" project of the emancipation of humanity.' For Lyotard, Auschwitz signifies the tragic end of modernity's grand vision of emancipation and a cruel indict-ment of the concept of history on which it was founded. After Auschwitz the 'grand narrative' of history dissolves into the 'small narratives (*petits récits*)' of particular knowledges and fragmented spaces of communication (Lyotard 1979). 'Auschwitz' therefore signifies the end of universalism and the end of the Enlightenment idea of progress. In short, Lyotard employs 'Auschwitz' as a metaphor for the failure of the whole enterprise of modernity. As he says, ' "Auschwitz" can be taken as a paradigmatic name for the tragic failure of modernity' (Lyotard 1988a: 32).[6] Hence the quote marks surrounding the name to designate its paradigmatic function.

For Lyotard, and for all those commentators mentioned above, 'Auschwitz' is not simply the product of fascist ideology but of a whole tradition of Western philosophy and history. The logocentrism of Western thought and the evolutionist concept of history inherited from Hegel (both of which are founded on binary oppositions) are two of the principal pillars propping up the modern edifice – which have produced dictatorships and democracies alike. There is therefore a 'contamination' (Derrida 1987) at a more profound level across modern conceptual and political structures which challenges the neat distinction between democracy and dictatorship. (This point will be developed later in this chapter; see 'History, memory, representation'.) The philosopher Philippe Lacoue-Labarthe (1988–1989: 484) employs 'Auschwitz' in the same way to castigate the West in general: 'In the apocalypse at Auschwitz, it is no more or less than the essence of the West that is revealed – and that has not ceased since that time to reveal itself.' The West is ultimately responsible for the attempted annihilation of 'the other' which took place at Auschwitz, and it is therefore the whole system underpinning the Enlightenment tradition which stands indicted. It is not simply Jews who died in the gas chambers but the very spirit of modernity itself.

Auschwitz becomes the metaphorical dividing line between modernity and postmodernity.

A significant aspect of this postmodern critique of modernity and the West is the link traced between rationality, Christianity and the Greco-Roman tradition of thought, within which Judaism has been a perpetual outsider and victim, and which reached its apotheosis at Auschwitz. Once again the critique is aimed not simply at those forms of modern political anti-Semitism which overtly stigmatized the Jew, but at modernity as a whole in its dealings with 'the other'. Lacoue-Labarthe gives a clear expression of this position:

> God effectively died at Auschwitz, in any case the God of the Greco-Christian West, and it is no coincidence that those who were the objects of extermination were the witnesses, in that West, of another origin of God, one which remains outside the Hellenic and Roman framework and which therefore impedes its programme of fulfilment.
>
> (cited in Mongin 1988: 91)

Here the Jew and Judaism are perceived as 'other' to 'Christian Europe', 'other' to rationality, logocentrism and the law, and 'other' to the autonomous and self-constituted self at the heart of Western 'Hellenic' humanistic philosophy. The Jew is that which, ultimately, gives the lie to the grand modern vision of totality, harmony, purity and order, and is the witness to modernity's reckless pursuit of uniformity. In this sense, 'the Jew' is equivalent to what Julia Kristeva (following Freud) calls 'the disturbing strangeness...which inhabits us all...the hidden face of our identity, the space which challenges our fixed nature' (Kristeva 1988: 9). Derrida, Lyotard, Lacoue-Labarthe and Jean-Luc Nancy have all mobilized the figure of 'the Jew' in this way: as a sign of otherness and strangeness, that which is left out, left-over, suppressed, eradicated in modernity's mad rush towards the creation of a rational order, and that which unsettles all attempts at fixing and recuperation.

'The Jew' is therefore a sign of otherness. In *Heidegger et 'les juifs'*, Lyotard writes 'jew' not only in inverted commas but also with a lower-case 'j' in order to distinguish these 'jews' – employed figuratively or allegorically – from real Jews. Lyotard's 'jews' are the sign of the challenge to the perfect autonomy and unity of the self. He says:

> 'the jews' are in 'the spirit' of the West...they are that which resists this spirit, in its wilfulness, the wilfulness of wanting, that

which impedes this wilfulness, in its accomplishment, project and progress, that which ceaselessly opens up the wound of what is unaccomplished.... They are that which resists domestication within the obsession to dominate, within the compulsive quest for the acquisition of property, within the passion for empire, recurrent since Hellenic Greece and Christian Rome. 'The jews' are never at home wherever they may be, they cannot be integrated, converted or expelled. They are always outsiders even when they are in their own place, within their own traditions, since at their very origin is exodus, excision, impropriety and respect for what has been forgotten.

(Lyotard 1988b: 45)

Nancy (1986) invokes 'the jew' as the allegorical marker of the interruption or disruption of myth and community. Lyotard (1993: 100) makes the same point when he observes that 'the jew' is the challenge to 'the blind narcissism of the community' or again when he designates Auschwitz as a sign of the impossibility of constructing an autonomous and unproblematic 'we': 'In the camps, there was no first person plural subject. The absence of this subject means that "after Auschwitz" there is no subject at all, no *Selbst* which might name itself in naming "Auschwitz"…. There is no collective witness' (Lyotard 1983: 146); 'the name "Auschwitz" is certainly not the total sum of Is, yous and hes, since this name designates the impossibility of any such totalization' (Lyotard 1983: 152). Kristeva's 'stranger' is also 'a symptom which renders any "we" problematic, perhaps even impossible' (Kristeva 1988: 9).

Hence, if 'Auschwitz' has been adopted as a sign of the end of modernity, the figure of 'the Jew' has been similarly appropriated as a sign of difference or otherness which modernity sought to eradicate. In the figures of 'Auschwitz' and 'the Jew' postmodern anti-humanist philosophy invests its challenge to instrumental rationality, the West (defined as logocentric and Eurocentric), history and representation. 'The Jew' is cast as other to history and representation, and as other to Christianity and the European Greco-Roman tradition of philosophy, as if 'Europe (or philosophy, or the Greeks, or maybe even Christianity)' (Bennington 1998: 189–190) formed an unproblematic whole. 'The Jew' personifies a new ethics as opposed to the law, open-ended interpretation as opposed to the incarnation of the word.[7]

The influence of Emmanuel Lévinas on the direction of French postmodern philosophy over the last thirty years should not be underestimated here. Mongin (1994a: 78) suggests that interest in

Lévinas during the 1960s was not entirely fortuitous since the nature of his thought reflected a growing preoccupation with the demise of a sense of history and a renewed interest in ethics at the expense of politics. Jacques Derrida had already devoted a long essay to the work of Lévinas in *L'Écriture et la différence* (1967: 117–228). Derrida's decision to quote from Matthew Arnold's *Culture and Anarchy* as preface to this essay reflects his use of the opposition between Hebraism and Hellenism as the two poles of influence of culture. For Derrida (1967: 123), the Greek tradition at the heart of Western philosophy, which is even to be found in the thought of Husserl and Heidegger, is profoundly challenged by the thought of Lévinas, for whom Hebraism is characterized by difference rather than reduction to the same. Susan Handelman, who adopts Derrida's terms uncritically, describes Derrida's fascination with Lévinas in the following way:

> In Lévinas, Derrida finds an attempt to 'dislocate the Greek logos' and thus to dislocate our identity and the principle of identity in general, which is a summons to depart from Greece, to liberate thought from the 'oppression' of the same and the one, an 'ontological, or transcendental oppression', which Derrida claims is the source of all oppression in the world.... As psychoanalysis was a species of parricide and giving of a new law, so Derridean deconstructionism will murder the father-founders of philosophy and disseminate a new writing, which, in the wake of the overthrow of the same and the one, celebrates pluralism, otherness, distance, and difference. Parmenides' disregard of the other is 'totalitarian' and tautologous according to Lévinas and Derrida, and the rebellion against the Greeks is a species of liberation.
>
> (Handelman 1982: 171)

Handelman demonstrates how Derrida's discussion of Lévinas has become a major element underpinning deconstruction and the celebration of the voice of 'the other' (especially in the 'Anglo-Saxon' world). In France, other influences (apart from the usual ones of Nietzsche and Heidegger) should be mentioned in relation to this particular preoccupation of philosophy in the wake of the Holocaust. Olivier Mongin (1994a: 80) mentions the importance of the translation into French of Yosef Hayim Yerushalmi's book *Zakhor* in proposing the same antithesis as that outlined by Handelman between the Hellenic and Hebraic traditions, for it showed how 'the Jewish imaginary has for long been distanced from historical rationality and has maintained a relation to memory which is not that of historical science'. Jean-Louis

Schlegel makes a similar point in relation to the work of Franz Rosenzweig:

> Even in relation to the Shoah, Rosenzweig explains why contemporary philosophy, in its most creative moment, has strong affinities with Judaism, with its 'reading without images', as Emmanuel Lévinas has said, which one could translate as the accepted presence of a principle of incompleteness, plurality, original difference, non-accomplishment, exteriority, and hence ethics, which Christianity (even Protestant Christianity) finds so distasteful. To paraphrase Paul Ricouer, Judaism today gives food for thought, whilst Christianity has very little to offer.
>
> (Schlegel 1990: 79) (cf. Münster, ed., 1994)

The suggestion here is that the attraction of Judaism, in the eyes of those for whom philosophy has become discredited through its association with totalizing systems of thought, is its difference from rationalism and its concern with the otherness and 'unknowability' of 'the other'. Pierre Bouretz demonstrates how the Hebraic tradition disrupts the rationalist concept of time and the Hegelian dialectic of history so important to the Christian West:

> The Jewish conception of a temporality outside history goes beyond a specifically Jewish experience. As the opposite to a Christian consciousness historicized within the State, it offers us the means of resistance to the Hegelian idea of History as 'serious, painful, patient and working through the negative'. Occupying an empty space in Hegel's version of universal history, the Jewish people give us the awareness of a plenitude of time removed from the dialectic of history. It is as if the experience of a time lived in exile has become the counterpoint to a temporality inscribed within the history of the kingdom. Exile and the kingdom: one day it will perhaps be necessary to explore the distance which separates these two symbolic spaces in Western culture.
>
> (Bouretz 1992: 128) (cf. also Ricoeur 1985)

Jewish exile is here the counterpoint to the Christian kingdom just as, for others cited above, Hebraism is the antithesis of Hellenism, and the Jew is other to the Greek. Ironically, the deconstructionist critique of a Western tradition founded on binary oppositions appears to be founded on a binary opposition of its own – between Hebraism and Hellenism, between Judaism and Christianity, and between Jew and

Greek. Susan Handelman's tendentious equation between the tradition of Rabbinic thought and deconstructionist literary theory is a good case in point:

> As Christianity severed its ties with Judaism and spread into the Roman Empire, later to conquer Europe, it became allied with Greek philosophy (and a variety of intellectual and religious currents prevailing in the Hellenistic era), and a link was formed which provided the matrix for Western culture.
>
> (Handelman 1982: xiv)

Handelman's thesis rests on a crude dichotomy in which Judaism is a cipher of otherness within the Greek logocentric tradition. She asserts: 'If Judaism is the experience of the infinitely other, it is precisely this irruption of the totally other that threatens the Greek logos, and the Christian holy family as well' (1982: 173).

The recruitment of Judaism as 'the other' to 'Hellenic Greece and Christian Rome' might be convenient as an allegory of anti-Western rationality, logocentrism, totalizing systems of thought, and violence but does not hold up to proper scrutiny in reality. Furthermore, it relies on a fairly monolithic, and even essentialist, view of both 'Hellenic Greece', on the one hand, and Judaism on the other. Martin Bernal's analysis of the 'Afro-Asiatic' roots of European civilization (Bernal 1987) undermines any such essentialist characterization of Europe.[8] More specifically, Mongin takes issue with Lacoue-Labarthe's caricature of the West, dependent as it is on the same sort of crude antithesis between Hellenism and Hebraism employed by Handelman:

> Surely the silencing of history does not simply lead to the philosophical questioning of the West? Is not the recourse to a philosophical representation of the West a confession of the weakness of thought whose only perspective on the West is that of its failure? And how accurate is it to conceive of the God of the Greco-Christian West and a God removed from Hellenic recuperation as opposites?
>
> (Mongin 1988: 92)

Gillian Rose also mounts an attack on French postmodern philosophy's demonization of rationality through the use of the opposition between the Greek and the Jew. In her fascinating book *Judaism and Modernity* (1993) she employs the term 'diremption' (forceful separation) to characterize the artificial construction of an antithesis between the two traditions, which she terms Athens and Jerusalem. She argues that to characterize the former in terms of philosophy and principled rationality and the latter as prophetic revelation is a false dichotomy. Her analysis of Halacha (Jewish law) and her critique of Jewish thinkers like Leo Strauss and Emmanuel Lévinas demonstrate that by misrepresenting, or stereotyping, both the 'Hellenic tradition' and Judaism, an over-simplistic dichotomy has been created (Rose 1993: 16). The effect of this misrepresentation is to obscure a far more complex reality. David Stern, a specialist in the Rabbinic tradition of interpretation of the Torah (midrash), also provides an important corrective to the crude binary terms that inform Handelman's thesis, and that of others (see, for example, Grosz 1990) who similarly conflate the Jewish tradition and contemporary deconstruction. Stern observes:

> Classical Rabbinic exegesis, like Rabbinic Judaism itself, was not so much completely 'other' to, or apart from, Western culture as it was a marginal presence on its borders, a tradition that developed by drawing on Western categories and transforming them without becoming wholly absorbed by them.... No attempt will ever be sufficient that presents midrash and its hermeneutics in simple opposition to logocentrism, with the latter being characterized as a Greco-Roman or Christian development and the former as a Jewish one. To read midrash as a rewriting of Derrida, Jacques Lacan, or Edmond Jabès is equally misguided.
>
> (Stern 1989: 134)

Stern's objection, like that of Rose, is that history is collapsed into an eternal tension between two opposing traditions – which danger-ously falsifies both. Judaism has not simply been other to Christian Hellenism but rather inside and outside, not simply exiled from the kingdom but straddling that ambivalent line between the two.[9] Bauman (1991a) demonstrates this ambivalence in relation to the Jew under modern conditions, just as Paul Gilroy does (1993) with regard to the formation of black intellectuals in the modern era. Indeed, deconstruction itself (in other areas) demonstrates the same ambiv-alence of so-called opposites. However, in this instance, the challenge to modernity presented by those who have celebrated 'the Jewish tradi-tion' seems to be founded on a crude manicheanism.

Not only does the opposition between Hebraism and Hellenism lead to essentialist definitions of both but, paradoxically, it tends to confirm the dichotomy between the two traditions constructed in the age of modernity. In employing an ethnic allegory to characterize the tension between order and disorder, reason and the resistance to reason, the self-constituted unified self and the heterogeneous self, the West of 'Hellenic Greece and Christian Rome' and its (Jewish) other, this post-modern theory would appear to overlap uncomfortably with the ethnic allegory employed in the Enlightenment version of progress. Both seem to work from a paradigm in which the anxious struggle between, on the one hand, reason, philosophy and the law and, on the other hand, the rootless, the nomadic, the cosmopolitan, the unruly, the discordant and the excess, is characterized in ethnic terms. The opposition between the Aryan and the Semite constructed in the nineteenth century, theorized in France especially by the religious historian Ernest Renan to form the basis of modern racial thought, and which then led to the catastrophic consequences of the twentieth century, reappears in postmodern theory in inverted form. Postmodern theory's adoption of an ethnicized allegory for portraying the tension between self and other, the nation and its others, therefore appears to concur, in a para-doxical way, with the problematic discourse of the era of modernity in which 'the Jew' was cast, precisely, across that anxious fault-line between order and disorder, and for which real Jews suffered with their lives (cf. Cheyette 1996: 296).[10] The judaizing of alterity in post-modern theory therefore reproduces the very binary terms which it critiques, but simply inverts the opposition so that what was formerly stigmatized is now celebrated.

Jean-Claude Eslin (1990: 117) questions the benefits of this manichean inversion: 'Must the contemporary presentation of European history now stigmatize not the Jew but the "Greek", the other actor in the partnership, and to close off all possible outlets to him so as finally to incur his wrath?' Taking issue with Lyotard's cari-cature of 'Christian Europe' (as Lyotard says, 'the whole social, political, religious and philosophical history of Christian Europe is evidence of a continuous enterprise, employing diverse methods – question, conversion, expulsion, censorship – to neutralize the message of the Jews and to banish the community of non-believers' 1990: 115), Eslin hints at the dangers of this type of misrepresentation: 'Should we depict the Jews, in manichean fashion, as radically other to Europe and therefore place them outside modernity?' (Eslin 1990: 117).

The representation of women has, of course, also been down this path. The celebration of emotion (as opposed to reason), body (as opposed to mind), indecipherability (as opposed to clarity), difference (as opposed to uniformity), and so on, merely reproduces essentialist stereotypes but posits positive rather than negative images to the feminine (see, for example, Annie Leclerc's *Parole de femme*, 1974, and Marie Cardinal's *Autrement dit*, 1977). It is interesting to note the similarities between the judaizing and feminization of alterity – and especially the extent to which the celebration of both today could be seen as an inverted form of some of the classic anti-Semitic images of the 1930s, which made prolific use of the opposition between a virile, 'male' France and a feminized Jewish other (cf. Birnbaum 1988).

In terms of the uncomfortable similarities between a postmodern philo-Semitism and a modern anti-Semitism, let us take for example the following statement by Lyotard:

> The Jews do not belong to 'the family' even though they have been 'resident', as one says, in Carpentras for more than a thousand years and in Prague, Budapest and the Rhineland for centuries. The Jews are not a nation. They do not speak their own language. They do not have roots in an essential *nature* like the European nations. Their source of origin is a book.
>
> (Lyotard 1990:114)

The unsuspecting reader of these words could be forgiven for thinking that they were written by Drumont, Barrès, Maurras, Daudet or any other of the anti-Semitic writers of the first decades of the twentieth century. It is the well-worn image of the wandering Jew who has no attachment to family, nation or language. Of course, Lyotard's use of 'the jew' here as a figure of non-fixity, diaspora and alterity differs profoundly from that of the anti-Semites mentioned above. Lyotard's purpose is to point up the impossibility and, most importantly, the *violence* of the modern project of fixing meaning and 'making the same', the Western metaphysical project of truth, reason and law, and the cultivation (in Bauman's terms, 1991a) of a well-ordered garden.[11] Lyotard's aim is to break with the modern obsession with the unitary nature of the self and to make a permanent space for what is *non récupérable*, sublime. The problem simply comes from giving this ambivalence the name 'jew', and thus valorizing what was previously deemed to be problematic.

Alain Stoekl (1995) makes a similar point about the thought of the writer Maurice Blanchot, who was an enormously influential figure in the postmodern turn with regard to writing and representation. Stoekl describes Blanchot's thought as having evolved from a pre-war anti-Semitism to a post-war philo-Semitism (largely through the influence of Georges Bataille) by simply rendering negatives – exile, exodus and speech (*la parole*) – as positives. Stoekl states that

Blanchot's affirmation of the Jews is mainly the flip side of the reactionary's condemnation: if a Barrès, or a disciple of Barrès, could decry their rootlessness, a [post-war] Blanchot could affirm it. Now their rootlessness is positive, but the terms remain the same.

(Stoekl 1995: 135)[12]

Here post-Holocaust allegories of 'the Jew' touch on much wider questions of modernity and postmodernity. For it could be said, more generally, that what was previously stigmatized and deemed subversive has been democratized and become the norm: difference is desirable, marginality has moved to the centre, hybridity and non-fixity are a sign of postmodern times. Scott Lash (Beck *et al.* 1994: 144), using the terms 'cognitive reflexivity' and 'aesthetic reflexivity' to refer to modern and postmodern modes respectively (see Chapter 3), also demonstrates how the postmodern valorization of contingency, marginality and nomadism simply inverts the hierarchy of terms established in the age of modernity: 'Cognitive reflexivity posed the calculating subject versus contingency, and the conceptual versus the mimetic. Aesthetic reflexivity's renewal of this hierarchy, with the embrace of contingency and mimesis, remain arguably located in the same metaphysical universe.'

We shall consider some of the consequences of this reversal elsewhere in this book. Let us just note here that the postmodern conditions leading to the celebration of difference do not automatically guarantee a protection of 'the other' from forces that would eradicate it; on the contrary, new conditions might well be as inhospitable to 'the other' as those in the modern era. Daniel and Jonathan Boyarin (1993) have raised a number of related questions in relation to postmodern philosophy's adoption of 'the Jew' as the site of 'the other'. First, the caricature of a Hellenic West, to which Hebraism is irredeemably other, suggests that real Jews were merely the passive victims of Christian Europe's constructions of 'the Jew'. As the Boyarins point out, this was the major problem with Sartre's conceptual framework in *Réflexions sur la question juive*:

Lyotard basically repeats Sartre's thesis about the production of the Jew by the anti-Semite. [He says] 'What is most real about real Jews is that Europe, in any case, does not know what to do with them: Christians demand their conversion; monarchs expel them; republics assimilate them; Nazis exterminate them.' But one might also add 'and philosophers allegorize them' and in doing so, they continue another particularly Christian practice with regard to uppercase Jews, one that begins with Paul.

(Boyarin and Boyarin 1993: 701)

The Boyarins' objection here is that 'the Jew' as allegorized 'other' is presented, as in Sartre's text, as simply an object of the Christian gaze, simply someone else's representation rather than having any subject-status, agency or history of its own. (For a critique of *Réflexions sur la question juive*, see, for example, Grosz 1990, Kritzman 1995b, Suleiman 1995.)

Second, and perhaps more important, in employing 'Jew' as a trope for alterity – including all real outsiders, strangers, Blacks, Arabs and real Jews – this use of 'the Jew' would seem to conflate all difference into an indistinguishable alterity and, in the process, eradicate the specificities of each group. Where are real Jews here, with a specific history, ask the Boyarins. They point out (1993: 699) that although Jean-Luc Nancy, for example, is motivated by the desire to 'unwork' the complicity between philosophy and twentieth-century violence, it is possible that 'his rhetoric is complicit in perpetuating the cultural annihilation of the Jew'. Within the thought of philosophers like Nancy, they continue, there 'lies a blindness to the particularity of Jewish difference that is itself part of a relentless penchant for allego-rizing all "difference" into a univocal discourse'. 'The Jew', then, simply becomes the figure (or trope) employed to define a new univer-salism, the reified marker of all resistance to rootedness, fixity and closure – the postmodern nomad *par excellence*. The problem of defining collectivities between this infinite dispersal of identity and its rooted-ness within a specific history is characteristic of the postmodern dilemma.

Jews and poets

Postmodern philosophy's adoption of 'Auschwitz' as an allegory of the tragic decline of the West and 'the Jew' as victim of and witness to this tragedy is also an allegory of the demise of Western forms of represen-tation. These (allegorical) 'Jews' bear witness not only to the absurdity of the modern political process of assimilation (uniformity and the reduction to the same) but also to the impossibility of the broader modern philosophical and cultural project of classification and repre-sentation of the real. They designate the 'unnameable', what is lacking in all representation, what cannot be spoken – since all representation is a form of absence from a source – the point at which language meets silence. In other words, 'the Jew' and 'Auschwitz' stand as a sign of the modernist challenge to referential realism. In *Le Différend*, Lyotard outlines clearly this interpretation of 'Auschwitz':

> The 'Auschwitz' model designates an 'experience' of language which questions all speculative discourse. Such discourse can no longer function 'after Auschwitz'. 'Auschwitz' is a name which denies the process of speculative thought. It is therefore not a name in the Hegelian sense, that is, a figure of memory which guarantees the fixity of the referent and its meanings even when the spirit has destroyed its outer signs. It is a name with no speculative 'name', irrecuperable in terms of a concept.
>
> (Lyotard 1983: 133)

Lyotard's approach (and that of Jacques Derrida) is here placed explicitly in an anti-representational line which would include Mallarmé and Blanchot (among others) but which then ethnicizes the silence/absence at the heart of representation by associating it with the genocide of Jews at Auschwitz. The silence beyond language is designated by the anti-nominalist name 'Jew', while Auschwitz becomes the present absence, that which lies behind all human discourse, whose traces (for that is all we have) we are obliged to interrogate. Blanchot extends Adorno's stricture on the impossibility of poetry after Auschwitz into one on the impossibility of narrative: 'I would suggest that there can be no fictional narrative of Auschwitz' (*Après-coup*, Minuit, 1983, p. 98). In *L'Écriture du désastre* (1980), he equates the disaster of Auschwitz with the disaster of meaning, for Auschwitz is the ultimate sign of the impossibility of language to speak the truth: 'This unknown name is beyond naming. The Holocaust, the absolute event of History, historically dated, this consuming furnace in which History was destroyed, is also the moment at which meaning was extinguished' (p. 80). Blanchot's 'Holocaust' is the absence inevitably present in all projects of knowing, writing and being. Lyotard (1988b: 83–84) extends the allegory by saying of 'Jews': 'They continue to bear witness, "after Auschwitz", to the impossibility for art and writing to bear witness to the Other.'

In being recruited for the anti-representational argument, these 'Jews' rejoin Roland Barthes' 'scriptible' or Julia Kristeva's 'semiotic' as other to institutionalized readings of texts and to the symbolic order. They become equated with the process of writing itself – that which bears witness to the perpetual displacement of meaning and the subversion of all forms of closure. This interpretation of 'the Jew' mirrors the contemporary shifts in focus from the perpetrators of violence to its victims/witnesses, from the voice of authority to the voice of 'the other', and from the (hi)story told to the problematic nature of telling, so that language itself becomes the real (anti-)hero of the text.

We do not need to rehearse the more general debate on poststructuralism here (which has been amply discussed elsewhere). What is more significant for our present discussion is the very use of 'Jew' and 'Auschwitz' for this purpose. We might describe this as a process of judaizing the site of 'the other' in an allegorical critique of Western forms of representation. 'Auschwitz' is the event which cannot be written (just as Talmudic tradition proscribes all representations of God) but must always be written *about* so as never to be forgotten. Lyotard says, in *Heidegger et 'les juifs'* (1988b: 50), 'to represent "Auschwitz" in images and in words is a way of forgetting', yet the imperative is nevertheless, as the philosopher Sarah Kofman was tragically aware, 'to write endlessly about writing about "Auschwitz", in order not to forget what happened at "Auschwitz"' (Marks 1995: 41; see also the same problems surrounding the question of 'witnessing' the Holocaust discussed in Felman 1990 and 'La parole contre l'extermination', *Le Monde des livres*, 25 February 1994).

Hence the Jew's condition, and especially the Jew's specific link with the Holocaust, is generalized to encompass the whole of humanity (we are all survivors of Auschwitz, according to Blanchot) and the very process of writing itself. The Jew is the witness of loss and absence and doomed to write and rewrite that message – which is precisely the essence of writing. The Jew is the poet/witness. Alan Stoekl (1995: 136) discusses this appropriation of Jewishness in the work of Maurice Blanchot. He observes that, for Blanchot, Jews ' "bear witness", and it is their internal exile, so to speak, along with their word, that communicates to us a state of "distance which defies the possibility of simple unification-through-communication" '. Writing after Auschwitz is essentially 'Jewish' in that it defies the Western utilitarian tradition of a transcendent sense and functions as perpetual displacement of truth and meaning. As Stoekl (1995: 135) again says of Blanchot's treatment of the Jewish question, 'the Jews are, in effect, exemplary in that they "bear witness" to a relation that itself is not specifically Jewish'. The Jew becomes emblematic of this wider lesson. This is mimicked in Derrida's *Circumfession* (in Bennington and Derrida 1990), as Lawrence Kritzman observes:

> In effect, the alterity that the Jew represents for Derrida engages the figure of the writer in a quest without closure, in an endless

pursuit of the 'other in me' which itself re-turns the possibility of revelation.... Jewishness becomes a somewhat precarious enterprise as it enters the realm of undecidability.

(Kritzman 1995b: 115)

Derrida had already traced this correspondence between the Jew and writing in the work of the poet Edmond Jabès ('Edmond Jabès et la question du livre', Derrida 1967: 99–116), for whom 'the difficulty of being a Jew *coincides* with the difficulty of writing; for Judaism and writing are but the same waiting, the same hope, the same depletion' (from *Le Livre des questions*, 1963, cited in Bauman 1991a: 157).[13] Bauman poses the essential questions about this correspondence, again invoking the example of Jabès:

Why do Jewishness and the universally human search each other out, define each other, blend? Why is it that Tsvetayeva, Borges, Celan, Joyce, trying to capture that void, that no-essence that is the first abode and the last retreat of universality, cannot but find the Jew in their net? ('First I thought I was a writer. Then I realized I was a Jew. Then I no longer distinguished the writer in me from the Jew because one and the other are only the torment of an ancient word,' confessed Edmond Jabès. Elsewhere he admits that the Jew is 'the figure of exile, errancy, strangeness and separation, condition that is that of the writer as well' (*Le Soupçon, le désert*, Gallimard, 1978, p. 85)).

(Bauman 1991a: 191)

This amalgamation of the condition of the Jew and the act of writing raises the same questions that we noted in the previous section regarding the amalgamation of 'the Jew' and the more general critique of Western rationality – for it is indeed part of the same logic. On one level, by transforming 'the Jew' into an allegory for a process which, in itself, has nothing to do with Jewishness (namely the process of writing), and by generalizing Jewish experience (or at least a particular version of it) into a universal truth, this theory is in danger of effacing any sense of Jewish specificity. Writing is 'Hebraized' while, on the other hand, the departicularized 'Jew' is thoroughly secularized. In a sense, this amounts to the ultimate form of assimilation of the Jew to a 'higher' cause. This is ironic – to say the least – given the professed desire of such theory to refuse to trap 'the other' within the oppressive logic of sameness and difference, and to return otherness to 'the other'. The universalizing of the Jew in this way moves perilously close, as

Daniel and Jonathan Boyarin (1993) argue, to eradicating the Jew all over again.

On a more general level, if the Jewish experience of the Holocaust becomes an allegory for the limits of language (that is, the impossibility of language to speak the truth) and the irreducibility of 'the other', then the Holocaust is detached from its context in history and politics and relocated within the realm of aesthetics. Elaine Marks (1995: 36) suggests that this reading of the Holocaust transforms 'the historical-social-ethical question of the extermination of the Jews into a philosophical-poetical-linguistic question of presence and absence'. The density of history is collapsed into the flat and immediate surface of story (narrative) beyond which language cannot go; experience recedes in favour of simulacra whose fate is to gesture obliquely towards that which cannot be spoken. There is a further irony here in that Adorno's warning *against* the aestheticization of the Holocaust ('to write poetry after Auschwitz is barbaric') ends up as a way of aestheticizing it – in terms of unspeakable and apocalyptic violence or as pure event, the point at which the end of history meets the end of philosophy (cf. Rose 1993: 257). Michael Bernstein (1998: 8) puts this paradox most clearly: 'To insist that the Shoah embodies some ultimate negative truth may represent the last, cunningly disguised bid of philosophical discourse to subject the multiplicity and heterogeneity of human experience to a single, all-encompassing standard.' Blanchot's appropriation of the Holocaust (1980: 80) would appear to confirm this paradoxical aestheticization (and hence reduction) of that which is beyond all aestheticizing and beyond all forms of reductionism: 'How should we maintain [a memory of the Holocaust] if not through thought; yet how should we construct a thought which could capture that event in which everything was lost, including "appropriating" thought?'

Does the deconstructionist use of 'Jew' and 'Auschwitz' therefore turn out to be another method of 'dislocating the memory of the Shoah from its past' (Kritzman 1995a: 6), obscuring the specificity of the Holocaust, and, ultimately, recruiting the Jew yet again for the purpose of a universal truth?

History, memory, representation

It is, of course, here that the discussion of the Holocaust meets the more general postmodern textualization of history and the problems of memorializing the past. Whatever concepts one employs for defining the distinction between history and memory (the historian François

Bédarida, for example, maintains that their trajectories are different, for 'the objective of memory is fidelity, whilst the objective of history is truth' 1993: 7), their common grounding in language and representation inevitably blurs the distinctions. Lyotard designates 'Auschwitz' as the end of the modern version of history in which language could recuperate reality through an expression of 'facts', and the dawning of an age in which the limits of language are to the fore:

> The historian must henceforward break with the accepted hegemony of the cognitive linguistic regime governing history and be bold enough to pursue a different regime according to what cannot be presented within a cognitive framework. All reality is subject to this exigency insofar as any reality is composed of an unknown number of possible meanings. In this sense, Auschwitz is the most real of realities. Its name defines that space in which the very competence of historical knowledge is rendered problematic.
>
> (1983: 92)

The 'end of history', in this sense, means the inevitable recognition of the interconnections between historical event and the spoken or written memories of that event. The description by the historian Pierre Nora of the difference between the 'old' and 'new' historian highlights this evolution:

> The traditional historian…fills in the gap which separates us from the past. He makes the past speak to us. He is, at one and the same time, notary and prophet. The new historian, on the other hand, is perfectly well aware that he is irrevocably cut off from the past. His task is simply to reconstruct the representation of the past. He has become intermediary and interpreter.
>
> ('Un entretien avec Pierre Nora', *Le Monde*, 29 November 1994)

In his enormous multi-volume enterprise entitled *Les Lieux de mémoire* (1984), Nora recognizes the fact that the contemporary obsession with the 'sites' of memory today marks, paradoxically, the unriveting of those links which moulded past, present and future into historical time, and the death of the historical mission of the nation which depended on this version of time. Reflecting on Nora's exposé of this 'shattering of temporality', Mongin (1993: 104) observes: 'The present, which has become more and more "historiographical" and less and less "historical", is reflected within a memory which has become more and more cumbersome.' Mongin had already remarked on the problems raised by this new historiography founded on memory in the context of 'speaking' the Holocaust:

> The 'historiographical' interrogation underpinning a certain interpretation of Nazism echoes the interrogation brought to bear on the memory of the Shoah: how should Nazism be interpreted historically? But also how should we speak of and remember the Shoah? These two different questions are in effect the same question for they both ask what 'narration' is possible to constitute the narrative of a crime whose specificity and uniqueness (*Eighenheit*) 'paralyses' the historian as much as the writer.
>
> (Mongin 1988: 85)

These difficult questions are explored in a fascinating and immensely profound way in Claude Lanzmann's monumental film on the Holocaust, *Shoah*. Through the apparently simple device of interviews between the director and survivors and witnesses of and accomplices to the Holocaust, Lanzmann traces the interconnections between memory, history and speech while, at the same time, dramatizing his own role in pursuit of this lost disaster. It is not, as Lanzmann has said, a documentary, but a work of art as much about memory and narration as history itself (or rather the inevitable interconnections between all three processes). As Todorov (1994: 288) has observed, 'the distance between past and present is abolished. Lanzmann does not film the past, which is impossible (no archival material is used in *Shoah*), but the way in which we remember – now.' The historian Pierre Vidal-Naquet has suggested that underlying Lanzmann's project in *Shoah* is the problem faced by all historians today:

> How to bring to history the teaching of Marcel Proust, the search for lost time as time lost and recovered at the same time. [In *Shoah*] we are presented with a single document where everything depends on the questions it asks today of its witnesses and on the answers it receives.... Between time lost and time recovered there is the work of art and the test which *Shoah* sets for the historian is his obligation to be both a scientist and an artist at one and the same time. Without this dual function in mind, the historian irremediably loses a fraction of that truth which he pursues.
>
> (Vidal-Naquet 1990: 208)

Shoah, as Michel Deguy says (1990: 36), is a work which is made in the spirit of Adorno's injunction on the impossibility of poetry and representation after Auschwitz.

Modernism's challenge to representational realism has now become the inescapable truth of history. Vidal-Naquet's reference to Proust underlines this fact, for it highlights the dilemma of the contemporary historian who can no longer be unaware of the problematic nature of recording the past. The historian's dilemma and that of the writer are the same, for both are subject to the present constraints of language and narrative (see especially the works of Hayden White). The textualization of history is also the conflation of the past event and the present of writing, the historian and the writer – all of which are part of the more general process of the flattening of history noted above (which, as we shall see in Chapter 3, is dependent on the spatialization of time). Also with Lanzmann's film in mind, Mongin shows how attempts to record the Shoah relate directly to the contemporary feeling of 'an exhaustion of the historical experience itself':

> The Shoah poses the question of the crisis of history and of the memory that one is obliged to privilege to remember the dead. This is why the suspicion which weighs on the experience itself gives rise to an interrogation of the very act of 'memorializing', that is our ability to make links with the past and, more importantly, with the dead whose deaths passed unnoticed.
>
> (Mongin 1994a: 80)

Lyotard's 'Auschwitz' (1983: 145–146) is precisely the problematization of experience itself: ' "Auschwitz" cannot have a speculative name because it is the name of a para-experience or even of the destruction of experience.' For Mongin (1991: 191), Lanzmann's *Shoah* inserts the Shoah and 'the Jewish question' at the heart of the whole modern enterprise, since the problems of recalling the catastrophe are intricately connected with the breakdown of Western reason: 'It is the failure of European political reason which is at the heart of these images of memory and the commemoration of the dead.' The invasion of the problems of 'subjective' memory into the field of 'objective' history, and of representation into the field of 'experience' is therefore akin to the judaizing of Western scientific method, given the dichotomy (for some) between a Judaism which values memory over history ('Zakhor') and a Christianity which has the opposite values. In the words of François Bédarida (1993: 8–9) 'the Christian tradition has been relentless in its desire to privilege history over memory, whilst the Jewish tradition, until quite recently, privileged and even exaggerated memory to the detriment of history'. In this sense the Shoah marks the transformation of the confident modern version of history into our contemporary scepticism, 'when the figures of evil and memory have replaced those of good and the Utopian imagination' (Mongin 1991: 192).[14] For Lyotard, this understanding of the Shoah signals the end of the project of modernity, while for the German political philosopher Jürgen Habermas (1996) it signals the need for the completion of the modern project in the light of the failure of instrumentalist rationality (cf. Mongin 1994a: 69–77). Mongin (1991: 192) concludes that 'history has lost its rhythm, it is running down...and the final glorious dream is in the process of becoming a bad memory'.

How to discuss the Holocaust in the light of the contemporary problematization of truth, objectivity and reality, and the conflation of history, memory and language? How to disentangle the Holocaust from the mass of images and words about the Holocaust now that the umbilical cord linking past to present has been cut and we appear to be adrift in a sea of simulacra? These are some of the important questions raised in recent years after two decades of relative silence in the immediate post-war period. Furthermore, in an advanced information society (*la société de communication*) in which, as Mongin (1993: 105) observes, we are both plunged into an 'autistic' present which undermines 'the idea of history' and beset by 'a cult of memory', how do we distinguish 'genuine' information from 'false' disinformation? The recording of the past in a postmodern age opens up a space in which, paradoxically, the 'reality' of the Holocaust is at once both more 'present' and direct (the spectator fused with the event as if beyond all forms of mediation) and more distant (a moment irrevocably lost in time and inevitably refracted through the prism of present consciousness and the intertextual web of language and image).[15]

The focus on the problematic nature of representing the Holocaust through language, and the transformation of the density of 'history' and 'reality' into the flat surface of the present (detaching us from a fixed version of the past) provide the context within which contemporary revisionist versions of the Holocaust can flourish. On the one hand, our sense of horror has been weakened due to over-exposure to images of violence. Following Jean Baudrillard's writings on the nature of evil, Geoffrey Hartman refers to the 'compassion fatigue' and accompanying feeling of 'unreality' that beset us today:

> Baudrillard, who extends Benjamin's insight on how technology invades sensibility, suggests that the later negationist obsession

with challenging the historical reality of the Holocaust is only another expression of our growing sense of the unreality of the past. This unreality fuses our horror of the Holocaust with an incredulity that comes from the awareness that we now live more and more among simulacra.

(Hartman 1995: 21)

In a climate of simulacra and pure relativism, negationism is simply one image of the past among others.

On the other hand (and as we noted earlier in this chapter) deconstruction's challenge to binary oppositions has subverted the manichean antithesis between democracy and dictatorship, good and evil, and confuses the previously clear-cut delineation of perpetrators and victims. The indictment of the West and modernity in general in terms of their involvement in the Holocaust therefore calls into question the neat distinction between Nazism (as the quintessential evil) and the Western democracies (as upholders of the moral order). Through what Henri Rousso (1987) has described as the 'Vichy syndrome', France has been profoundly divided in recent years over the question of the relationship between fascism and democracy. The repressed connections between republicanism and fascism have returned with a vengeance (not least in the figure of François Mitterrand). In *De l'esprit*, Jacques Derrida discusses the inevitable 'contaminations' traversing all artificial demarcations established in Western philosophy, rendering problematic those discourses which would wish to see Nazism as a species alien to Western forms of thought:

Nazism was not born in the desert. We know this but it must be constantly repeated. And even if it had sprouted like a mushroom, far from any desert, in the silence of a European forest, it would only have been able to do so under the shade of tall trees, in the shelter of their silence and their indifference, rooted in the same soil.... They would bear the names of religions, philosophies, political regimes, economic structures, religious or academic institutions. In short, they would be what we confusingly call 'culture' or 'the world of the spirit'.

(Derrida 1987: 179)

Lyotard (1988a: 83) also remarks on the interconnections and 'contaminations' between Nazism and Western forms of liberal democracy. Capitalism, he suggests, 'keeps house with despotism, as we can see with Nazism'.

Derrida and Lyotard both challenge us to consider our own position when rushing to judge others, and ask us provocatively how we can so easily condemn Nazism without realizing the complicity of the West. Lyotard, for example, seems to equate republican assimilation and Nazi genocide as if there was little to choose between them in terms of their respective forms of violence to 'the other'. The 'will of the people' guiding the reign of Terror of the French Revolution and the spirit of the *Volk* underpinning Nazi genocide might not be identical but neither are they opposites. The mythology constructed around the *Volk* could only flourish because the ground had already been prepared by 'democratic' thinking:

> Nazism replaced the idea of the citizen with the name 'Aryan'. It founded its legitimacy on the myths of the Northern race and abandoned the modern horizon of cosmopolitanism. It succeeded because it implanted within the idea of the sovereignty of the people, 'democratically' in the Kantian sense, a desire for a 'return to origins' which could only be satisfied by myth. Nazism provided 'the people' with the names and narratives which allowed it to identify exclusively with German heroes and to heal the wounds produced by defeat and crisis.
>
> (Lyotard 1988a: 68)[16]

Lacoue-Labarthe and Nancy (1990: 312) also blur the dividing line between Nazism and democracy when they state that Nazi myth-making 'belongs profoundly to the character of the West in general, and more precisely, to the fundamental tendency of the *subject*, in the metaphysical sense of the word'. The challenge to the oppositions between universalism and particularism, assimilation and difference, democracy and totalitarian rule, undercuts the manichean moral universe employed to legitimize the West.

This theoretically sensible position only poses problems when the questions of responsibility, guilt and justice are pursued to their logical extreme. As Gillian Rose (1993: 257) has pointed out, the danger of making the Holocaust the benchmark for the limits of modernity, 'the measure of history as such, of truth as such, of reason as such', is that it removes the Holocaust from the realm of human action and opens the way for more thoroughgoing revisions of Nazi genocide. These problems were highlighted at the time of the Paul de Man affair. When it was revealed that the celebrated literary critic had written for a collaborationist and anti-Semitic paper during the war, Derrida was accused of casuistry (and worse) in defending de Man according to the

type of argument outlined above.[17] Shoshana Felman adopted a typically Derridean stance in her own defence of de Man:

> The easy judgments made on de Man's historical misjudgments
> provide not insight but relief: in passing judgment on de Man, we
> distance and disown his dangerous closeness to us, in an attempt
> to distance history, the Holocaust, as past, *his* past, which, as such,
> remains foreign and exterior to our present. We blind ourselves to
> the historical reality of that past by reducing its obscurity to a
> paradigm of readability – an easily intelligible and safely remote
> manichean allegory of good and evil...de Man was 'Nazi': in
> denouncing him as one of 'them', we believe we place ourselves in
> a different zone of ethics and temporality; 'we' as opposed to
> 'they', are on the right side of history – a side untouched,
> untainted by the evil of the Holocaust.
>
> (Felman 1989: 706)

But virtually the same argument as Felman's was subsequently used
by Jacques Vergès in his defence of Klaus Barbie, the 'butcher of Lyon'
at the time of Germany's occupation of France during the Second
World War. At the time of the Barbie trial, Simone Weil condemned
this confusion of right and wrong, which she claimed constituted a
'banalization of the Holocaust' (quoted in Chaumont 1994: 80).[18] Le
Pen, too, is particularly adept at equating all sorts of 'catastrophes'
(Islam, Aids, the Holocaust, and so on), a tactic which has the same
effect of reducing everything to the same and consequently down-
grading the particular value of anything. Mongin observes that this
leaves us with an impossible choice:

> If the world is composed of victims and there is no difference
> between different crimes, the risk that we run is to lock ourselves
> into a stark alternative: either the most extreme of crimes is down-
> graded or, on the other hand, it becomes reified.... And if we
> therefore oscillate between a 'dumbing down' and a reification of
> evil, we thereby lose our capacity to perceive any gradation in
> crimes, and hence our capacity to judge.
>
> (Mongin 1991: 193)[19]

A further example of this less overt postmodern revisionism (which
also demonstrates the revisionist potential of the deconstructionist
argument, cf. Marks 1996: 13–20) can be seen in the famous
Historikerstreit (*querelle des historiens* or 'historians' debate') in Germany.

The comparative approach of Ernst Nolte was criticized not only because it placed Soviet practices of extermination alongside those of the Nazis (and therefore challenged the uniqueness of Nazi genocide) but also because, in so doing, it establishes a 'slippage in meaning' which exonerates Germany from the sole responsibility for the atrocities of the war (Bédarida 1997: 221). Nolte's approach therefore had a specific function in the present: it allowed Germans to reappropriate their past by providing them with the gratifying knowledge that their history (Nazism) was really no worse than other forms of barbarism (see Friedländer 1987 and Dominick La Capra's argument in Friedländer, ed., 1992).

From the Pandora's box of postmodern textuality, the challenge to binary oppositions and the demise of history comes an assortment of reappraisals of the past with unpredictable political and moral consequences. Can French postmodern philosophy's challenge to modernity and objectivity be said to collude with negationist statements on the Holocaust? Does the poststructuralist refusal to equate the word with the truth in realist fashion reproduce the Nazis' deliberate camouflage of the truth?[20] Conan and Lindenberg wonder whether the use of the word 'Shoah' in the 1980s might itself be an indication of an implicit negationism:

> To name this monstrous event 'Shoah'...is possibly symptomatic of a slippage (which certain commentators have theorized) towards the abdication of reason in the face of the Unfathomable and the Indescribable or Unbearable. This manoeuvre constitutes the reverse side of negationism since it removes the event from any history which would attempt to 'explain' it.
>
> (Conan and Lindenberg 1992: 15)

Elaine Marks asks a similar question:

> Were the Nazis poststructuralists and deconstructors *avant la lettre* in their desire 'never to utter the words that would be appropriate to the action being taken'? Or, more worrisome still, were and are the Heideggerians and poststructuralists, as has been asserted in France and the United States during the recent debates concerning the politics and the philosophical and/or literary theories of Martin Heidegger and Paul de Man, engaged in an intellectual enterprise that involves inherently dangerous modes of thought?
>
> (Marks 1995: 37–38)

However, rather than equate poststructuralism and deconstruction with Nazism – which is as rash a judgement as the unproblematic conflation of democracy and Nazism under the broad banner of 'modernity' – we should perhaps be aware of both the similarities and differences between these so-called 'opposites'. Todorov adopts a more nuanced perspective on this question:

> I have no sympathy with those who view Auschwitz as the inevitable end-point, the essential truth unfolded, the scarcely more extreme manifestation of our modernity. If the term 'modernity' can cover such different realities as democracy and totalitarianism, then I doubt its usefulness as a concept. However, precisely because it is the extreme limit of modernity...totalitarianism can teach us much about democracy.
>
> (Todorov 1994: 307)[21]

Without collapsing all differences into a monolithic concept of modernity and the West (which leads precisely to the sort of problems raised above) we should nevertheless be responsive to the question of 'contamination' between so-called 'opposites' announced in postmodern philosophy. The break with binary oppositions and the demise of a transcendent truth do indeed signal a more complex and messy value system, and a problematization of history. Furthermore, the connections between modernity, Jews and the disaster of the Holocaust cannot be overlooked if a new ethics is to emerge beyond totalizing systems of thought and political practice (whatever the problems might be of allegorizing 'Auschwitz' and 'the Jew' for this purpose). We can no longer live with the same Utopian illusions that guided a modernity founded on reducing 'the other' to the same; nor can we be unaware of the sense of loss, absence and exile from an original source or transcendent meaning which underpins all our actions and our language. We are condemned to a life devoid of the certainty of the past and constrained within the walls of our own images of experience. In one sense, this is a tragic vision for, as Olivier Mongin observes, being cut off from the past signifies the demise of the modern concept of 'Man':

> This idea of a possible loss of a link with the past inevitably weighs heavily on our conception of history and destroys the possibility of historical experience. If this link is well and truly broken, then, by the same token, humanity is in crisis.
>
> (Mongin 1994a: 81)

But it is also a necessary prerequisite for the creation of any new being – less hubristic and intimately acquainted with contingency. Living with uncertainty and with no fixed idea of history and progress is a double-edged sword.[22]

New ethics, new dangers

The contemporary rediscovery of the Holocaust therefore brings with it both new chances and new dangers. The passage from relative silence about the Holocaust to a frenzy of talking may have shattered past taboos and brought to the surface what was formerly repressed, but the plurality of voices now raised may not, for all that, have provided a cure. As Todorov has pointed out (1998: 13) 'memory is no longer threatened by the suppression of information but by its over-abundance'. The constant stream of Holocaust-talk of recent years might simply have buried the Holocaust once again beneath a plethora of interpretations. Geoffrey Hartman (1995: 15) suggests that 'this hyperknowledge about both perpetrators and victims, this wish to disclose and expose everything, may be no more remedial than the conspiracy of silence that used to exist'. In particular, the mobilization of 'Auschwitz' for the cause of the wider indictment of modernity might be the path towards the contemporary 'banalization of the Holocaust' rather than towards a more profound understanding of its import. 'Auschwitz' as the end of history and the end of philosophy opens up the space for a resurgent revisionism dressed up in the clothes of a 'respectable' relativism.

It would therefore be premature and foolhardy to celebrate unequivocally the post-Holocaust and postmodern era as a new dawn. If we are all (allegorical) 'Jews' today – all non-rooted, diasporic, nomadic and cosmopolitan – it does not necessarily follow that we have entered a realm of new freedoms and new ethics for all beyond the constraints of modern concepts of self and other. If the particular state of the Jew under modern conditions has become the general state of us all under postmodern conditions (with the sole difference that stigmatization of difference has now given way to celebration of it) then this might be a cause for concern as much as rejoicing. In the following chapters we will explore the consequences of this process of democratization of marginality, not the least of which is the commodification of difference, hybridity and cosmopolitanism.

However, it would be equally foolhardy to dismiss the possibilities on offer now that we have seen through the Utopian illusions of modernity and can reflect on modernity's hubris. Living in the shadow of the Holocaust can open the door to another way of viewing 'the other', founded on the recognition of the absence of totality in the self and the parallel recognition of (and responsibility for) this absence in others. Is this a Jewish ethics as opposed to the ethics of 'the Christian West', or is such a formulation a simplification of the distinction between Athens and Jerusalem (Rose 1993)? Whatever the answer to this question, it is certainly a vision of otherness which is not confined within modernity's binary straitjacket of same/other, uniformity/irredeemable difference.

Yet any new ethics needs a new politics to make such a vision a reality. Unfortunately, postmodern life is not always conducive to the realization of either.

2 New racisms

Modern 'logics' of racism

Although the term 'racism' was not formally invented until the inter-war period, the practice was a product of modern social structures and modern ideas which pre-dated the 1930s. In his path-breaking analysis of racism and anti-racism of the modern era, Pierre-André Taguieff (1988a) outlines two major discourses of racism. The first was linked to the universalizing and civilizing mission of the modern nation-state which found its major forms of expression in colonialism abroad and assimilationist social engineering at home. This was a racism that aimed at eradicating the difference of 'the other' by reducing 'the other' to the same. The second was a particularist form of racism founded on the concept of the essential and absolute differences between groups. This was a racism that aimed at excluding 'the other'. In Taguieff's terms, the first is 'heterophobic', 'mixophilic' and in-feriorizes the other, the second is 'heterophilic', 'mixophobic' and differentiates 'the other' (for a more detailed discussion of these terms, see Silverman 1992).

In his introduction to a recent collection entitled *Racisme et modernité*, Michel Wieviorka adopts the same terms as Taguieff (Wieviorka 1993a). However, Wieviorka suggests that it is more useful to see these discourses as two 'logics' of racism which are not mutually exclusive but are frequently co-present in different forms of racist behaviour and action (cf. Wieviorka 1991 and 1994, and Lapeyronnie 1993). Zygmunt Bauman (1993: 163–165) uses the terms employed by the French anthropologist Claude Lévi-Strauss in *Tristes tropiques* (1955) to define the same strategies: anthropophagism is the cannibalistic and ingestionist racism of assimila-tion, and anthropoemism is the expulsion of 'the other' or 'vomiting out' racism of apartheid or (in its genocidal form) Nazism. The two broad types correspond to universalistic and particularistic modes respectively.

In a general sense, these two strategies or 'logics' define the modern paradigm for apprehending difference. Difference was a problem, or rather a task: it had either to be fixed for ever or removed completely. On the one hand, new scientific method used skull sizes (and other equally 'reliable' evidence) to divide the human race into a hierarchy of races, thus grounding the difference of 'the other' in the immutable laws of nature. On the other hand, difference could (indeed must) be transcended in order to bring about the Utopian society of equals. The first saw difference as an essential characteristic of humanity; the second saw difference as an irritant, a stain, a sign of parochialism, backwardness and tradition which needed to be removed in the name of civilization, enlightenment and progress. Here we have the classic dichotomy of the modern period between the deterministic idea of the *Volk* and the voluntarist concept of the free individual: that is, between biological essentialism and assimilationist rationalism.

But Wieviorka's warning not to see the two 'logics' of racism as mutually exclusive is an important corrective to Taguieff's schema. What was frequently presented as a choice between opposites (and is often presented in the same way today) was, in effect, a far more fluid relationship between universalism and particularism, assimilation and difference, ingestion and expulsion of 'the other'. Tzvetan Todorov's wide-ranging appraisal of some of the great French thinkers of the modern period (from Montesquieu and Rousseau to Barrès and Péguy) in his book *Nous et les autres* (1989) highlights the ambivalence of the opposition between the rational belief in the perfectibility of 'Man', on the one hand, and the biological determinism of human essences, on the other. Is it possible to say with any certainty that the racialized nationalism and anti-Semitism of Maurice Barrès at the end of the nineteenth century, based on the *volkisch* principles of soil and blood as determinants of belonging to the community, were any more instrumental in suppressing the claims of 'the other' than Michelet's patriotic nationalism, based on the Enlightenment principles of reason and truth, whose ideology underpinned Jules Ferry's confident 'civilizing' colonialism of the 1880s (see Girardet 1972)? The dividing line between universalists and relativists is sometimes rather blurred when viewed from the standpoint of their treatment of 'the other'.

The modern project of assimilation is a good case in point. Despite its continual flirtation with racial thinking through the second part of the nineteenth century and the first part of the twentieth century, France, as we know, officially chose the course of assimilation, based primarily (although not exclusively) on the *jus soli* (*droit du sol*). Assimilation viewed identity as pliable and transformable. It gave modern society its ultimate rationale: to undertake a civilizing mission to nurture a higher form of humanity. The dream was to make all the same, irrespective of origin, race, religion or creed: uniformity in the name of equality. The institution which would put this mission into practice was the nation-state. Nation, state and culture would be fused indissolubly to form 'the single and indivisible Republic (*la république une et indivisible*)'.

The problem was that some differences turned out to be particularly resistant to change. Some 'peasants' needed a fair degree of disciplining to transform them into 'Frenchmen' (Foucault 1976, Weber 1976). Indeed, there were even those who were so backward that no amount of cajoling and coercion could bring them into the realm of light. What is more, even those who made the effort, who shed all signs of their parochial garb and jettisoned all that baggage in the name of progress, could always be *suspected* of harbouring secret attachments to their origins. Jews were the example *par excellence* of this double-bind (cf. Bauman 1991a). They were in fact mimics or impostors, not exactly the real thing.

Here, of course, the binary line between racial and assimilationist thinking, between the essential and transformable nature of identity, and between the so-called ethnic and political models of the nation which arose from this dichotomy ('French' and 'German' respectively) appears less clear. Is it the *droit du sol* which underpins this perspective or the racialized *droit du sang* (*jus sanguinis*)? The notion of a manichean opposition between a French universalist and German particularist model can only be maintained if the 'contaminations' between the two are rigidly policed, and troubling interferences (like French anti-Semitism, Vichy racial policy, and so on) are classified as anti-republican and Germanic in origin (see Sternhell 1983). As we noted in Chapter 1, this type of dichotomy simply effaces the ambivalence of (and therefore interconnections between) both terms. As Gil Delannoi remarks, 'Rousseau's model of the nation is not as far removed from Herder's model as one might think' (1994: 90). Elsewhere I have attempted to show how the seminal text eulogized by defenders of the republican political model of the nation – 'What is a nation? (*Qu'est-ce qu'une nation?*)' delivered as a lecture at the Sorbonne in 1882 by Renan – demonstrates, in fact, a constant slippage between a determinist essentialism and a rationalist voluntarism in terms of a definition of the nation (Silverman 1992: 20–24). The slippage is obscured especially by the use of the word 'culture', for Renan can both reject the criterion of 'race' as the foundation of the nation and yet introduce an equally essentialist definition (through the back door, so to speak) by transposing questions of biology on to questions of language, history and psychology. Renan can thus look both ways at the same time: the individual is at once (pre-)determined by his/her membership of a collectivity with a past comprising specific traditions and customs *and* free to associate with others according to his/her own rational choices. This Janus-like quality makes Renan's text classically modern, for it is caught between past and future, remembering and forgetting, the conflicting paradigms of fixing *and* changing 'the other', categorizing 'the other' in immutable terms *and* transforming otherness into the same.[1]

At a deeper level than the conventional (and often manichean) oppositions between rationalism and determinism, *Lumières* and romanticism, universalism and particularism, and assimilation and difference, there is therefore an ambivalent attitude towards otherness which characterizes the modern mind. In one sense, the two 'logics' outlined above converge in terms of their quest for a unitary self. Assimilation seeks to fix 'the other' just as much as racial determinism. The psychoanalyst and writer Daniel Sibony (1988: 118) has defined the assimilationist project in the following terms: 'Assimilation means making the same...either assimilating oneself to the other or assimilating the other to oneself, dissolving the other in oneself or dissolving oneself in the other.' The dissolution of 'the other' and the immutable fixing of 'the other' both deny the unsettling, unnameable and irrecuperable difference of 'the other': 'There is always a left-over which cannot be recuperated. Whether one believes that one can master it or not, it is always *there*' (Sibony 1988: 118). Elsewhere Sibony (1997: 36) suggests that the two 'logics' of racism are really one and the same: 'The two manoeuvres of the "racist" – designating the other as *inferior* or as *different* (therefore fixing him in his difference) – is really one single logic.' He maintains that 'assimilation is only possible in conjunction with its opposite, namely the most extreme form of differentiation' (1997: 142). Ingestion and expulsion of 'the other' could therefore be seen as two sides of the same process of fixing the boundaries of the self in relation to 'the other', that same Utopian dream of ordering the world according to the new scientific 'evidence' concerning humanity. Both contained the seeds of a violence to 'the other' which, when allowed to flourish fully through a developing industrial and bureaucratic complex, resulted in apocalyptic violence (cf. Bauman 1988). It is precisely these seeds that anti-humanist philosophy of the post-war period has attempted to uproot (see Chapter 1).

It is not my intention here to discuss racism and modernity

exhaustively (see, for example, Wieviorka (ed.) 1993; Rattansi 1994) but simply to provide the context for considering forms of racism in France today. The 'logics' of modern racism are a product of that brief period in the history of 'Man' in which the confident and proselytizing message of Western patriarchal thinking was converted into the universal aspirations for the whole of humanity. Modern forms of racism are an integral part of a process which included the scientific classification and hierarchical ordering of groups according to Western values, the nationalization of society through the developing institutions of the state, the conquest of foreign lands through a mixture of military, administrative and ideological power, and the Janus-faced contextualization of identity within a mythologized past and a brave-new-world future.

However, if racism is inextricably linked to modernity, then might one expect that in the age of the end of modernity (if that is indeed the period we inhabit today) racism itself would disappear? If universalism has broken down, if Western values have been relativized in the wake of the empire's fightback, if the rivets which fused nation, state and culture have come apart through globalization and localization of capital, culture and communications, and if 'the other' has been released from its subjection to scientific laws on human nature (on the one hand) and the creation of 'Man' (on the other), then should racism not also have withered away in the process? Unfortunately, we know that the answer to this question is 'no'.

Culture, difference and identity

For more than a decade, a number of analysts have used the term 'new racism (*néo-racisme*)' to describe forms of racism which are substantially different from those of the modern era (Barker 1981; Balibar in Balibar and Wallerstein 1988; Bauman 1991a; Gilroy 1987; Guillaumin 1991, Taguieff 1988b). It is generally agreed that the major defining feature of this new racism is its abandonment of the old discourse of racial purity and racial hierarchy in favour of one based on cultural difference and cultural essentialism. Racial discourse is too closely associated with a discredited Nazism and condemned colonialism to be respectable today, whereas under the banner of 'culture' and 'nation' the stigmatization of particular groups can be couched in a more acceptable form. Taguieff (1995a: 305) emphasizes the more indirect and implicit nature of this discourse, in which racist sentiment can be 'expressed without being declared, a substitute for direct and declared (or assumed) racism. The new discursive modes of racialization operate on the level of what is understood, implicit, connoted and presupposed.' Jean-Marie Le Pen's infamous description of the Holocaust as a 'detail' in the history of the Second World War is a good example of this, as is his apparently innocuous and 'common-sense' remark, cited by Georges Kiejman in *Le Figaro* (12–13 May 1990), that 'the Jews have too much power in the press just as the Bretons have in sea-faring and the Corsicans in custom controls'. Etienne Balibar has described this indirect form of racism as a 'racism without races' (Balibar and Wallerstein 1988: 32–33). It could be argued that the whole discourse on 'immigration', the 'problems of the suburbs' and 'national identity' is symptomatic of this discursive shift (Silverman 1992). It is within the context of these areas – new migrations, the changing city and the crisis of the nation-state – that concepts of self and other, and insiders and outsiders have been rearticulated in contemporary France, employing a language of cultural difference (religion, language, traditions, food, and so on) far more than the more overtly racist language of racial superiority and inferiority based on biological differences (cf. Gilroy 1992: 53).

Of course, the discourse of cultural difference is not entirely new, as we have seen in the case of Ernest Renan. Todorov (1989) demonstrates convincingly how, in the writings of a number of other prominent philosophers and historians of the second half of the nineteenth century (Taine and Le Bon, for example), the notion of race is transposed from the physical to the cultural plane. In the hands of these authors, culture (employed in an absolutist or essentialist way) can compartmentalize peoples in much the same way as race. Daniel Sibony (1993: 141) suggests that the ethno-cultural base of racism has a much longer pedigree still, for hatred of 'the other' has always had a cultural component. In the modern era, most racisms have combined biology with culture to stigmatize others. Indeed, in France, as Balibar has observed (1991: 79), 'cultural difference has always received at least as much, if not more, attention than the strictly biological discourse'.

However, the long-standing tradition of ethno-cultural racisms should not blind us to the function and status today of 'the cultural turn'. The contemporary discourse of cultural difference is not related to the universalist project of modern society or the scientific and hierarchical classification of peoples but, on the contrary, to the breakdown of that project, the shift from a hierarchical to a relativist perspective, and the rise of ethnic and cultural identities. In other words, the new racism of cultural difference is a symptom of the new times in which we live. As such it is bound up with those larger transformations of Western democracies that we have termed 'postmodern'. Indeed, the rise of cultural difference is probably one of the most potent signs of postmodernity. We need to consider some of the ways in which recent developments have produced new forms of discrimination and new modes of racist expression.

On one level, the rise of cultural difference needs to be seen within the post-Holocaust and anti-colonial context of the 1940s and 1950s. It was at that time that the contemporary notion of the right to difference made its first major intellectual and political impact on French universalism.[2] The desire to delegitimize the scientific status of race after the Second World War was accompanied by a search for a new understanding of the relationships between peoples. UNESCO played an important part in this project through its declarations from 1949 onwards which effectively announced the death of scientific theories of racism (Taguieff 1995a: 272). The crucial task was, as Colette Guillaumin observes (1991: 11), that of 'dissociating somatic from social and mental characteristics, and of breaking the links between these two areas which had hitherto constituted the meaning of the term "race" itself'.

An influential text which came out of this prodigious effort was *Race et histoire* (1952) by Claude Lévi-Strauss. In this work Lévi-Strauss detaches culture from race and suggests that the former is not determined by the latter (although he does not question the very concept of race itself as a valid category for the classification of peoples). His text is a plea for the recognition of the diversity of cultures which is threatened by Western assimilationism's quest for uniformity. He critiques the ethnocentrism of Western universalism and proposes a respect for different cultures founded on a relativism of values. Taguieff (1995a: 284) defines the three central characteristics of this 'culturalist' and anti-Western post-war anti-racism (cf. Leiris 1969): 'the autonomy of cultural phenomena, culture as the major determinant of mental structures and forms of life, and the equal value of all cultures'.

In the hands of Franz Fanon and Albert Memmi, the anti-Western thrust of Lévi-Strauss's argument and the call for a right to cultural difference of subjected peoples (underpinned by an obsessive engagement with Sartreian existentialist philosophy) became the centrepiece of anti-colonial theory in the 1950s. Anti-ethnocentric and 'culturalist' anthropology and anti-Western colonial struggles therefore played a major role in transforming post-war thinking from a belief in the hierarchy of races to the recognition of a diversity of cultures. The new social movements of the 1960s exploited the calls for diversity and difference in their attack on the centralizing and unitarian nature of the state. The recognition of culture as what people do and the customs they practise (the conjoining of the anthropological and socio-logical definitions of culture – see Chapter 4) became the rallying cry for anti-authoritarian liberation struggles, civil rights movements and counter-cultural movements across a range of social strata.

These developments are well documented and need little expansion here. Where they are crucial to the rise of new racisms is the New Right's adoption of the same categories of cultural difference for the purpose of exclusion. Colette Guillaumin (1991) has discussed the appropriation by the New Right of a discourse which had its roots in the anti-colonial and civil rights movements of the Left. Pierre-André Taguieff has been an even more assiduous analyst of the ways in which the New Right has made this discourse its own. His detailed study of the philosopher Alain de Benoist in the context of New Right discourse (Taguieff 1994) demonstrates the way in which Lévi-Strauss's formula for the preservation of cultures endangered by the imperial-istic universalism of the West (see, for example, the preface to *Le Regard éloigné*, 1983) also provides the perfect *raison d'être* for the defence of a European civilization which is threatened today by global capitalism and the incessant mixing of cultures and peoples.[3] There are clearly echoes here of the fears of mixing, miscegenation and hybridity expressed by the Comte de Gobineau in his classic study of 'the races' between 1853 and 1855, *On the Inequality of the Human Races* (*Essai sur l'inégalité des races humaines*). Yet Benoist's ideas (which are character-istic of a particular type of New Right thinking intent on preserving 'European civilization') have little to do with the scientific racism of Gobineau's time, founded on the hierarchical distinction between higher and lower races.[4] Benoist's position is based on the postmodern anti-universalist platform of the right to cultural difference in the name of cultural pluralism and diversity. As we shall see, this appro-priation of the anti-racist discourse of difference makes this new racism not only 'respectable' but also far more difficult to confront than theo-ries grounded in a morally discredited biological essentialism and hierarchy.

If modern forms of racism were generally centred first and foremost on a stigmatization of 'the other' ('altero-referential' racism), then postmodern forms of racism founded on cultural difference are more centred on the definition of the self and an exclusion of 'the other' ('auto-referential' racism; cf. Taguieff 1988a).[5] In other words, we can detect here the end of the confident assimilationist logic of high modernity (which was indeed the clearest example of an 'altero-referential' racism, the self not even identified as a 'race'), and the signs of a retreat into a relativist cultural essentialism, founded on a definition of the particular characteristics of the 'home' community and its differences from other communities.

Contemporary racialized nationalism is preoccupied with self-protection, not self-aggrandisement. As the philosopher and cultural critic Gilles Lipovetsky (1990: 267) remarks, it has no connection with the nineteenth-century ideological project of assimilation of people to form a grand collectivity: '[Today] nationalist ideology is of secondary importance, or even of no importance at all, compared to our expectation that everyone belongs in their own place [*chacun chez soi*], and our individualistic requirement for protection by the powers that be.' All the major slogans of the Front National are indications of this particularistic concern with defining and preserving the cultural/national boundaries of this community.[6] The nationalism of the Front National fits the postmodern paradigm of defensive and particularistic nationalisms in a fragmented world, rather than the modern paradigms of assimilationist or differentialist nationalisms (despite the obvious similarities with the latter). As Lyotard observes:

> The multiplication of independence struggles since the Second World War and the recognition of new nations seem to indicate the reinforcement of the concept of local legitimacy and the end of the grand horizon of universal emancipation.... As the slogan of the Front National proclaims, 'French first [*les Français d'abord*]'.
>
> (Lyotard 1988a: 54)

New nationalisms coincide with the end of *le roman national*, that is the end of the classical modern nation considered in terms of historical time and universal emancipation.

Yet this brief description of the appropriation of the discourse of cultural difference by New Right ideologues – dislodging it from its previous articulation within the 'left-wing' anti-universalist, anti-ethnocentric and anti-state discourses of the post-war period, and rearticulating it within a discourse of cultural essentialism, non-mixing and the separation of groups – itself needs to be contextualized within a wider consideration of forms of identification and difference in contemporary France. As Balibar observes (1991: 79), it is not sufficient simply to outline a shift in discourse without also considering 'which structural changes have taken place in our societies which can account for this shift'.

The framework proposed by Michel Wieviorka does precisely this by situating the rise of new racisms in the context of the crisis of the structures of modernity and the advent of a post-industrial society. In

L'Espace du racisme (1991) Wieviorka argues that the contemporary racism of cultural difference acquires its significance in the context of the crisis of universalism and the decline of the strong social relations established in industrial society. The breakdown in the ability of the modern institutions of industrial society and the republican tradition (state education, secularism in the public sphere, trade unions, political parties, the army, and so on; cf. Nicolet 1982) to integrate people around the common projects of equality and *solidarité* ('an industrial, republican and universalist France', Wieviorka 1993b: 202) has opened up a new space for the clash of cultural identities. The end of industrial society has led to the break-up of the former hierarchical class structure in favour of a model based on individualism and consumption and characterized by the 'dualization of society': 'you are either *in* or *out*' (Wieviorka 1992: 29). It has also produced new urban degradation mimicking the model of the American ghettos in which 'social exclusion can be seen to be reinforced by a spatial exclusion' (Wieviorka 1992: 31). Religion has returned as a major player in the stakes for communal construction of identity, as the secular and 'neutral' ideal of the Third Republic and the homogenizing aspirations of the nation-state falter in an age of pluralism and new ethnicities.

Yet religion is but one example of the rise of particularist cultural identities which have come to fill the gap left by the breakdown in social relations and the decline of social movements.[7] The political scientist Sami Naïr proposes a similar analysis to that of Wieviorka:

> Today's civilization is founded on the unfettered globalization of the economy, the general deregulation of social systems and the institutional breakdown of the nation. These processes have undermined traditional forms of collective solidarity, accentuated selfish individualism and provoked irrational defensive reactions in which ethnic membership re-emerges as social identities disappear and religious affiliation is consolidated as ideological and collective identifications fragment. In this situation, ethnicity is of crucial importance as in ex-Yugoslavia.
>
> ('Où va la France?', *Le Monde*, 16 June 1993)

The framework employed by Wieviorka and other sociologists who form part of the CADIS (Centre d'analyse et d'intervention sociologiques) at the Ecole des Hautes Etudes en Sciences Sociales in Paris (cf. Touraine 1992 and 1994, Dubet and Lapeyronnie 1992, Lapeyronnie 1993, Wieviorka, ed., 1997; see also Naïr 1992) is an important model for understanding contemporary racism. First, such an approach eschews the dominant perspective on popular racism which conflates racism and the Front National. The demonization of Le Pen simply marginalizes racism by situating it within a manichean concept of good and evil, and allows others to adopt (too easily and conveniently) the moral high ground (this is precisely what Jean Baudrillard has argued in 'La conjuration des imbéciles', *Libération*, 7 May 1997). Second, by situating contemporary racisms within the recent transformations of Western societies, these commentators avoid viewing racism today as a simple repetition of ideologies and practices of the past.[8] Taguieff has frequently made both these points in his numerous critiques of anti-racism.

However, if the model of post-industrial society is indispensable for understanding new racisms, other aspects of postmodern society should also be considered. For example, the wider cultural effects of social and economic upheaval are also crucial to the nature of difference today and the creation of new types of identity formation. The de-industrialization of the West ('less and less industrial and more and more based on technology and information', Naïr 1992: 221), the globalization of economies and communications, and the migration of peoples in the post-colonial era have certainly shattered the two major forms of identification of the modern period, those of class and nation. It is also true that the state no longer has the power (or indeed the will) to indulge in the social engineering of a homogeneous nation that characterized the centralizing state of the Third Republic; nor is it the focus of all aspirations to power now that power relations are dispersed across a range of local and global networks. Foucault's analyses of the multidimensional (rather than monolithic) nature of power flows (and also identities) are an important insight into the more fragmented and pluralist nature of postmodern societies within which contemporary racism flourishes (see also Chapter 5).

Yet the globalization of the economy and communications has also had a remarkable effect on cultural flows and time–space perception which impinge directly on identities and communities. Time–space compression (Harvey 1989) has confused the distinctions between places and times. What was distant now appears close; the frontiers separating one place from another appear to be porous; the globe has become compressed into a flat and undifferentiated space. Similarly, the ubiquity of the image (see Chapter 4) has flattened the distinction between past and present; simultaneity has converted chronological time into a ceaseless present. The specificity of geographical place is no longer commensurate with the free-floating nature of mental space, while the connection between a common past and a shared present has been severed for good.

On the one hand, this seems to be a process of reducing everything to the same, a new uniformity produced by the superimposition and condensation of disparate elements (hence the calls by some for a fixing of boundaries and a recreation of differences). On the other hand, it is quite the opposite process which seems to be at work, one in which nothing can stem the ceaseless tide of fragmentation, discontinuity, rupture and dislocation (hence the calls by others for a new universalism and a halt to ceaseless differentiation). Given this massive acceleration in change (is postmodernity simply accelerated modernity?), cultures and identities have been disembedded in a far more radical way than was ever possible in the classical period of modernity. Dislocated from specific times and places, the 'signs' of culture are free-floating, no longer solid or fixed, juxtaposed and rearranged in a weightless space (you don't have to be a Jew to eat a bagel). Cultures are in a state of constant flux, identities have lost their anchorage in anything solid.

In Chapter 3 we will describe this development (following Lyotard, Bauman and others) as the triumph of aesthetic spacing over cognitive or rational spacing: that is, the breakdown in the hierarchical rational planning of societies in favour of a market-led play of seduction and consumption. In this context, relationships are fleeting, contractual, temporary and contingent. As we will see, there are two broad responses to this state of affairs which depend, ultimately, on new relations of power today – but which are both crucial for an understanding of new racisms. On the one hand, there are those who have the means to 'go with the flow', the nomads whose pleasure is derived from the hybrid nature of identity and the contingent nature of postmodern life. On the other hand, there are those for whom the absence of guidelines and boundaries is a profoundly anxious and fearful moment. For them, any raft in the sea of flux is a small mercy. The ever more desperate search for a fixed, pure and uncontaminated culture, and the obsession with community, fixed frontiers and a sense of 'home' are therefore the flip-side to the dislocation and fragmentation of cultures and identities that we are experiencing today. As Etienne Balibar (1998: 115) has observed, we are caught between two extremes: 'a monolithic and univocal sense of identity and a floating identity which has no specific ties or traditions'. (For a tragi-comic fictional exploration of these extremes, see Hanif Kureishi's novel *The Black Album*.)

The first of these responses might more obviously be connected to new racisms, yet the second response is not completely exempt from any connection. Free-floating identity founded on ceaseless differentiation can lead to a depersonalization every bit as troubling as the depersonalization of monolithic concepts of self and other. Furthermore, the celebration of difference can easily flip over to the fear of it. Even if Daniel Sibony (1988: 10) is surely correct when he states (rather broadly) that 'racism means not accepting difference', we should be equally aware of the extent to which the apparent acceptance of difference today is not altogether unproblematic. This is not simply a question of the forms of cultural differentialism employed by the New Right which we discussed previously, which utilize an essentialist form of difference to preserve the 'purity' of the home community and exclude others. It is more a question of the narrow dividing line between celebration and fear and the fact, as Bauman observes, that postmodern tolerance is not that far removed from postmodern intolerance (1993: 238). The Italian psychoanalyst and social theorist Alberto Melucci (1996: 50) puts this ambivalence in the following way: 'The defensive resistance to the "other" is easily transformed into an aggressive attitude against the threat that the other represents. But also the claims to reciprocal understanding and communication are not entirely free from defensive attitudes.' In other words, these two responses are not opposites but are interrelated products of postmodern aesthetic spacing. 'The other' can be left as unprotected with the first response as with the second.

This ambivalence around difference is a product of the new individualism and the new communitarianism of contemporary life. It arises from a situation in which the task of creating identity has fallen on to the shoulders of the individual and where more 'organic' communities have broken down. In the high period of modernity (especially after 1870 under the Third Republic) the project of constructing identity was a fundamental aspect of the role of the state. It was the state's duty to fix the frontiers (territorial and imaginary) of the national community (cf. Noiriel 1988). Rootedness within a particular land and the consequent fixing of the frontiers between self and other were increasingly institutionalized, thus to a large extent removing that responsibility (and the moral consequences which resulted from it) from the individual. Today, the unriveting of that link between nation and state through the accelerating privatization of the state and the globalization of flows of capital, culture and information (which respect no national frontiers) means that the task of constructing identities and communities has, effectively, been deinstitutionalized. The individual has been left with the lonely task of self-improvement and self-construction.

In this context, difference is no longer a stain which states are required to remove, a stigma in the blinding light of rational thought, emancipation and progress, what we must lose in order to achieve equal status with fellow citizens; the state no longer indulges in that form of cultural crusade. On the contrary, difference is today what we must achieve as a demonstration of identity. We are all required to proclaim our own difference. But, abandoned by institutions which could ground it in something solid, dependent on our own efforts to bring it into existence, identity today is a flimsy affair. It is contingent, rudderless and insubstantial. The privatization of identity-construction which has accompanied 'the reflexive, artificial and constructed character of social life' (Melucci 1996: 43) means that communities must be imagined by a force of will on the part of the members alone. These postmodern imagined communities, unlike their modern counterparts (Anderson 1983), are not underpinned by the institutions of the state (or, if at all, only in symbolic fashion like the derisory political announcements of national sovereignty).

The sociologist Michel Maffesoli has characterized such communities as 'neo-tribes'. These are collectivities which show all the signs of postmodern developments and are therefore not to be confused with the grand collectivities of the age of modernity, such as the proletariat or the bourgeoisie who were ' "historical subjects" who had a mission to perform' (1988: 22). Neo-tribes are ephemeral groupings, dependent for their existence on affective ties, feeling and empathy, and on the dissolution of the distinction between self and other, subject and object (and other binary oppositions). Using a model which echoes the distinction mentioned above between cognitive/rational spacing and aesthetic spacing, Maffesoli describes this development as the substitution of 'rationalized *social* planning by a *"sociability"* founded on empathy' (ibid.: 23). The former was defined by precise contours, 'clear demarcations, a plan and a goal' (ibid.: 111); the latter is imprecise, hybrid, unstable and contingent. Neo-tribes are postmodernity's response to aesthetic space (*socialité*) in the way that the classes were modernity's response to cognitive space (*un social rationalisé*).

Maffesoli (1986: 94) emphasizes the importance of technological advances in the multiplication of networks today. The new heterogeneity and polyculturalism of social spaces (which Maffesoli describes as the dominance of Dionysiac forces) is underpinned largely by 'communication, pleasure in the here and now and the incoherence derived from emotional responses...which produce both contact and rejection at one and the same time'. Here, then, we see once again the double-edged nature of contemporary encounters which can slide between the poles of attraction and rejection. Maffesoli observes that this ambivalence, which is familiar within the realm of psychology, needs to be considered more fully in terms of its social manifestations.

Gilles Lipovetsky uses a similar analysis to that of Maffesoli and also emphasizes the differences between this postmodern form of 'tribalization' (founded on the self-construction of identity) and the modern system of classes:

> Postmodern 'tribalization' has nothing to do with the socialization of classes. What is significant today is the heterogeneous fragmentation of groups and the manifestation of ethnic and cultural signs as markers of identity. Neither is tribalization the communitarian reaction to contemporary neo-individualism. In fact, it is the other face of neo-individualism, both violent and unattached to class. The ethnicity which informs youth culture is not received from outside but is an 'autonomous' reconstruction of social ties, a *bricolage* made up of heterogeneous borrowings and traditions specific to urban everyday life. The flaunting of identity and ethnicity is a postmodern pick-and-mix culture. It is all about self-designation, affirmation of an identity in opposition to others, creating new networks of solidarity, manifesting one's sense of self [through] a patchwork of ethnic, graphic and vestimentary signs.
>
> (Lipovetsky 1991: 115)

New racisms could therefore be said to be largely the product of the clash of neo-tribes, in the way that modern forms of racism were the product of the historical mission of nations and races. They are born from the fragmentation of the clear and rational structures of modernity, a loss of rootedness, a need to (re)invent an ancestry and to construct one's own existence in a deinstitutionalized age. The difference which is celebrated today in the name of 'identity' or 'community' is brittle and fragile, more froth than substance, dependent on marketing, self-proclamation, visibility in the media, yet lacking the firm foundations to make it 'stick', and liable at any moment to dissolve into nothing. However, in a world where difference is the badge of identity (at the same time, as we noted above, that global capital, culture and communications have produced uniformity on an unprecedented scale) nobody can afford to be without their difference and their own specific history. Consequently, difference needs to be imagined and reimagined, invented and reinvented, constantly in search of itself. The construction of cultural identity and difference today lacks the confident, universalizing and proselytizing aspirations of modernity. It is a defensive project, staking out its space in a world splintered along ethnic, religious and cultural lines.

It is precisely the fragile and precarious nature of these neo-tribes, their need to reaffirm their identity (their difference, their distance, their territory) that makes conflict between them more likely and breeds a violence aimed at the most visible signs of 'otherness': for example, headscarves, synagogues, mosques, gravestones and so on. Bauman has highlighted the *symbolic* significance underlying the imagining of communities today:

> In the world of imagined communities, the struggle for survival is a struggle for access to the human imagination. Whatever events therefore succeed in gaining such access (street battles before and after football matches, hijacking of planes, targeted or haphazard acts of terrorism, desecration of graves, daubing offensive graffiti on cult buildings, poisoning or contaminating supermarket food, occupying public squares, taking hostages, stripping in public, mass marches or city riots) do so first and foremost in their semiotic, symbolic quality. Whatever the damage actually visited upon the intended or accidental victims of display, it is the *symbolic* significance that counts – the capturing of public imagination.
>
> (Bauman 1992: xx)

Recent reports on racist violence in France reinforce this aspect of violence today. For example, the 1991 report by the National Consultative Commission on Human Rights (Commission nationale consultative des droits de l'Homme) suggested that although acts of physical racial violence had not increased, there had been a significant increase in acts of 'symbolic' racial violence (Silverman 1995a). The desecration of Jewish graves in Carpentras (9–10 May 1990) was the most publicized example of symbolic racist attacks in recent years, but the increase in graffiti, the desecration of other graves (Jewish and Muslim), racist tracts, revisionist history denying the Holocaust, anonymous telephone calls, and so on, are other examples of what has been termed the 'banalization of racism'.

Here, we are back once again with today's more 'casual' racism, employing the discourse of cultural difference, that we discussed earlier in this chapter. Taguieff also calls it a symbolic racism: 'Symbolic racism manifests itself, in public political discourse, by strategies of presentation and representation which correspond to the conditions of legitimate and acceptable behaviour in the public arena appropriate to the specific historical conjuncture' (1995a: 306).

Lipovetsky too believes that the essence of the new racism lies in its symbolic nature:

> Antisemitic and xenophobic violence is more symbolic than aimed at particular people. Herein lies its novelty: at a time when threats, graffiti, insults, tracts and grave desecrations are increasing in number, open and explicit violence of a racist or xenophobic kind is on the decrease. Social hatred of the other is aimed less at people and more at symbols, less at the living and more at the dead.
>
> (Lipovetsky 1992: 157)

The detour that we have taken has hopefully enlarged upon the nature of the 'specific historical conjuncture' which underlies this 'symbolic racism'. The 'banalization of racism' is a result of the breakdown in modern oppositions discussed by Maffesoli, the end of a 'strong' moral order, the flattening of history, the relativism of values and the break with old taboos. It emerges with the rise of postmodern democratic and pluralist society whose divisions and exclusions are founded on a retreat into an individualistic sense of belonging and an indifference towards others (cf. Lipovetsky 1992: 158–159). We can no longer be shocked; often we cannot even tell the difference between real and imagined violence. Jean-Pierre Le Goff makes the association between this new indifference to violence and our 'society of spectacle':

> When the intolerable becomes a spectacle or is transformed into a 'social fact', then indifference is the result. What can one do in the face of the daily spectacle of catastrophes, horrors and misery in the world? The repetition of images of suffering devalues their significance and renders us powerless to do anything about it.
>
> (Le Goff 1996: 219) (see Chapter 4)

The down-side of the thirst for and acceptance of difference is therefore the onset of indifference, or, as Charles Newman remarks (1984: 9) in relation to an 'anything goes' artistic culture, 'a tolerance which finally amounts to indifference'.

Difference is no longer to be effaced; it is desirable. But, as we have noted, the desire for difference is not that far removed from the fear of ceaseless difference. Henry Louis Gates Jr observes, in relation to the way in which black culture has become youth culture in contemporary London, that the fact that it is hip for young working-class white kids to speak with a Jamaican inflection does not mean that racism has disappeared: 'Imitation and enmity have an uncanny ability to coexist' ('Black flash', *Guardian*, 19 July 1997). It is this slippage between the two which characterizes contemporary France. The multiple encounters and interactions of contemporary life produce equal mixtures of celebration and fear of difference, and can ultimately anaesthetize us to the plight of 'the other'.

In which case, the otherness of 'the other' (*altérité*) which is simply not recuperable (*non-récupérable*), always 'unmanageable, threatening, explosive' (Baudrillard and Guillaume 1994: 13) – what Julia Kristeva (1988) has termed 'strangeness (*l'étrangeté*)', Jean Baudrillard and Marc Guillaume (1994) 'radical otherness (*l'altérité radicale*)', Zygmunt Bauman (1991a) 'ambivalence' – might be as elusive a (non)product today (if not more so) than it was in the modern era. If, as Guillaume says (Baudrillard and Guillaume 1994: 19), 'otherness always constitutes a provocation', then we might ask (as we will in Chapter 4 regarding the end of the shock of the new, and the end of the avant-garde) whether we are today in an age when *altérité* has died another death (just when we thought that the end of the modern, assimilationist and colonialist era would liberate us from this 'normalizing' and ethnocentric project), not because it has been obliterated through assimilation but simply because we have become anaesthetized against its power to provoke. In other words, are we at the end of our ability to be 'radically provoked' because, in an age when anything goes, nothing really matters and therefore nothing is shocking or transgressive – even though, as Baudrillard and Guillaume point out (1994: 13), 'what has been embalmed or normalized can come to life at any moment'?

The 'ends' of anti-racism

A number of the above remarks are clearly not only applicable to contemporary France but are relevant to other modern democracies as well. Globalized capital and communications and the postcolonial migrations of peoples have created new contacts and a new sort of hybrid life (especially in the cities) in many such societies. The new individualism has profoundly undermined older forms of social collectivity and has led to the atomization of passions and the privatization of identity formation. As Sami Naïr (Naïr and Lucas 1996: 46) has observed, 'the crisis of individuality, the displacement of the meaning of norms and values, the ambiguities of diversity and the unsettling nature of difference are all signs of the emergence of problematic identifications'. It is in this context of fragmentation of identity, the break-up of established time–space structures, and the creation of new cultural fusions and syncretisms that difference (celebratory or hostile) acquires its contemporary significance (cf. Rattansi 1994: 27–28). The ubiquitous and ambiguous use of cultural difference has blurred the divisions between Left and Right, and between 'racists' and 'anti-racists' in a number of countries.[9]

Where France is perhaps different in relation to these transformations is in the stark discrepancy between a powerful republican political culture (Nicolet 1982) and contemporary everyday life, between institutions and ideologies fashioned during the Third Republic and practices which have little to do with that era. Sami Naïr (1992: 219) talks of 'a republican model which has run out of steam' and asks, 'Are we not in the process of breaking definitively with the Third Republic?' (1992: 222). The arena of racism and anti-racism is a good case in point. Elsewhere (Silverman 1992) I have tried to show how the racisms and anti-racisms which have emerged from the politicization of immigration are profoundly connected with a republican (and highly mythologized) model of the nation founded on universalism, individual assimilation, secularism (*laïcité*) and the neutrality of the public sphere, and in which signs of difference are stigmatized as contrary to the French tradition (cf. Blatt 1997). This classical Enlightenment perspective was highlighted at the time of the headscarf affair of 1989 when three Muslim girls breached the secular code of French schooling by wearing their Islamic headscarves in class (Gaspard and Khosrokhavar 1995; Dubet 1997). Yet the same focus surfaces routinely in the context of the question of 'immigration' and the 'problems of the suburbs'. In the discourse of many, the 'invasion' of cultural identities into the supposedly neutral political sphere (conflating the particular with the universal) is a recent phenomenon which must be resisted if social cohesion is to be preserved. The rise of cultural/ethnic identities is attributed to a confusing variety of sources: the 'invasion' of the cultural difference of the new 'immigrants' (used euphemistically to signify 'North Africans' and their children); the 'invasion' of the American-inspired differentialist discourse of anti-racism into the assimilationist sphere of the French republican tradition; the 'invasion' of the racist discourse and practices of the Front National into the 'anti-racist' republican tradition. This demonization of difference by republicans often goes hand in hand with the view that any concession to 'Anglo-Saxon' concepts of ethnic identity is simply a reinforcement of Le Pen's exclusivist brand of cultural nationalism, or, worse still, an endorsement of the racial policies of Nazi Germany and South African apartheid (Todorov 1995). In the republican tradition, multiculturalism is therefore too closely associated with racist forms of segregation to be considered as an acceptable path towards increased rights and protection from discrimination.

The more liberal proponents of this version of French universalist republicanism (for example, Dominique Schnapper and Tzvetan Todorov) are simply guilty of re-enacting the Dreyfus affair in an age when the clear oppositions between republican and 'ethnic' nationalists can no longer be creditably maintained. But the more extreme proponents of a similar argument are far more dangerous. In the worst cases of this (mis)reading of French history, France was 'race-free' before contemporary immigration and it is new forms of anti-racism (especially that of SOS Racisme of the 1980s) which are responsible for racializing French society, and the 'right to difference (*le droit à la différence*)' which is responsible for the ghettoization of communities in the manner of 'the Anglo-Saxon world (*le monde anglo-saxon*)'; (see, for example, Yonnet 1990 and 1993, Béjin and Freund 1986, Finkielkraut 1987 and Todd 1994).[10] Here 'cultural difference' – a product of what Agnes Heller and Ferenc Fehér (1988: 6) have termed 'the breakdown of the grand narrative of secularization' – becomes a euphemism for 'anti-France'.

It is true that many countries have experienced a similar backlash against 'multiculturalism' and the relativism of values introduced through the recognition of cultural difference. It is also true that the discourse of 'multiculturalism' risks reproducing the very discourse employed (in essentialist fashion) by the New Right to separate 'communities' for the purpose of exclusion (Silverman 1995b). One of the major questions for all Western democracies today is how to harness a respect for multidimensional differences to the need for common rules and social solidarity. Yet few have presented this problem in quite such manichean terms as France, since few pursued the modern universalist and Utopian dream of emancipation with quite the same rigour, enthusiasm and confidence as under the Third Republic. Today a republican political culture still profoundly attached to those modern ideals is frequently at odds with the post-colonial and postmodern reality of contemporary France.

Alain Touraine points up the contradiction when he considers the anachronistic and misleading nature of the belief that ethnic and other communities are simply

> a leftover from the past destined ultimately to disappear. This was the illusion fostered by rationalism: the Enlightenment would remove the shadows cast by the family, the nation and religion.

However, today's modernity is very different: we are immersed in
it body and soul, reason and memory at one and the same time.
(Touraine 1992: 348)

The inability to confront this new reality means that difference is
immediately inserted into the classic modern paradigm of the hierarchical opposition between universalism and particularism, and
consequently castigated as an undesirable foreign import to France (cf.
Wieviorka, ed., 1997: 5–8). This reveals a frightening discrepancy in
France between official discourse and that of republican social
commentary, on the one hand, and everyday life, on the other, in which
cultural/ethnic difference is ubiquitous. It also indicates an anachronistic republican rearguard action to maintain the division between the
(universalist) public and the (particularist) private spheres when they
have manifestly broken down. But, more worrying, it also leaves the
path clear for the Front National to disseminate unchallenged its own
vicious brand of differentialism. Numerous commentators have made
this point, but the political classes and certain social commentators
have shown no real signs of breaking with a cliché-ridden republicanism.

So, at a time when a new social landscape has clearly emerged in
which identities are shifting and multidimensional, and difference is a
fact of life, the tired formula of integration (frequently a euphemism
for assimilation) is still the major political and intellectual response
(cf. Bertheleu 1997). Anti-racism, too, seems incapable of breaking out
of the old paradigm of universalism and difference inherited from the
modern era.[11] Taguieff (1988a) has demonstrated how the two major
forms of anti-racism – differentialist and assimilationist – simply
shadow the two major forms of racism – assimilationist and differentialist respectively. Recently, anti-racism has swung between equality
and difference, or has adopted a mixture of the two. Cornelius
Castoriadis ('Notations sur le racisme', *Connexions*, no. 48, 1987,
quoted in Taguieff 1995a: 530) has denounced 'the euphoric
schizophrenia of the intellectual boy-scouts of recent decades who sing
the praises of both universal human rights *and* the radical difference of
cultures which would forbid any value-judgement to be passed on
other cultures'. Castoriadis is surely right in his criticism, but this is
only because the two poles between which anti-racism has swung are
the extremes of universalism and particularism established in the
modern era as opposites. The real problem here is that equality and
difference are still conceptualized within the modern antithesis of
universalism and particularism. In that framework, it is not difficult to

see the problems with both a concept of universalism founded on Western ethnocentric norms and values (which rejects difference), and a concept of cultural relativism which denies the possibility of any value judgements of other cultures (and therefore has no means of ensuring equality). That is why it is the framework itself which needs to be radically overhauled so that the concepts of universalism and particularism are no longer presented as opposites. The more complex structuring today of culture, difference and identity, discussed above, requires concepts which will be commensurate with the more fragmented and hybrid nature of contemporary life, rather than ones which simply try to fit old formulae to new times.

In a book ambiguously and provocatively entitled *Les Fins de l'antiracisme*, Taguieff (1995a) analyses in depth what he depicts as the confused aims of anti-racism while, at the same time, hinting at the end of anti-racism as we know it (cf. Gilroy 1992). Taguieff criticizes the media-oriented anti-racism of the 1980s (especially that of SOS Racisme) and its political manipulation by a 'mainstream' political class eager to capture the moral high ground and demonize Le Pen and the Front National. Anti-racism became a suitable logo either for selling products (for example, the Benetton adverts) or selling political parties (for example, the ex-Vichy functionary François Mitterrand joining the march against racism – in a suitable blaze of publicity – after the Carpentras desecrations in 1990). Taguieff is particularly acute in his analysis of the confused strategies and discourses of anti-racism. Yet his views on the 'ends' of anti-racism are, ultimately, disappointing. He argues, in effect, for a revamped universalism in which human rights would not simply be seen as a sign of 'the rationalizing and conquering West' (Taguieff 1995a: 532) but as beyond all particularisms (whatever the provenance of the codes themselves) and genuinely applicable to all and sundry. This is not so much a revamped universalism as a restatement of the conventional (Dreyfusard) republican position in which any renunciation of the separation between 'the public and private spheres, the state and religion, the social and the sacred' is tantamount to a surrender to the demands of 'Catholic reactionaries and "revolutionary" Islamic fundamentalists' (1995a: 532). Not only does this vision reproduce the sort of die-hard republicanism which was so visible at the time of the headscarf affairs, but it also flies in the face of the *de facto* reality of contemporary society in which modernity's demarcation line between the public and private spheres has been breached. In an essay entitled 'Culture, société et démocratie', Michel Wieviorka (in Wieviorka, ed., 1997: 21) highlights the reality of contemporary French society which Taguieff resolutely sets himself against, namely the blurring of the opposition 'between the spaces of political and personal life, between those of men and women, between work and the family, between the collective and the individual, etc.'.

Elsewhere, Taguieff shows the same faith in the ability of the republican nation-state to withstand the assaults on it from supra-national and sub-national forces. In the final section of a recent article entitled 'Par-delà communautarisme et nationalisme: la nation républicaine redécouverte', he extols the virtues of the traditional methods of 'integration' which are still capable of producing a cohesive community of citizens:

> The education system continues to carry out the function of cultural integration, and political action is still the path towards national citizenship, whether it be action of the more traditional sort (working in a political party) or of the newer sort (participating in charity or humanitarian associations). In short, citizenship has not been denationalized and, in spite of everything, the nation has remained the 'community of citizens'. The history of the French Republic is not over yet.
>
> (Taguieff 1995b: 28; see also Taguieff 1996)

This sort of universalist republicanism appears more and more anachronistic today and hardly constitutes a realistic way forward for anti-racism. Michel Wieviorka (1993c: 70) also thinks that 'the idea of the post-national society is premature' and, like Taguieff, fears the breakdown of social integration and the rise of 'worrying differentialist nationalisms, somewhat sinister populisms and claims for ethnicity' (1993c: 22). Nevertheless, he is far more willing to recognize that simple demonization of difference in terms of the rise of fundamentalisms (as in the quote above by Taguieff) is not a realistic proposition in a postmodern landscape:

> More often than not, France, much more than other countries, is wary of sanctioning the presence of difference anywhere outside the private sphere. Rather than accepting it as an element of democratic life, encouraging it to become a source of debate...we prefer in France either to deny difference, or repress it, or demonize it.
>
> ('Pour une politique de l'altérité', *Libération*, 21 December 1994)

Wieviorka situates this attitude to difference (and here he makes the distinction between France and other Western democracies) in the context of the powerful 'republican model of integration' in France. Describing what is specific to 'the French malaise' in his essay 'Culture, société et démocratie', he observes, 'it is still the case that the French feel intensely that their national culture is under threat, both from outside...and from within with the rise of particularisms' (Wieviorka, ed., 1997: 38). Wieviorka believes that, instead of simply demonizing 'Anglo-Saxon' multiculturalism, commentators, activists and policy-makers in France must recognize the realities of cultural difference today. This recognition is especially imperative for the recomposition of the Left in France today and the reconstruction of a democratic platform (see Wieviorka, ed., 1997). He argues for a blending of universalism and particularism, of common goals and the recognition of cultural/ethnic identity: 'I advocate a combination of the right to difference and integration within the framework of the universal values of reason and the law. A certain concept of ethnicity could be compatible with this articulation' ('La France des tribus: un entretien avec Michel Wieviorka', *Témoignage Chrétien*, 28 November 1992). Alain Touraine ('Et quand les banlieues exploseront', *Globe Hebdo*, 5–11 May 1993) takes a similar line, although with typically Gallic reservations about the worst consequences of ethnic identities: 'Nobody would want to encourage a politics of the ghetto with catastrophic consequences, but the fundamental aim of social integration cannot be achieved without some recognition of "cultural identity".'

Yet despite their belief that the reinvention of social democracy today must break with the abstract universalism of the modern era and consider the material aspects of people's lives (including cultural/ethnic identities), both Wieviorka and Touraine seem unwilling to adopt more radical concepts of identity which have been proposed more recently in 'the Anglo-Saxon world'. Wieviorka shows his 'modern' concerns, and the limits of his acceptance of cultural identity, when he views social cohesion as dependent on reducing demands for cultural difference:

> Popular racism is less than before associated with social relations as such, and more with cultural differentialism. This will be even more the case in the future unless the societies in which it occurs prove capable of reformulating the social question, reconstructing social debates and conflicts and preventing unfulfilled social demands from being subsumed within the proliferation of references to identity.
>
> (Wieviorka 1993a: 18)

Wieviorka is surely correct when he claims that it is the attention (and hostility) to the surface signs of cultural difference which underlies the shift of focus of popular racism. This is what I have argued above. Yet his belief that a reformulated social order depends on the reduction in demands for cultural identity appears to contradict his own criticism of the French approach to difference (quoted above), and to reproduce the very scenario which he critiques of a hellish descent into social disintegration and 'ghettoization' along lines of ethnic separatism characteristic of the 'Anglo-Saxon' world.

Wieviorka's theorization of the rise of contemporary cultural identities remains a profound contribution to the analysis of new racisms in post-industrial societies. Similarly, his efforts in liberating the concept of difference and 'multiculturalism' from its demonized representation within the universalist French paradigm (cf. Roman 1995 and Bertheleu 1997) is admirable in terms of the necessary search for a new social contract. However, one has the impression that his acceptance of cultural identity is ultimately constrained by a 'modern' (rather than postmodern) model of society. Fragmentation is conceived through the familiar binary opposition between universalism and particularism. As I suggested above, anti-racism as a whole is caught on the horns of this dilemma. Certainly, one should not underestimate the importance of the reinvention of social ties and social democracy today, as Touraine, Wieviorka and others constantly argue. But it seems misleading to suggest, as Wieviorka does, that the 'space' of racism necessarily decreases in proportion to the 'strength' of social ties. After all, the 'strong' social ties of the modern era did not prevent the rise of virulent forms of racism. In a world in which the modern project of universalism is in crisis and where violence can spring from the struggle for difference, it is the dichotomy itself between universalism and particularism which needs to be reconsidered if new forms of solidarity and democracy are to emerge.

The radical concepts of identity mentioned above that have more recently taken shape in Britain and America – for example, Stuart Hall's version of 'new ethnicities', Homi Bhabha's ideas on hybridity and a 'third way', the search by numerous commentators, activists and practitioners for non-essentialist and non-exclusivist forms of difference – at least have the potential to retheorize racist (and other) exclusions within a 'postmodern frame' (Rattansi 1994): that is, through a recognition of the *inevitable* fragmentation and multidimensional nature of identities in a transformed economic, political and social landscape. Of course, the translation of these ideas into a radical politics which can refashion the 'social' from the new 'sociability'

(Maffesoli 1988) and avoid a neo-liberal new individualism, on the one hand, and a neo-tribal new communitarianism, on the other, is not at all assured. Hence the view (as stated in the introduction to this book) that postmodernity is, in Zygmunt Bauman's words, both chance and menace (Bauman 1991b).

Yet at least there exists (as we suggested in Chapter 1) the impetus to break out of the modern dualism of sameness and difference, and seek a new ethics *vis-à-vis* 'the other' – an impetus derived (paradoxically) largely from French postmodern philosophy but adopted in a more far-reaching way in Britain and America than in France. The 'end' of old anti-racism could signal the beginnings of new anti-racisms whose 'ends' would be more local and multidimensional, and which would be responsive to the transformations in culture, identity and difference that have taken place in recent times.

3   City spaces

The modern city

Most major aspects of modernity can be discovered in the development of the city and city life. Paris, for example, would epitomize the Utopian dream of the 'city of light (*ville lumière*)', the ordered city, the centre of civilization (Roncayolo 1994: 36), in Walter Benjamin's memorable phrase, 'capital of the nineteenth century'. Like the new republican social order being constructed in the second half of the nineteenth century, the city would be founded on the Enlightenment principles of rational design, uniformity and equality. The rhetoric that was to characterize this grand project – especially that of bringing clarity to where there is darkness, order to where there is disorder, coherence to where there is chaos – gave rise to a new vocabulary of metropolitan life, one that would 'make sense' of the city, frequently through the metaphors of the body or the machine (Donald 1992). The Marxist historian and prolific writer on cities Henri Lefebvre shows how the rationale behind the modern ordering of the city could exploit the medical imagery of the unhealthy body which required healing:

> Rational organization perceived the problem as one of constructing order out of chaotic confusion. Disorder is abnormal. How should it be normalized?... Disorder is unhealthy. The doctors of modern society saw their role as doctors of a sick social space. What is the remedy? *Coherence*. The rationalist wanted to restore coherence to a chaotic reality.
>
> (Lefebvre 1968: 27)

However, as with modernity in general, the pursuit of the eradication of chaos, of the ultimate cure for all social ills and of a blueprint for a coherent, ordered and uniform city proved a Herculean and impossible task. Not only did the illusion of equality (produced especially through the uniformity of façades, cf. Loyer 1994: 39) hide real social and economic differences but there were always bits that refused to fit in, leftovers, dirt, unruliness, an excess of meaning, the ambivalence that is the inevitable underside of all such projects for coherence (Bauman 1991a), the ' "refuse" of a functionalist administration (abnormality, deviance, sickness, death, etc.)' (Certeau 1990: 144). Concepts of order bred new concepts of disorder – those troubling bits of waste (dangerous classes, women, foreigners, and so on) which either had to be cleansed and brought into the realm of light (through the process of assimilation), or disciplined and put under surveillance to regulate their behaviour (Foucault 1976), or simply dispensed with. Christopher Prendergast highlights the essential paradox of the modernization of cities:

> the clearer, cleaner and more uniform the city came to appear physically, the more opaque and mysterious it came to seem socially, as governed by a contingent and chaotic play of forces, transactions and interests, to which one could not attach a correspondingly clear description.
>
> (Prendergast 1992: 11)

The classic Janus-face of modernity (brightness and darkness, order and disorder, Nietzsche's Apollonian and Dionysiac forces) was clearly at work in the construction of the modern city. The city's human, civilized public spaces, founded on the principles of rational design, which could bring together and unify a disparate population (especially through new forms of mobility 'which both brought people into close contact with each other and allowed them to move very quickly from one place to another', Roncayolo 1994: 37) coexisted with the dark seething mass of ghettoized slums inhabited by 'the dangerous classes' (Chevalier 1978) – and no amount of policing the frontiers between the two realms could prevent the spillage of one into the other. In other words, the contradictions of modernity lie at the heart of city life. The development of capitalism and rapid industrialization had social effects which no amount of state-led social engineering could contain. The rational mapping of the city was not only incapable of harnessing diversity into a single blueprint for a 'concept city' but inevitably produced its own 'unreadability'. Michel de Certeau, one of the most perspicacious commentators on this tension between order and disorder in the modern city, observed: 'beneath the discourses which ideologized the city proliferated the streets and the multiple combinations of power networks which had no readable identity, could not be mapped conceptually, escaped rational transparency, and which were, in short, impossible to manage' (Certeau 1990: 145).

Beyond the imposition of the single vision, the modern city was therefore transformed into a cornucopia of new sights, sounds and sensations which made it a source of rich cultural, sexual and aesthetic pleasure (and pain) and provided new ways of conceiving of and exploring identity. In Walter Benjamin's terms, the disenchantment of the social world brought about by progressive rationalization (that one sees most clearly, for example, in the Haussmanization of Paris) was accompanied by a re-enchantment brought about by the very by-products of that same process. The new cities became reworkings of the mythological labyrinth in which the clarity of line and the maze, order and disorder, coherence and those elements which inevitably escaped rational control and Utopian planning progressed in tandem. It was this rich tapestry constituted by metropolitan experience which fascinated writers like Balzac, Baudelaire, Flaubert, Zola, Apollinaire, Breton and Aragon, and painters like Manet, Degas and Van Gogh throughout the nineteenth century and into the twentieth. One might even say that the new aesthetic of modernism was essentially an urban phenomenon in that it was, at heart, a response to the movement, the diversity, the random and transitory nature of encounters, and the juxtaposition of disparate elements that characterized life in the new metropolis (cf. Bradbury 1976).

Unlike any other topography, the city provided a complex network within which the tensions between self and other, the individual and the crowd, past and present, near and far, movement and stasis, desire and control – to be found at the centre of the works of many of the above artists and, indeed, at the core of modernism – could be worked out. Modernism explored the interface between the new forms and wonders of the metropolis and human sensibility and desire, for these went hand in hand. As James Donald has said:

> rationalizing plans had unexpected and unintended consequences. One was an emerging aesthetic of modernism: that is, a distinctively new sensuous perception or experience of metropolitan life that was formalized in new techniques of representation and new – modern – artistic movements. These often revealed the products of the reformed cities to be, not just more efficient, but also phantasmagoric, grotesque, and even inhuman.
>
> (Donald 1992: 423)

The Baudelairean figure of the *flâneur*, the gentleman stroller, so brilliantly dissected by Walter Benjamin (1983), is the archetypal manifestation of this fascination with the new and re-enchanted spectacle provided by the modern city. The *flâneur* was to the ordered and regulated city what modernism was to modernity: that is, the counter-culture, the other face, the flip-side which disrupts the circumscribed and institutionalized 'coherence' of rational planning, defies the controlled meanings of modern social spacing and transforms the clarity and 'legibility' of the city into an opaque and magical labyrinth. Fundamental to the pleasure attained by the *flâneur*'s perambulations in the city is the delight taken in the transitory and fleeting nature of the moment, the absence of any attachment to a fixed sense of place or to specific goals, the detached nature of the look (a form of male voyeurism) as opposed to engagement in social relationships, and hence a fascination with the *spectacle* of everyday life. The *flâneur* poeticized and mythologized the new, the transitory and the 'bizarre'. Indeed, Baudelaire maintained that the new poetry must be constructed from the material provided by the new cities. In the figure of the *flâneur*, city space and its everyday life are treated as a way of exploring the inner turbulent life of the looker/poet. The pleasure of the *flâneur* is derived from the transgression of social boundaries, while a new poetry is born from the aestheticization of everyday life in the city.

However, the extent to which the *flâneur* – and indeed modernism as a whole – transgressed social boundaries needs to be put into the wider context of prevailing class and gender relations (among others). The *flâneur* identifies with the marginals of city life, but is also distanced from them in that he is a member not of the impoverished classes but of the leisured class. He is a bourgeois gentleman. Apollinaire's narrator in the poem 'Zone' (the first poem in his 1913 collection *Alcools*) can return to Auteuil, a posh suburb of Paris, after his wanderings in the less salubrious parts of the city. His class therefore allows him a freedom which is not available to those with whom he identifies. Furthermore, the *flâneur*'s aesthetic response to modern city life is profoundly determined by male desire in the public sphere ('a masculine freedom', Wilson 1995: 65), for, as Katherine Gibson and Sophie Watson point out (1995: 4), 'The male gaze of the modernist *flâneur* eroticized life in the city, sexualizing the spaces it viewed' (see, for example, Baudelaire's poem 'A une passante'). As Janet Wolff and Griselda Pollock have both demonstrated convincingly, Baudelaire's figure of the *flâneur*/artist can function as an observer in the crowd, and 'can look without being watched or even recognized in the act of looking' (Pollock 1988: 71) only by dint of his sex (and, as Pollock points out, by his class). Wolff (1985) writes of the invisibility of the female *flâneuse*, a point which is substantiated by Pollock:

> Women did not enjoy the freedom of incognito in the crowd. They were never positioned as the normal occupants of the public realm. They did not have the right to look, to stare, scrutinize or watch.... They are positioned as the *object* of the *flâneur*'s gaze.
>
> (Pollock 1988: 71)

Elizabeth Wilson (1992, 1995), on the other hand, has problematized this view by suggesting that women were not simply objects of male desire and control, not simply denied access to the public sphere in any other form than that of the prostitute (and even then, she wonders, 'could not the prostitutes themselves be seen, ultimately, as the *flâneuses* of the nineteenth-century city?' (1995: 71)), that they were also able to transgress the social/sexual boundaries inscribed in the city, and that the *flâneur* himself represents 'not the triumph of masculine power but...masculinity as unstable, caught up in the violent dislocations that characterized urbanization' (1995: 74).

Gender and class critiques of the *flâneur* highlight the fact that he cannot simply be celebrated unproblematically as transgressive of modern social boundaries since he is himself predicated on the different (though not necessarily fixed) locations with regard to public and private spaces of men and women, and the leisured and working classes (cf. Rifkin 1993: 66). The *flâneur* occupies, instead, an ambivalent position with regard to dominant social norms (an ambivalence which is most apparent when viewed in the context of the commodification of social relations in the developing nineteenth-century metropolis). Cultural modernism in general might therefore more accurately be viewed as the ambivalent counter-culture to rationalizing modernity. It was not completely 'other' to the new social and economic processes of modernity, yet it challenged some of its fundamental tenets. The modern city exemplified this tension between 'determined opposites': between the forces of order and disorder, between the totalizing gaze of the planner and the fragmented and transitory sensations of individual everyday experience, between the 'readable' and the 'unreadable' (Prendergast 1992: 16). The city of light and the public sphere of citizenship, constructed under the ideology of equality, fraternity and liberty, were founded on the social marginalization of women, the proletariat, foreigners and others who could only be represented, within this paradigm, as a problem to be regulated. The Utopian projects of Haussmann in the previous century and Le Corbusier in this century (the city of light and the *machine à habiter* respectively) thus both contained their own inevitable contradictions.

Today cities have been transformed yet again in line with post-industrial and postmodern changes. Debates about the possible death of the city therefore have a resonance that goes far beyond urban questions, for they are symptomatic of a crisis in modernity itself. Olivier Mongin (1995) wonders whether, after the classic European city and then the grand urban Utopias, we have now entered the phase of 'the third city', founded on a new understanding of time and space and the recognition of the fallibility of past Utopias. In his introduction to Mongin's book, entitled *Vers la troisième ville*, the architect Christian de Portzamparc (whose expression 'third city' Mongin has adopted) puts contemporary 'democratic' developments in the city in the context of past experiments and asks the fundamental question as to whether the changes that have taken place in recent years signify an advancement in human freedom or a regression:

> It was assumed that the city could be planned, shaped, controlled by the dominant powers. However, in our contemporary democracies, the city appears to be the result of a multiplicity of contradictory and incoherent processes. It escapes control and unity. Attempts to treat this problem inevitably fail to deal with large areas of city life. Is this unpredictability, multiplicity and disorder the sign of greater freedom? Has the city finally rid itself of its mathematical 'frock-coat', of its architectural 'straitjacket', of the principles of order and intimidation which Georges Bataille so detested since they symbolized a profound suppression of freedom and life?
>
> (cited in Mongin 1995: 9)

The following discussion considers whether the tensions constitutive of modernity have indeed given way to a rather different paradigm for the regulation of city life (more fragmented, more contradictory, more pluralist), and whether this 'democratization' of the city heralds a genuine freedom or whether, instead, it merely announces oppressions of a different sort.

From time to space, from the social to the aesthetic

In his important book on 'the reassertion of space in critical social theory', Edward Soja cites Michel Foucault's description of the change of paradigm that has occurred in recent times, from one concerned with time to one concerned with space:

> The great obsession of the nineteenth century was, as we know, history: with its themes of development and of suspension, of crisis and cycle, themes of ever-accumulating past, with its great preponderance of dead men and the menacing glaciation of the world.... The present epoch will perhaps be above all the epoch of space. We are in the epoch of simultaneity: we are in the epoch of juxtaposition, the epoch of the near and far, of the side-by-side, of the dispersed. We are at a moment, I believe, when our experience of the world is less that of a long life developing through time than that of a network that connects points and intersects with its own skein.
>
> ('Of other spaces', *Diacritics*, 16 (1986), 22–27, cited in Soja 1989: 10)

Foucault clearly sees this shift from time to space as crucial to the shift away from modern forms of organization. The linear and chronological mentality, with its clear distinctions between past, present and future, which is fundamental to the modern notion of progress, collapses into a present space consisting of diverse elements from different 'times' and 'places'. Clearly this movement from time to space was already announced by the revolutionary techniques of cultural modernism. Marcel Proust's *A La Recherche du temps perdu*, like many other works of the period, flattens the chronological life-process of realist narrative by discovering connections across time; it breaks dramatically with a positivist definition of subjectivity by positing instead the power of the unconscious mechanism of memory to transcend purely temporal demarcations; and it announces the classic modernist elision between the past life of a 'character' with the present act/space of the 'writer'. The past is conflated with the present within the space of writing itself. The *flâneur*, as we have seen, operates a similar 'spatialization' of time with regard to the city. His pleasure comes from juxtaposing and rendering simultaneous elements which rational design wishes to confine to separate realms. Like Proust's, his is a metaphorical imagination (see also, for example, the works of Claude Simon). In other words, a diachronic perspective (with its grounding in history) is replaced by a synchronic perspective (with its grounding in the simultaneity of the present) (cf. Kumar 1995: 146–147).

Today's spatialization could therefore be seen as the democratization of connections formerly perceived only by a narrow elite of avant-garde artists and philosophers. But quite clearly the democratization of the spatial imagination is not due to the fact that more people have taken to reading Baudelaire or Proust recently! Numerous processes have contributed to the shift in paradigm noted by Foucault and have affected us all, most notably the globalization of capital and culture and accelerated patterns of migration and forms of travel. In her immensely stimulating (though at times rather reductive) book on the reordering of French culture in the 1950s and 1960s, Kristin Ross (1995: 19) highlights the way in which the car – whose 'production, transformation into discourse (i.e., advertising, media representations), and consumption and use' she takes as exemplary of twentieth-century modernization – institutes a mode of mobility which 'freezes time' and nullifies history. She cites Jean Baudrillard, writing in 1967, on the way in which the mobility of the car collapses time into space:

> Mobility without effort constitutes a kind of unreal happiness, a suspension of existence, an irresponsibility. Speed's effect, by integrating space and time, is one of leveling the world to two dimensions, to an image; it loses its depth and its becoming; in some ways it brings about a sublime immobility and a contemplative state. At more than a hundred miles an hour, there's a presumption of eternity.
>
> (Ross 1995: 21)[1]

This spatialization of time is possibly even more profoundly in debt to the revolution in information flows and communication. Film became the perfect medium for transforming the 'density' of time into the simultaneity of a two-dimensional space, captured on celluloid. Today, the world has shrunk still further to the size of the TV screen and the computer terminal. Never before has such a simultaneity of diverse elements been possible, and never has the juxtaposition of elements separated in time and space been achieved so completely as with the advent of recent technological developments. David Harvey (1989) has coined the term 'time–space compression' to define this phenomenon.

These processes have had a profound effect on the topography of cities and consequently on the nature of the social relations that are produced in the city. The new movement, new encounters and new classes which characterized the new cities of the nineteenth century, and were associated especially with modern forms of industrialization, have today been transformed under the influence of post-industrial late capitalism. The technologization of flows of capital and communications has disrupted the links between place, culture and identity (Massey and Jess, eds, 1995), producing a process of deterritorialization (uprooting our former sense of place and identity) and reterritorialization (positioning us within different time–space networks). The local is itself more and more global: that is, a hybrid space composed of a mosaic of diverse pieces from diverse places.

The juxtaposition of disparate elements in the postmodern city is at the expense of the Utopian search for uniformity and coherence that characterized the modern city. In this transformation we can detect all the tensions between new opportunities and new dangers for social relations that are a feature of the contemporary period. On the one hand, this evolution signifies the end of all blueprints for the regulation of city life, and the possibility of a flowering of new types of expression and encounter. Fragmentation of a 'master' plan (founded on rationalism, coherence and social engineering) heralds the age of diversification and pluralism and the possible emergence of the sort of heterogeneous site (beyond the hierarchies and binaries of 'Cartesian' space) that Foucault (1986) defined as a 'heterotopia'. It is clear that the de-centring of metropolitan experience has seen the emergence of new styles and voices and the cross-fertilization, or hybridization, of culture. What was formerly located at the margins (both in physical and in cultural terms) is now at the centre; or, more properly, the break with universalist, egalitarian (and ethnocentric) norms has flattened the hierarchies of old and dispersed the centre across the surface of the metropole. As Jill Forbes has remarked in relation to new cultural practices in the city:

> The art of the 1980s and 1990s celebrates a different city, one which belongs to the marginal and the underground as the perhaps paradoxical source of creativity and energy.... The hidden or obscure places under and around the city and their eccentric denizens are now taken as its defining locus, its source of meaning and *lieu de vérité*. More than this, the artist no longer observes from a fixed point.... In the 1980s and 1990s [they] are in transit or displacement across the city; their point of view is mobile and fragmented, not all-embracing.
>
> (Forbes and Kelly 1995: 256–257)

Examples of this cult of underground, hidden and exotic Paris can be found in the films *Diva*, *Subway* and *Les Amants du Pont Neuf*. The works of postcolonial writers, film-makers and musicians are also a sign of the new cultural pluralism challenging the Eurocentric norms of old (see Hargreaves and McKinney, eds, 1997). In this sense, the postcolonial and globalized postmodern city could be seen as the locus for an awakening and celebration of previously hidden, stigmatized or repressed voices and the emergence of counter-cultural forms occupying new spaces of resistance to established order (although to what extent they remain marginal and transgressive once they are brought into the realm of the commodification of the cultural 'exotic' is open to debate – see Chapter 4).

However, despite the new opportunities today for voices which were formerly marginalized, it would be naïve to celebrate the virtues of this new democratic and heterogeneous space (in the manner, for example, of Gilles Lipovetsky 1983, and Paul Yonnet 1985) without pointing up also the limitations to freedom imposed by the new order. The optimism of the post-war project of social housing (which saw the construction of the big council estates, or HLM, in the suburbs of the big cities) has more recently given way to the apocalyptic prognostications which have accompanied the 'problems of the suburbs' and the explosive violence of those who feel economically and socially excluded from participation in society. In France, *la banlieue* (the suburbs) has become the major euphemism for the racialization (and fragmentation) of city space, symbolically representing the anxieties and sense of crisis of our age, from the fear of drugs, violence, AIDS and religious fundamentalism to the more general 'malaise' of Western democratic societies. It is as if what was once categorized as the 'underside' of city life, which planners and visionaries of a previous age attempted to order, regulate and control, has now broken free from its former constraints and threatens to 'pollute' the body politic (a vision that Sophie Body-Gendrot has characterized as the ' "third-worldization" of the national space', 1993: 81).

The opening up of a more pluralistic sense of city space therefore carries with it the danger of new forms of fragmentation and segregation along racialized (and other) lines. It is no coincidence that today's social problems are conceptualized less in terms of inequality following class domination and more in terms of marginalization and exclusion (cf. Genestier 1994: 197), for these reflect the *spatial* dimension to disparities in social organization today (cf. the discussion of social exclusion, and the analysis of Alain Touraine, in Chapter 5). This process of spatial fragmentation both fuels new racisms (as we saw in the previous chapter) and is a genuine cause for concern for all those worried by the breakdown in social solidarity and the rise of new forms of exclusion (see Chapter 5). As Jacques Donzelot and Joël Roman have remarked,

> there is no longer an organic link connecting the popular suburbs to the city. The suburbs now exist outside the system, as if they no longer have any *raison d'être* and have simply been left to their own devices. They have become synonymous with exclusion.
>
> (Donzelot and Roman 1991: 6)

Olivier Mongin (1995) highlights two general features which characterize the contemporary crisis of the city: the disjunction between civic culture and urban life and the failure of urban Utopias. Recent developments which have brought about this disjunction between *urbs* and *civitas* are numerous and complex. Lipovetsky (1991) claims that it would be wrong to use nineteenth-century terms to understand this crisis. He suggests that it is the new individualism and narcissism characteristic of postmodern social and cultural developments which provides the major context for an understanding of the contemporary city. The public spaces which were formerly places of sociality and mixing have given way to a privatization of individual needs and desires. Individualistic hedonism has taken over from civic duty and the public interest. He writes:

> the traditional city dominated by the creation of a public sphere is dead. Now the city is constituted by a multiplicity of networks in which individuals associate intermittently according to their personal trajectories and their private interests, motivations and desires.
>
> (Lipovetsky 1991: 108)

The atomization of the social, leading to new freedoms for some but new tensions and antagonisms for others, is a general feature of the contemporary city which most commentators describe. New city spaces clearly intersect (and always have intersected) with questions of the social and citizenship (hence the title of the conference and book, 'Citoyenneté et urbanité', of which Lipovetsky's essay forms a part).[2] But the new individualism is only a general feature of this reconfiguration of social spaces. Paul Virilio's essays on contemporary city life deal largely with the effect of the information and communications revolution. He describes the growing divorce between the virtual space of the new electronic highways and the physical space of geographical sites, and hence between those who do or do not have access to the new technology. In *Vitesse et politique* (1977) Virilio considers the links between movement, immobility and power (see also Balandier 1985: 155–161). In the nineteenth century, the bourgeoisie controlled the movement of the masses, hence immobilizing their disruptive potential through the imposition of social and institutional structures. This clearly has links with Michel Foucault's carceral, disciplinary and surveillance society, or Michel de Certeau's centralized society whose immobilizing tactics are actively resisted by the creative acts and 'pedestrian rhetoric' of ordinary citizens. According to Virilio, the rise of the electronic city rearranges the relationship between mobility and power, yet still works to deny freedom to large numbers of people. Now it is those who are cut off from access to the electronic highways who are removed from the locus of power, for today power is less connected with the physical spaces of the city than with the virtual spaces of (invisible) global electronic networks (cf. Graham 1997).

The new division between physical and virtual spaces has therefore created new inequalities in society. As Manuel Castells has said, we are witnessing 'the historical emergence of the space of flows', which supersedes 'the meaning of the space of places', and although 'people live in places, power rules through flows' (cited in Donald 1992: 452). The advent of global information processes means that mental space has become more detached from its link with physical territories. This means that for some a sense of place has become less and less dependent on physical locus, while for others – constrained to live within the confines of specific places ('the suburbs' in particular) – space and place are still more tightly connected. In an interesting comparison of Certeau and Virilio, Verena Andermatt Conley (1996) points out that Certeau's belief that walking is a way of 'rusing' with the regimes of power that regulate the city seems wildly optimistic, given the changed nature today of regimes of power. Virilio's analyses suggest, on the contrary, that, if power operates more and more through the invisible flows of fibre optic channels, then those who are not networked and are confined to the physical space of the city are once again 'immobile in their mobility' (Conley 1996: 168). Commenting on Conley's analysis in the same collection, Michael Sheringham puts this succinctly:

> If for Michel de Certeau the everyday practices of mobile, individual citizens maintain habitability, the analyses of Paul Virilio suggest that the city street is no longer the locus of power and

wonder, and that citizens cut off from the networks engendered by advanced technology may be as immobile as sitting ducks.

(Sheringham 1996: 7)

The work of the anthropologist Marc Augé on the changing topography of the city from modern spaces to those regulated by what he terms 'supermodernity (*surmodernité*)' – see also Balandier 1994 – suggests a similar division of citizens in metropolitan areas, and a breakdown in socialization. Notwithstanding the continuous process of change and 'disembedding of the social system' characteristic of modernity (Giddens 1990: 21), the modern space, or *lieu*, was nevertheless, according to Augé, a site in which culture and identity remained relatively localized within a constrained spatio-temporal context. They were places of social meeting and mixing. But advanced technology, migration and new forms of travel have created different spaces characteristic of 'supermodernity', which Augé (1992) calls 'non-places (*non-lieux*)'. These spaces – examples of which are airports, the banking system, shopping malls, motorways, supermarkets (cf. Chemetov 1996) – 'interpellate' us as individuals (rather than as members of a wider collectivity) and produce the anonymous identity of the fleeting passenger or the customer. In the 'non-spaces' we are no longer bound by a fixed and stable structure governing relationships but enter into a purely contractual arrangement which lasts only as long as the moment itself (Augé 1992: 127–128). For some, the 'non-space' might be a place of freedom: the floating and weightless experience of (s)he who is cut loose from all restrictive ties. For others, they are places of anonymity and fear: the frightening experience of (s)he who has no bearings and no fixed structures. But although they claim our attention as if we were all equal individuals, all equally able to enter the contractual relationship on the same basis (we are all interpellated equally), these spaces elide the social differences which are a feature of postmodern life. And furthermore, by their very nature, they deny social mixing by producing merely 'a meeting with one's self' (1992: 131; cf. Sheringham 1995: 218).

Augé, like Virilio, believes that modern spaces still exist but they are threatened by the new processes regulating city life:

The modern place is still a social, distinctive and historical place; it is not a post-modern space. As for the circuits and the freedom of improvisation so beautifully expressed by the *flâneur*, in the modern place they mesh perfectly with both technique and technology. On the other hand, the *dissociation* between the means of transportation and the ways of communication (highways on the one hand, pedestrian streets on the other) brings about a new aesthetics and another logic, which are not those of modernity.... Supermodernity is characterized by the acceleration or enhancement of the determining constituents of modernity, and by a triple excess (of information, images and individuality), which, in the technologically most advanced areas of modernity, creates the practical conditions for immediacy and ubiquity mentioned by Paul Virilio. Non-places are the contemporary spaces where supermodernity can be found, in conflict with identity, relationship and history. They are the spaces of circulation, communication and consumption, where solitudes coexist without creating any social bond or even a social emotion.

(Augé 1996: 177–178; see also Segalen 1993: 220 who adopts a similar perspective to that of Augé)

Virilio's analyses highlight the shifting patterns of power in these recent developments. He does not simply demonstrate that advanced technology signifies an erosion of 'an art of the eco', as Conley puts it, but seems to be announcing a radical departure from the modernist dialectic (which can be traced from Baudelaire to Certeau) between the concept city and the lived reality, between the centralizing and controlling gaze and the subversive intervention by *le peuple* faced by this 'imposed immobility' (Conley 1996: 170). This tension between unity and fragmentation, order and transgression, was operative in an age when controlled boundaries guaranteed temporal distance and spatial separation. But the audio-visual revolution has effaced these distinctions and has collapsed them into the single space of 'Real Time in which there are no boundaries.... Hence the former *tyranny of distances* between geographically dispersed subjects has progressively given way to this *tyranny of real time*' (Virilio 1995: 31). In this transformed landscape individual perambulations in the city (or even mass protest on the streets) might not be an effective means of challenging the sites of power today. Pierre Sansot's belief that 'the city is composed and recomposed at each moment by the moves of its inhabitants' (Sansot 1996: 139; see also the poetry of Jacques Réda) might need to be revised in the light of new networks of information, exchange and power in the city. We should also remember how Certeau's romanticized image of the walker as one who disrupts the power regime of real estate (*immobilier*), ignores the fact that for those who roam the streets today with 'no fixed abode (*sans domicile fixe*)', ' "walking"...reflects less a challenge to the power of those who own the city than one of the miserable effects of that power' (Prendergast 1992: 211).

This divorce between physical space and power flows also announces a split between the visible city and the 'work' or productive aspect of city life. The era of global information and capital flows and post-Fordist modes of economic production (in which the production of products or the dealings of capital frequently go on 'elsewhere') has loosened the 'organic' link between external appearance and internal reality. (Can one even talk of 'inside' and 'outside' any more, in an era in which that distinction has been progressively effaced?) The external appearance has been transformed into a depthless façade which gives no indication of what takes place 'behind' or 'beyond'. Hence the proliferation of surfaces – detached both from what they 'contain' and from each other, yet similarly bland and uniform – which are nothing more than fronts announcing their own reality. As Jill Forbes has observed:

> In Paris it has not only become less and less possible to discern from the exterior appearance of a structure what its function is, but façades have in some sense become functions. It is as though Haussmann's concern with imposing uniformity in the height and design of façades had been translated to the entire city, turning it into one immense façade which, like its many modern buildings faced with reflecting glass, tells us nothing about what goes on inside.
>
> (Forbes and Kelly 1995: 254)

Françoise Choay (1990: 314) describes this development in terms of a transformation of the city from a *place* of exchange (*lieu*) to a simple *object* of exchange for the promotion of products. Urban marketing has therefore replaced the sense of lived space. Choay's perspective clearly owes much to the earlier critiques of 1960s consumer society by Henri Lefebvre, Jean Baudrillard and others. Eleonore Kofman and Elizabeth Lebas (1996: 19) describe how Lefebvre's *Le Droit à la ville* (1968) already signalled the way in which 'the logic of the market has reduced...urban qualities to exchange and suppressed the city as "oeuvre" '. The loss of the complexity of the city as *oeuvre* is also central to the concerns of the contemporary poet and writer on cities, Jean-Christophe Bailly, whose book *La Ville à l'oeuvre* (1992) is a passionate defence of the multilayered city in the face of the uniform logic of the market. Elsewhere Bailly contrasts the contemporary city as an object of exchange with nineteenth-century Paris, and suggests that today the effacement of the material life of the city (the city as 'a meeting place') has gone hand in hand with the banishment of the city's 'problems' to the suburbs:

> It is not only the 'dangerous classes' who are banished, as far as possible, to the edges. It is also the visibility of the process of work. This progressive banishment of productive activity means that goods are only presented in their final state, that is, as objects for sale. Nineteenth-century Paris was not only a city of shop-fronts but was also a city of workshops.... Today, everything that is unfinished, perishable, cumbersome, noisy, in short everything that presents us with the spectacle of its fabrication seems to have been removed from our gaze.
>
> (Bailly 1994: 274)

No longer offering 'the spectacle of fabrication', cities are increasingly offering spectacle alone. They have ceased to function as a world of interweaving signs which exist on different layers or levels and have been converted into a disconnected alignment of surfaces. Using an argument that mirrors the attack on the self-reflexivity and surface play of postmodern art, Bailly bemoans the fact that representation of spectacle has become dissociated from its truth value: 'representation has ceased to be the presentation of another reality and has become pure sign...that is, stripped of impurity and the weight of meaning' (Bailly 1994: 276–277). The one single criterion that regulates the flow of signs today is that of instant readability, so that complexity and ambiguity are sacrificed at the altar of accessibility. Bailly detects two trends as part of this new reductive 'language' of the city: on the one hand, a plethora of surface signs, and on the other the impoverishment of signs linking different spaces (Bailly 1994: 273).

Bailly's vision of the contemporary city is that of a world of signs divorced from the world of signification, the spatial equivalent of the post-structuralist description of language in which signifiers float free of their attachment to specific meanings. Bailly (1992: 40) develops the comparison between the 'language' of the city and language itself in a manner which pays homage to the tradition of the Baudelairean *flâneur* and to Certeau's 'rusing' with the regimes of power in the city: 'We speak *in* language and we walk *in* the city.... Both language and the urban world are animated by the multiple movements which are engendered in this process' (cf. the section entitled 'Le parler des pas perdus' in Certeau 1990: 147–154). Like Virilio and Augé, Bailly – undoubtedly a modernist at heart – regrets the disappearance of a complex but interconnecting language of the city, for bland surfaces ultimately represent an impoverishment of life. Like each *parole* in language, walking in the streets should be about making connections between individual subjectivity and outer 'reality', between personal memory and (public) history. Walking in the streets should be a bridge between the physical topography of 'outer' space and the imaginary topography of 'inner' space. For the city is, in Bailly's words, 'a veritable patchwork in the most literal sense of the word, that is, a composition of woven material' (Bailly 1992: 73). Using another metaphor for the city – that of the body – he states, 'just as, in acupuncture, a needle inserted next to the tibia can help cure neuralgia, so there exists a similar circulation of messages in the city' (1994: 278).

The effacement of these interconnections, or 'body' of meaning, leaves in its wake an array of dazzling but sanitized and disconnected surfaces, what Henning Bech has termed 'telecity':

> The screen mediated world of the telecity exists only by way of surfaces; and, tendentially, everything can and must be turned into an object for the gaze.... There is, by way of 'readings' of the surface signs, opportunity for a much more intense and changing empathy in and out of identities, because of the possibilities of uninterfered and continual watching.
>
> (quoted in Bauman 1996: 27–28)

Baudrillard interprets this free-floating space as the end of the public sphere in the city:

> When space is simulated and representation has ceased to exist, the city implodes as a public and political space. We have the impression that this is no longer a public space but a space for publicity, whose dimensions are not at all the same.... This space of publicity is a space regulated by the image.
>
> (Baudrillard 1991: 157–158) (see also the work of Régis Debray to be discussed in Chapter 4)

It is now the eye which is bombarded with visual stimuli at the expense of a complex *language* of the city. For a number of the commentators mentioned above, it is this shift from word to image, the spoken to the visual, which is crucial to the contemporary disaggregation of city space and the social habitus of the city. Françoise Choay puts this process in the following terms:

An urban space is not simply a visual space but concerns the whole body. To view city space simply in terms of a visual aesthetic is therefore a highly reductive manoeuvre. Our everyday reality does not correspond to the bird's-eye view but is lived on the ground. Furthermore, this approach fails to appreciate the fact that an urban space cannot be fixed at any one moment but is the sum total of a succession of fragmentary sequences and different times and trajectories.

(cited in Mongin 1995: 44)

Although modernity clearly transformed the 'language' of the city – disrupting and reformulating the connections (pursued by modernist writers and artists) between place, the past, memory and identity – it also established, in the process, a complex interweaving of different layers of 'reality'. However, the fear expressed by Choay, Bailly, Augé, Virilio, Réda and others is that recent changes have effaced that complex and layered language, banishing, at the same time, a 'lived' sense of place (*lieu*), and replaced it with *representations* or *simulations* of that reality (which in fact simply signify the disappearance and loss of that reality).

Hence, the cult of the preservation of heritage (*le patrimoine*) is an indication of the anxiety that surrounds the loss of the past and a sense of time, and the need to fill that absent space (cf. Choay 1992). Lived place, with its popular and private memories which were frequently at odds with official history, is replaced by the idealized (often kitsch) reconstruction of the past, driven by 'media systems, capital and politics in order to be consumed as a heritage myth' (Westwood and Williams 1997: 3). Marc Augé (1992: 95) suggests that these glib reconstructions of time and place 'are merely a way of articulating present space'. The outer appearance of the city, therefore, takes on the form of a painted but empty shell, or a bland façade presenting a two-dimensional version of history (while the 'work' of the city takes place through the hidden networks of fibre optic channels of communication). As Augé comments elsewhere (1996: 179): 'The whole world is nowadays transformed into images and shows. This is particularly true in big cities: renovated housefronts, floodlit monuments, protected areas inexorably turn the city into a life-size stage set' (cf. Kofman 1993). Mongin (1995: 50) calls this 'the museified city' and contrasts it with that other image that we have today of the city, one of violence and excess ('the jungle city'). 'The museified city' is accompanied by the transformation of the *flâneur* into the tourist:

The more the city is transformed into a museum, the more we run from one museum to another, from one city to another, in search of what the city can no longer offer us as tourists who have forgotten how to be pedestrians.

(Mongin 1995: 75; cf. Urry 1990 and Bauman 1996)

Augé (1992: 138) compares the contemporary 'museification' of the city with the complex patterning of modernity: 'Baudelaire's modernity was characterized by a continual mixing...an interweaving of the ancient and the modern. Supermodernity, on the other hand, has made the ancient (and history itself) into a spectacle.'

According to Jean-François Lyotard (1993: 31, 33), this process which has transformed the lives of those living in 'the megapole' is that of a 'generalized aestheticization' in which style has become the ultimate value. Zygmunt Bauman (1993: Chapter 6) uses the same terms when he defines the passage from modern to postmodern sensibility as the evolution from cognitive social spacing to aesthetic social spacing, that is, viewing the city today not as rationally planned space but as spectacle. Baudrillard (1991: 162) describes this phenomenon thus: 'It is no longer a social space, rather a space which is liberated and expanded but where, in fact, there is no distance.' Distance is linked to cognitive spacing which separates out and defines boundaries between elements. It is associated with the teleological and scientific modern mind. Aesthetic spacing, on the other hand, signifies the abolition of distances, the collapse of the 'density' of the social into the flat and undifferentiated space of surface and representation.

It was precisely the aesthetic spacing of the *flâneur* which disrupted the 'social coherence' of the modern city. As we have noted, the juxtaposition of disparate elements from diverse places and times produced a flattening of the hierarchies and dichotomies which underlay rational (or cognitive) social spacing. The fascination with what is fleeting and contingent (rather than fixed and rooted) disrupted a teleological sense of time by questioning the very fabric which ties moments together in a chronological sequence, hence allowing those moments to float free in an unfettered space. In this sense, we can see once again how the postmodern norms of contingency, simultaneity and the sense of an endless present could be defined as the democratization of the spirit of cultural modernism. We are all *flâneurs* today (although we do not all have the same means to indulge our habits). Or, as Bauman has said:

The stroller and the strolling waited at the periphery for their hour to arrive. And it did arrive – or rather it was brought by the postmodern avatar of the heroic producer into playful consumer. Now the strolling, once the activity practised by marginal people on the margins of 'real life', came to be life itself, and the question of 'reality' need not be dealt with any more.

(Bauman 1996: 27)

But if the 'art' of the *flâneur* has moved from the margins to the centre (just like marginal or sub-cultures in general) this democratization of his aesthetic – and especially its commercialization – has radically affected its status. The fascination and wonder of the city for the *flâneur* were derived from the unconventional connections he made between his imaginary desires, on the one hand, and the outer topography of the city (including, of course, its inhabitants) on the other hand (see, for example, Louis Aragon's *Le Paysan de Paris* or André Breton's *Nadja*). The richness of the experience comes from the interconnections between subjective and objective, past and present, (public) history and (private) memory, the everyday and the eternal. As Michael Keith and Steve Pile (1993: 8) say about Walter Benjamin, his work as '*flâneur* immersed in the urban experience...is about the intertwining of experience, knowledge and spatiality'. However, it must be recognized that the policed boundaries and hierarchies of modernity were a necessary prerequisite for the nourishment of this sensibility (and for the art of transgression to which it gave rise), for they brought into existence the marginal realms which enabled the poet/*flâneur* to act as an outsider to social convention and morality, and ally himself with the otherness of rationally ordered society. As Michael Sheringham says, commenting on Benjamin, Breton and the poet Jacques Réda,

> for all three writers the experience of urban wandering involves temporal dislocation. But if the future is suspended as the present becomes suffused with the past, we always remain in a border zone, between now and then, and between the city's own historical archive and that of the individual.
>
> (Sheringham 1996: 112)

But the postmodern conflation of these oppositions, the 'normalization' of what is transitory (our 'throw-away' culture), 'exotic' and transgressive, the reduction of everything to surface and an endless present are in danger of eradicating this 'border zone' (and, in the process, effacing the modern poet at the same time) by eradicating the very distinctions between the different spheres themselves.

Ironically, what was the source of that rich texture explored by modernist poets and artists is now the source of the eradication of texture. The blurring of dichotomies (the aestheticization of the social domain) was only transgressive in an age when those binary oppositions were the pillars of social spacing. The surrealists, for example, 'sought what was most disquieting in the streets of Paris or at the fleamarket, in the unusual juxtapositions and coincidences that made up everyday life. Art and life were here and now' (Lipovetsky 1983: 129). But the blurring of art and everyday life today – so dear to the surrealists – threatens the very existence of a texture composed of *different* planes. 'The city is a handful of secrets thrown to the forbidden winds', says Thierry Paquot (1990: 135). This poetic vision of the modern city might be purely illusory in the light of postmodern developments.

Encounters in the city

The democratization of the art of the *flâneur* today – no longer confined to the margins but now 'life itself' – has, as Zygmunt Bauman indicates above, been achieved through the conversion of the stroller into the consumer. Of course, the playful look of the gentleman stroller (the *metteur en scène* of life's vicissitudes), the fascination with the contingent, the transitory and the evanescent, and with the spectacle of the city, were never far removed from the seductive lure of the commodity for the customer. Was it not in the arcades – those temples of consumption – that Walter Benjamin located the equivalence between the desire of the *flâneur* and the seduction of the consumer?[3] As Joël Roman observes (1996: 34), 'the development of the city goes hand in hand with its economic corollary, the development of the market'. Yet if the *flâneur* formerly occupied a border zone between controlling and being controlled by the object of his gaze, just as he occupied that other border zone between 'objectivity' and 'subjectivity', then it is possible that today that border zone has been thoroughly commodified, so that the lure of the spectacle of city life signifies the final act in the metamorphosis of the *flâneur* into the customer:

> From the start, there was money to be made out of the *flaneur's* affliction. Wittingly and premeditatedly, these spaces [the arcades] *sold* pleasurable views to look at. In order to attract the customers, though, the designers and the owners of those spaces had to buy them first. The right to look gratuitously was to be the *flâneur's*, tomorrow's *customer's*, reward. Pleasurable display, fascinating view,

the enticing game of shapes and colours. Customers bought through the seduction of the *flâneur*; the *flâneur*, through seduction, was transformed into the consumer. In the process, the miraculous avatar of the commodity into the shopper is accomplished. At the end of the day, the dividing line has been blurred. It is no more clear what (who) is the object of consumption, who (what) is the consumer.

(Bauman 1993: 173–174)

For Bauman, this development heralds not the extension of freedom (as the liberal free-marketeers would have us believe) but a further constraint upon it:

The most cherished of *flâneurisme* seductions – the right to write the script and to direct the play of surfaces – has been expropriated by the designers and the managers and the profit-makers of the shopping malls. The scripts are now ready-made and expert-made, discreet yet precise...leaving little to the imagination and less still to the spectator's freedom.

(1993: 177)

To what extent, then, has the (male) looker become a victim or object of consumption (in the way that women habitually were) rather than the detached observer of its specular delights?

This is a far cry from Jean-Christophe Bailly's modernist vision of the city: 'The history of the city is that of a permanent combat between the production of a constantly displaced excess of meaning and the control of all social forms which reproduce this excess by those in society who exercise or maintain their power by naturalizing these forms' (Bailly 1992: 27). If Bailly is right about the history of the city, then Bauman's comments on recent developments (which echo Bailly's own fears) might make us wonder whether, in the passage from modern to postmodern forms of organization of the city, post-industrial societies like France have not jumped from the frying-pan into the fire: that is, that by breaking with the rational, Utopian language of urban and social design (which in its day strove to contain and control the free flow of meaning in the city), they quite possibly find themselves in thrall to a different master, that of late capitalism whose exploitation of the 'excess of meaning' is for the purposes of selling, rather than challenging social convention. Does the ludic quality that Henri Lefebvre talks of still exist today, or has the democratization of this 'playfulness' been achieved under the banner of consumption (with its consequent inequalities of access built in) rather than under the banner of genuine democratic access to new spaces?

If it is true that the democratization of 'strolling' is best epitomized today by the customer's perambulations in the sanitized environment of the pedestrian precinct and shopping mall, and if (as Bailly suggests) the proliferation of endless surfaces is at the expense of a network of meaning in the city, then this has both moral and political consequences of a profound nature. Today the fragmentation and speed of city life have converted the eye into a ceaselessly mobile instrument, compelled to flit from one surface to another but not allowed to rest long enough to see further than the surface itself. We have thus become more and more detached from any involvement in 'meaningful' relationships (in the same way that the *flâneur*, in order to indulge his playful aestheticization and eroticization of the city, had to distance himself from the crowd and, in one sense, function as a voyeur). The aesthetic space which we inhabit today – with its emphasis on the affective, the pleasurable, the gratification of instant and constantly renewable sensation and desire – is, as Bauman points out (1993: Chapter 6), not conducive to a responsibility for 'the other' which is at the heart of any *moral* spacing.

The aesthetic space of the postmodern city works to transform us from social beings – with a sense of living with others – into 'nomads' for whom others are objects of our transitory gaze but with whom we have no time to establish a relationship. Encounters with others in the city therefore involve little or no sense of attachment. Fleeting encounters stimulate the senses but are not conducive to long-term contracts, as Augé's descriptions of 'non-places' confirm. But, then, the nomad is not concerned with long-term contracts, for (s)he has no sense either of being attached to the past or of what might happen in the future. It is only the present that matters to the nomad. As Keith Tester has pointed out, drawing on the work of Gilles Deleuze and Félix Guattari:

> the whole point of the nomad, of course, is that as an individual or a group the nomad simply travels. The journey has no point; it has no place of origin and neither, for that matter, does it have a destination. The nomad has no fixed identity, rather his or her identity is simply something which emerges out of the transient play of roles, resources and relationships. But, and as Gilles Deleuze and Félix Guattari have realized, to the extent that the travelling of the nomad has no point, and to the extent that the nomad moves in a milieu which has no boundaries and therefore no places and

no directions, the nomad is historically stationary. 'The nomad distributes himself in a smooth space, he occupies, inhabits, holds that space; that is his territorial principle. It is therefore false to define the nomad by movement...the nomad is on the contrary *he who does not move.*' (*Nomadology: The War Machine*, trans. B. Massumi, New York: Semiotext(e), 1986, p. 51)

(Tester 1993: 75)

Uprooted from an attachment to temporal chronology, the nomad occupies a free-floating space. This concept of the nomad who is immobile in his 'smooth space' recalls Paul Virilio's description of the immobility of those for whom the virtual space of the new electronic networks has replaced the 'real' space of geographical sites (see also Jonas 1984). It is worth insisting on the part played by advanced technology in the creation of this new 'nomadic' space. But the point that I wish to make here is one that concerns the ethics attached to nomadic aesthetic space. We noted in Chapter 1 how the replacement of a 'Hellenic' rational order with a 'Hebraic' nomadism signalled, according to a number of philosophers, the end of the modern urge to assimilate or annihilate 'the other', and heralded a new ethical stance *vis-à-vis* 'the other'. Yet the rejoicing at such a development is perhaps premature in the light of what we have said above; namely, that this deregulated space might be a consumer's paradise (for some) but a moral backwater (for most) (cf. Rose 1993), and that the fragmentary and transitory nature of encounters in the city might be as damaging to moral life with others as modern forms of obliterating individual responsibility (cf. Bauman 1996: 32–35).

Marc Guillaume (Baudrillard and Guillaume 1994) uses the term 'spectrality' to define the dispersal and simulation of identity which characterizes city life today (and which can be seen in its purest form in contemporary forms of communication, ibid., 25). In breaking 'the stable ego' and the (supposed) unity of individual consciousness, the processes which regulate communication flows in the city have channelled relationships into a ceaseless stream of differentiation which ultimately leads, paradoxically, to the meaninglessness of difference and an 'eclipse' of 'the other':

In our control societies, the management of otherness no longer functions principally through discipline and normalization but through transformation and 'spectralization' of the masses. Consumption, communication, transport and mass urbanization produce the cohabitation of millions of selves who are in proximity with each other yet do not see each other, who enter into exchanges with each other without having dealings with each other, who meet each other without confronting each other. 'The other' is eclipsed.... This industrial processing of differences renders difference meaningless and monotonous and reduces it to specks of otherness. Our innumerable encounters and exchanges are fragmentary and 'spectral'. They leave no room for troubling otherness and therefore contain no risk of unsettling our selves. Conflicts are transformed into 'problems' and arbitrations into 'solutions'. This is how a multitude of interactions are routinely managed. This is the relatively efficient solution to Kant's question of 'unsociable sociability', of the unsociable urban phenomenon of big cities today.

(Baudrillard and Guillaume 1994: 13)[4]

Guillaume (Baudrillard and Guillaume 1994: 34) detects two possible emotional responses inspired by 'spectrality': on the one hand, a fear of ceaseless differentiation which results in a retreat into imaginary shelters for identity; on the other, the (orgasmic?) pleasure derived from the dispersal, dissemination and hybridization of identity. As we saw in the preceding chapter, these two responses are at the heart of our strategies for negotiating difference today. They are also crucial to the new division in the contemporary city described by Virilio, that is, between those who have the means to 'go with the flow' and those who are locked more and more firmly into their 'Euclidian space' (Conley 1996: 170) and obliged to invent ever more feverishly their bearings. Those in the suburbs are not only physically situated outside the gates of the city; they are also cut adrift from the wider networks enjoyed by their fellow city-dwellers. Can one then even talk of belonging to the same community of city-dwellers when the gulf between those inside and those outside the walls seems ever-widening? Mongin (1995: 108) suggests that this phenomenon calls into question the very possibility of representing urban society: 'There is much talk today of civic society...but recent developments have provoked a serious crisis in cities in that many people are no longer full citizens, that is individuals who belong symbolically to the same collectivity.'

The postmodern city is a space of seduction and circulation but is it, or can it also be, a space of sociality? If the modern city was (ideally, it should be emphasized) a meeting-place for a diverse population around the common principles of uniformity, equality and civic order, are we witnessing today a fracturing of the population according to who has and who lacks the means to survive in a world of ceaseless differentiation? The result of detaching looking and circulating in the city from its institutional and social grounding threatens the very sense of sociality and poses serious ethical questions about relationships and political questions about solidarity. What chance is there for ethics when 'face-to-face' contact is disappearing beneath a proliferation of simulated encounters? And what chance is there for a renewed sense of citizenship when the (social) citizen is increasingly in danger of being transformed into the (atomized) consumer? (See Chapter 5.)

Or do these bleak hypotheses underestimate the new possibilities on offer today? After all, if the rationalized and 'coherent' social spacing of modernity could neither disenchant the world completely nor eradicate the ambivalent affective life of individuals but, paradoxically, led to a re-enchantment of both through different forms, then could it not be the case that postmodern aesthetic spacing will also achieve a reworking of myths and a renewal of meaningful imaginary identifications through different modes? Michel de Certeau's optimism with regard to modern city spacing might serve well with regard to the current age:

> It would be superficial to believe that rationalization has abolished myth, for the notion that the streets have been 'disinfected' of myth is mistaken. On the contrary, myth is dominant. It implants into surface images society's dreams and what has been repressed. It reappears everywhere but through different channels to those of the past.
>
> (Certeau 1993: 36)

Making connections

Many of these questions about living in the city today are raised in a fascinating book by the writer and left-wing ex-publisher François Maspero, *Les Passagers du Roissy-Express* (1990), which records his journey through the suburbs of Paris accompanied by a friend and photographer, Anaïk Frantz. François (as the narrator is called in the text) treads in the path of Baudelaire, Apollinaire and Breton in the sense that his pedestrian wanderings among the marginal inhabitants of 'the zone' (those who have been excluded from the centre of Paris both physically and socially) are an exploration of the dialectic between inner self and the outer topography of the city. Yet, unlike the *flâneur* who disrupts the order of modern social spacing by his aestheticization of city life (with no commitment on his part to those he objectifies),

Maspero's narrator, on the contrary, seeks to *make connections* in a space which has become fragmented, diversified and uprooted from its anchorage in a spatio-temporal and social context. As François says (p. 21), 'nothing connects dispersed localities which are thrown together as if by chance like jumbled letters in the alphabet. Space has disintegrated and is in fragments.' Walking through the suburbs has become a forgotten pastime – except, of course, for those who live there and have been rendered immobile in their ghettos.[5] For those who have the means, these are simply spaces which one passes through:

> People don't journey in the Paris region any more. They move or jump from one point to another. What is in between is the undifferentiated spatio-temporal site of the train or car journey, a grey continuum which nothing links to the outside world.
>
> (p. 22) (cf. Virilio 1989)

Rather than cultivate the fleeting image based on the transitory nature of the chance encounter and the non-committal nature of the aestheticizing and voyeuristic gaze, François tries to *enter into dialogue*, therefore breaking the first taboo of all voyeurism. He transgresses the frontiers between different city spaces, not in the form of the gentleman of leisure whose pleasure comes from his freedom to rove where he pleases and from his aestheticization of 'the other', but in the form of an anxious and self-conscious outsider attempting to make connections: one who neither reduces 'the other' to the same, nor exoticizes the other's difference, but who gropes towards a different understanding of and relationship with the stranger. François brings out his baggage (rather than hiding it in voyeuristic fashion) and expects others to bring out theirs. The encounters which then ensue are consequently determined not by the non-committal look of the so-called 'free' and unencumbered observer (in a position of power over his subjects) but by a certain sense of dialogue, involvement, responsibility (commitment even?) and morality.

This can be seen most clearly in Anaïk's photos. Anaïk photographs 'frontier' people (p. 18) – marginals, tramps and so on, that 'world of frontiers' which casts back an anxious reflection on our own world. She cannot sell her photos because they are non-functional: that is, they are no good as commodities in the market. Rather than show a surface gloss they reveal instead the 'anxieties' of her subjects (p. 19). She refuses to objectify her subjects ('I'm no good at postcards,' she explains; p. 297), preferring instead to send them her photos so that the whole photographic experience itself becomes a *dialogue* between photographer and photographed rather than an impersonal and objectifying experience. (She realises, at one point, that she has transgressed her own rule when, during the journey, she photographs some Malians without knowing them and without having asked their permission: that is, precisely in voyeuristic fashion, pp. 127–128.)

The photographs, like the encounters as a whole, are not simply records of a momentary event during the journey but are an attempt to incorporate into that moment of freezing and fixing a sense of depth, dialogue, responsibility and moral weight – all things which are resolutely effaced by the fleeting image today. They are a snapshot which links this moment with others (with a past) in the same way that the journey on foot through the hinterland of the suburbs (rather than simply flashing through them via the motorway) is an attempt to reintegrate space and time, memory and history, which have become disconnected fragments. The text is therefore an attempt to reinstate a certain density of experience beyond the spliced image to counter the play of depthless surface and perpetual present.[6]

Maspero resolutely refuses the journey of the morally disengaged stroller of the contemporary city who is in thrall to the seductive surface of the commodity. He refuses to eulogize what Gillian Rose has termed 'nomad' city, the postmodernist paradise of the maze whose so-called freedom and infinite choice, according to Rose (1993: 51), simply masks 'the idol of the market-place'. Nor does he withdraw into the imagined communitarianism of a home retreat, safe from the stranger. Instead, he challenges the segregated, ghettoized, fragmented nature of postmodern city life, challenges the concept of the city as a differentialist spacing of disconnected 'zones' or disconnected surfaces. In short, he refuses to aestheticize difference, either through an unequivocal celebration of 'the other' or through the erection of a wall to keep out 'the other' – the two classic modes, or 'siamese twins' as Zygmunt Bauman has called them, of postmodern differentialist thinking.

Similarly, the fragments of personal memory, political and social history, and cultural works which intertwine during the course of the journey (in which the distinctions between private and public, subjective and objective, are always indistinct) are not juxtaposed in simple relativist fashion, but are drawn together, put into dialogue with each other, made to question each other, encounter each other in the same way that different city spaces are made to connect, thus challenging their distinctness and separateness. In both a temporal and a spatial sense, the text becomes a sort of mosaic of interlocking pieces but one that never finally coalesces into a glib and totalizing whole (cf. also Rolin 1996).

Here is just one example of this process. One of the stops on the line on the way in to the centre of Paris from Roissy is Drancy. The Cité de la Muette housing estate in Drancy started its life as one of the most innovative designs for social housing in inter-war Europe. The intervention of the war and the occupation of northern France by the Nazis in 1940 meant that the estate remained unfinished and was then used as the main camp for the round-up of Jews by the French police prior to their dispatch to the concentration camps in the east. Maspero interconnects a detached and 'factual' description of these events with a commentary on Jews, a commentary on the architecture of the building and its relevance in terms of social housing, the nature of social housing in the 1960s, and then the inhabitants today, most of whom are first- and second-generation immigrant families. In other words, Maspero constructs his own architecture, composed of multilayered discourses across time, space and genre, and invites us to ponder on the connections between these different layers. When talking of the present inhabitants he states that the wartime history of the Jews in Drancy is not *their* history: that is, the history of the people who live there now. Whose history is this, then, and how should it be recounted? What is the link between past and present and between different 'communities' – the North African and other immigrant inhabitants today and the Jews who passed through fifty years before on their way to the gas chambers? And what is the relevance of this multilayered account of Drancy to the city as a whole and to France in its bicentenary year?

Maspero refuses to give us clear answers to these questions. His technique is rather to draw together different fragments and make them 'speak' to each other so that at least these difficult questions are on the agenda. We are left with a sense that the only possible history of Drancy (like other places described on the journey) is a multifaceted one in which the past is not simply a fixed and monolithic entity, the same for everyone, but neither is it simply a fragmented collection of entirely different stories. Similarly, this place does not exist in a vacuum but is connected with other aspects of the city and the nation. However, the connections have to be made through the journey itself and through the telling of the stories. Past and present fragments and different city spaces are made to connect only in the *process* of journeying and memorializing. These are connections which are not 'out there' waiting to be resurrected but can only be produced and constituted through the human effort of walking, talking and writing. Jeffrey Weeks' general comment on the construction of human solidarity fits well with Maspero's project in the text:

Human solidarity [is] a project not of realising what already is there, undiscovered beneath our noses, but of constructing bonds across the chasm of difference...the universal is itself relativised, becoming not an unproblematic given but an articulation of a variety of social discourses and logics around an evolving project.

(Weeks 1993: 196)

History here, then, is not a question of the revelation of hidden truths beyond the disconnected surface images: the past cannot be fitted to the present in such a deterministic way. It is rather a quest for connections, the quest itself, the journey, as an integral part of the historical process.

Maspero's effort seems to be to seek *reconnections* through *dialogue*, rather than submit either to the atomization of disconnected voices, moments and images, or to the simplistic construction of new imagined communities speaking, each one, with a single voice. What he does is to walk, talk and write. As we noted above, this might be anachronistic in an age of advanced technology. Yet it does express an overwhelming desire to reconnect and rediscover solidarities in a fragmented world. Walking and talking, involving face-to-face interaction, are the forgotten arts which Jean-Christophe Bailly and Paul Virilio also advocate as a way of resisting the relentless process of the atomization and de-moralization of social relations. Maspero's text embodies Bailly's search for a language which can renew the links, once again, between centre and periphery:

Whilst at the centre an over-abundance of urban signs (deprived of any substance) seems to produce the slow suffocation of the city, on the margins it is the chronic absence of these signs (and their substance) which stifles life.... An organic link attaches the problems of the centre to those of the periphery, for those within and those outside the walls are connected like two communicating channels, but whose points of contact have been smothered. We must reopen these channels.

(Bailly 1994: 278)

However, if the problems of reconnecting in a fragmented world are clearly visible, the new moral and political language of living with difference is still in its infancy.

4 Cultural debates

Probably the most over-used word in recent French debates about culture is 'crisis'. Clearly a sense of crisis is not particular to France alone, for the fragmentation and decentring of the notion of a universal culture is a major feature of contemporary Western societies. Yet in France the crisis is felt particularly acutely. Culture is so intricately connected with the nation and with the civilizing mission of the state (in both metropolitan France and the colonies) that the transformation from Culture (in the singular and with a capital 'C') to 'cultures' (plural and lower-case) touches profoundly on the more general crisis of the nation-state today and the question of difference and pluralism.

However, the sense of crisis goes further still. For what is really at stake – beyond the belief in universal culture as a cornerstone of national and social integration – is the demise of the Enlightenment dichotomy between the transcendent world of the spirit (*l'esprit*) and the beautiful (*le beau*) and the more worldly sociological and anthropological spheres, or in other words between art and everyday life. This process (inherited from cultural modernism but extended dramatically over the last few decades) has blurred the distinctions between creation and life-style, and between culture, leisure and entertainment. Most significantly, the breakdown in the dichotomy between art and everyday life has confused the distinction between culture and commodity. This chapter seeks to explore these aspects of recent debates about culture.

From *Culture* to *le culturel*

In the age of modernity, culture was at the heart of the Enlightenment project to haul people out of their particularist and parochial ghettos and bring them into the world of light and reason. Culture – meaning classical or high culture founded on a concept of creation and the life of the spirit – was a major weapon in the state's armoury in its mission to civilize and socialize its citizens. Alain Touraine demonstrates the connection between culture, reason and social integration in relation to the principal institution of the state required to carry out this function of social engineering, namely the school:

> The school...sought to detach the child from his particularist background and put him in touch with Reason, either through scientific culture or by bringing him as close as possible to the great works of the human mind, to philosophy and art. From the German concept of the *Bildung* to André Malraux's construction in France of cultural centres (*maisons de la culture*), one can trace a continuous effort to link the inculcation of the ways of reason and beauty with the task of social integration.
>
> (Touraine 1992: 405–406)

The cultural policy of André Malraux, during his period of office as Minister of Culture in the 1960s under Charles de Gaulle, represents the last attempt by the state to disseminate and democratize the classical universalist concept of culture. Since then, and especially during the 1980s when Jacques Lang was the Socialist Minister of Culture under François Mitterrand, the classical version of culture has been joined by a wider sociological or anthropological definition (an inheritance of post-war anti-ethnocentric anthropology and the counter-cultural movements of the 1960s) which treats culture as what people do, their customs and their life-styles. Under Lang, the state definition of *Culture* was transformed into *cultures* and embraced, in the process, not only the traditional arts but also diverse forms of popular culture, from popular music to tagging.

Ironically, this belated recognition by the state of cultural relativism and diversity did not noticeably dampen either its enthusiasm for political intervention or its obsession with the national function of culture. David Looseley has pointed up the continuities in cultural policy between the Socialist regime of the 1980s and the Gaullist regime of the 1960s, despite the evident expansion in the definition of the term:

> A further continuation with the de Gaulle era is this perennial preoccupation, despite all the talk of diversity and eclecticism, with fostering a national culture, visible in a host of other ways: the insistence on maintaining the state's role as harmonizer when the decentralisation laws were being implemented, the promotion of French mass culture in opposition to American, the stress on

collective fun, and the idea of a national multiculture enshrined in the Goude procession.

(Looseley 1995: 241; see especially Chapter 7, pp. 135–154)

Panivong Norindr (1996) traces the continuities back further still by showing how François Mitterrand's *grands projets* of the 1980s and 1990s – including especially the Louvre pyramid, the grand arch and marble cube at La Défense and the new French national library – can be viewed as part of a long-standing association (from the Second Empire redesigning of Paris via the International Colonial Exhibition in Paris in 1931) between state-inspired cultural projects and the construction of *la plus grande France*. Thus, in one very important sense, the traditional contextualization of cultural policy within the framework of national and social integration remained as firm as ever during the 1980s. What changed was the evolution from a concept of universal (high) Culture, to which all citizens should aspire, to a concept of diverse cultures which constituted the mosaic which was France. The latter concept has been termed (usually pejoratively) *le culturel* (or *le tout culturel*) in which more or less anything can count as culture.[1]

The two interlinked strands of the definition of culture and the role of the state in fostering it have been major aspects of cultural debates in contemporary France. Jacques Lang's cultural policy of the 1980s was criticized mercilessly as a sign of postmodern times by those who regretted the decline of universal high culture. The most sustained assaults came from the philosopher Alain Finkielkraut (1987) and the cultural historian Marc Fumaroli (1992). Finkielkraut's book, *La Défaite de la pensée*, is not aimed specifically at Lang's policies themselves (see, however, his more forthright attack on Lang in 'Finkielkraut persiste et signe: c'est la défaite de la culture!', *L'Événement du Jeudi*, 19–25 April 1990) but is a historical critique of the expansion and eventual dissolution of the term 'culture' (of which Lang's policies form a part) into a meaningless relativism. Finkielkraut's depiction of the crisis of culture will be familiar to all those who have followed the general debates around culture in recent years: the decline of a notion of culture founded on the intellect, solitary reflection, meaning and a concept of *l'esprit* (hence 'the death of thought') and the emergence of an anti-intellectualist version of culture founded on an easy hedonism and instant gratification of the senses; the elevation of mass and popular cultural forms (television, rock music, fashion and so on) to the same status as classical culture (hence, to take one of Finkielkraut's examples, 'a pair of boots has the same value as Shakespeare', 1987: 135); the connivance of education in this debasement, or 'dumbing down', of culture so that the pedagogic, social and national function of the school, so dear to the Enlightenment republican project, is jettisoned in favour of an approach which simply indulges the individualistic whims and desires of young people;[2] the appropriation of culture by the audio-visual media and the leisure and entertainment industries so that culture becomes indistinguishable from mass consumption; and the infantilization of society which this debasement of classical culture entails. In this scenario, May 1968 is generally depicted as the symbolic moment at which this infantilization took place. In the words of Pascal Bruckner (1996: 47) 'May 68 was the moment in European history at which youth was elevated to the realm of the sages, and when it became the ideal state in opposition to adulthood.'

Although informed by a similar attitude towards mass cultural pursuits as that expressed by Finkielkraut, Fumaroli engages more directly with the cultural policy of the state, not only to lambast Lang's pluriculturalist approach but also to critique Malraux's failed attempt to bring high culture to the masses through the *maisons de la culture*. He abhors the ways in which successive post-war governments have imposed a particular notion of culture on the people, used culture for political and propagandist ends and, in the process, not only debased culture itself but abused the freedom of individuals to choose their own forms of culture. He notes that 'state culture has more and more profoundly functionalized and commodified the Arts and, with its politico-media music-hall, has compromised them more than in any other country in the world' (Fumaroli 1992: 60). A state-led democratization of culture is none other than the reduction of culture to spectacle and to consumer demand. The noble spirit of the French tradition is sullied in the process: 'Should one be surprised if a nation which carries the name of France, one of the most noble of all names, dabbles a bit in the age of democracy?' (Fumaroli 1992: 27).

If one can get beyond the barrage of elitist, ethnocentric and unreconstructed-humanist pronouncements which run throughout these books, their depiction of postmodern culture can be seen to connect with more serious and balanced accounts of the contemporary situation by other commentators, especially with regard to the shift from the word to the image and from the contemplative to the spectacle. These will be discussed in more detail later in this chapter (see ' "The democratization" of the image'). What is of interest here, in terms of a distinctive French purchase on the contemporary debate, is the way in which national traditions (or myths?) are constructed and utilized in the formulation of a critique of postmodernism.

Despite their differences, both Finkielkraut and Fumaroli offer a similar explanation for the evolution from *Culture* to *le culturel*, or from the Enlightenment classical tradition to that of postmodern multiculturalism. A major part of Finkielkraut's book is taken up with reading the history of France in terms of a binary opposition between the French universalist tradition, founded on the rationalist precepts of the Enlightenment, and the German particularist tradition, founded on the romantic notion of the *Volksgeist* (or spirit of the people). If the former offers emancipation from ethnic, religious or national attachment and is open to all humanity, irrespective of origins, then the latter enshrines culture in the community of origin. Finkielkraut replays the classic modern antithesis between rational free will, on the one hand, and the predetermined nature of race and environment on the other, classifying the former as French and the latter as German.

In this schema, the contemporary decline of a classical version of Culture is interpreted as the infiltration of the German model of *Kultur* into the French tradition. Not simply is France being invaded by Germany (yet again!) but today the foreign virus is transported primarily through 'Anglo-Saxon' (meaning American) practices, for it is in 'the Anglo-Saxon world' that the heretical anthropological or sociological definition of culture now finds its quintessential form of expression. It is no surprise that Finkielkraut couples his critique of postmodern culture with a critique of multiculturalism (as we saw in Chapter 2) for, according to his simplistic and manichean divide between French universalism and German or 'Anglo-Saxon' particularism, any acceptance of particularist differences in the public sphere can be interpreted as an invasion of foreign ideas into the pure universalism of the French.[3]

Fumaroli also interprets the decline of humanist culture and the rise of *le culturel* according to monolithic national models:

> Culture, in the sense officially recognized in France today, is a sociological and ethnological idea which derives part of its meaning from the German *Kultur* but none of it from the French version of civilization. *Kultur*, like Anglo-Saxon 'culture', has little ability to define its target because it is too wide a concept. It attempts to encompass a vague and general order of things, a hazy and impersonal collection of 'ways of thinking' or 'practices' which blurs the contours, renders objects indistinguishable and reduces everything to the lowest common denominator. The social sciences have endowed this notion with intellectual legitimacy and have provided it with its tools of analysis.
>
> (Fumaroli 1992: 229)

For Fumaroli (1992: 223–224) the sociological and ethnological definition of culture which is hegemonic today clearly represents an assault on a 'certain idea' of France and French heritage (*le patrimoine français*), one in which *la chanson* had words you could understand (instead of the torrent of contemporary rock) and in which the function of the state was not to guarantee 'a social security for imported leisure pursuits' but to preside over 'the good health of its language and its education' and to guarantee 'the integration into the nation of its immigrant citizens, the moral salubrity and social amenities of its towns and the preservation of its natural environment and its countryside'.

Fumaroli's vision is one in which the state has adopted a vulgarized form of culture as a new religion (or drug) aimed at diverting attention from the post-war decline of France and the loss of empire (cf. Debray and Fumaroli 1993: 7). In this sense, Mitterrand's *grands travaux* might be seen not so much as testimonies to the continuation of *la plus grande France* but as symbolic of its demise. In a less polemical and less nostalgic vein, Pierre Nora also puts the contemporary obsession with heritage (especially by the state) in the context of the *malaises* and anxieties of a crisis-ridden, post-empire France. These comprise:

> the feeling of having departed from the grand course of history, the 'national identity crisis' provoked by the construction of Europe, the problem of decentralization which inflicts on a very centralized, Jacobin country another form of loss of identity, immigration and the threat to the tradition of assimilation posed by a large number of foreigners who seem more difficult to 'digest'.
>
> ('Un entretien avec Pierre Nora', *Le Monde*, 29 November 1994)

Nora's approach to this phenomenon is to reveal the symbolic import attached to society's construction of particular 'sites of memory (*lieux de mémoire*)' (Nora 1984). Fumaroli's approach is, on the contrary, more straightforwardly ideological. For him, the 'cultural state' is simply a perversion of the true 'French nature'. Jean-Pierre Rioux (1992: 61) characterizes Fumaroli's approach as one which stereotypes contemporary cultural developments in France in terms of a mixture of an Anglo-Saxon 'sociologico-anthropological' definition of culture and a German 'Hegelian-Bismarckian' version of *Kultur*. Rioux contemptuously dismisses Fumaroli himself as an archaic upholder of the Enlightenment version of 'eternal France', mired for ever nostalgically in a bygone age (Rioux 1992: 61).

The sort of sociological revisionism of culture Fumaroli has in mind which has destroyed this French idyll, and which characterizes the mind-set of those who now set the cultural policy agenda, would be epitomized by the theories of Michel de Certeau and the legacy of 1968, consisting of 'social and moral stereotypes invented in Greenwich Village' (Fumaroli 1992: 223). Certeau's pluralistic vision of culture converted culture from acts of genius into the acts of us all in everyday life, for culture consists not in receiving from on high but in discovering and developing the creative potential within us all (Certeau 1993: iii). This individualization and democratization of culture (culture as individual expression, or what Finkielkraut refers to as 'my culture' as opposed to Culture) is part of what Olivier Mongin (1994a: 175), among others, has termed 'the rise of identity – a highly polemical theme today because it brings together ethnic belonging, the arts, creation and aesthetic invention'. It is precisely this rediscovery of the individual subject (his or her customs, community or 'ethnic' traditions and so on, which the idealized and abstract Enlightenment philosophy of 'Man' deemed backward and parochial, cf. Touraine 1992), and the subsequent conversion of these 'anti-republican' principles into cultural policy by the *soixante-huitard* Left who came to power in the 1980s, which Fumaroli and Finkielkraut interpret as an assault on the fundamental spirit and heritage of France herself.[4]

Culture and society

Not only do the analyses of Finkielkraut and Fumaroli rest on a mythologized and nostalgic (not to mention elitist and ethnocentric) view of France and the Enlightenment tradition, but they also constitute a hopeless rearguard action in the face of contemporary developments.[5] Such a critique of the perspective offered by Finkielkraut and Fumaroli does not necessarily imply that, in the wake of modernity's dream of universal culture, the only option on offer today is total cultural relativism and unremitting doses of market-led kitsch and hackneyed pastiche (although this might well be the case). But it does suggest that the realities of the transformed relationship between culture and society and between art and everyday life cannot simply be wished away by a return to a lost golden age in which culture would be, in Matthew Arnold's terms, the salvation from anarchy, or that one can simply dismiss the anthropological concept of culture as 'tradition' and replace it with the pedagogical concept of culture as learning (*formation* or the German *Bildung*; cf. Todorov 1996: 180).

A view which is diametrically opposed to that of Finkielkraut and Fumaroli is proposed by Gilles Lipovetsky. Although he defines a similar trajectory to that outlined above as regards the evolution from modernity to postmodernity, Lipovetsky sees contemporary culture not as the antithesis of the Enlightenment tradition but, on the contrary, as the logical extension of the democratization of Western societies from the Revolution onwards, and the inevitable outcome of the Enlightenment pursuit of freedom and equality. Rather than bemoaning this state of affairs (like Finkielkraut and Fumaroli), he welcomes the more democratic notion of culture which has ensued from the breakdown in the hierarchical and elitist relationship between high and popular culture.

In *L'Ère du vide* (1983) Lipovetsky emphasizes not the differences but the similarities (at a profound rather than superficial level) between modernity and modernism. Following the thesis proposed by the conservative American political philosopher Daniel Bell in *Cultural Contradictions of Capitalism* (1976), he suggests that modernism simply pursued the republican message (being spread liberally elsewhere during the nineteenth century) *jusqu'au bout*. Modernism was the cultural development of the modern democratic project to realise the sovereignty of the individual, emancipated from all external control and freed from all attachments to the past and to tradition:

> Whatever the intention of the artists involved, modernism should be understood as the cultural extension of the revolutionary dynamic. The analogies between the revolutionary process and the modernist project are evident: the same desire to institute a radical and irreversible break between past and present; the same devalorization of tradition...the same secular consecration of the new era in the name of the people, equality, the nation in one case and art itself or the new 'Man' in the other; the same obsession with extremes, the same desire to raise the stakes, either on the level of ideology and terrorism or according to the passion for extending ever further the frontiers of artistic innovation; the same desire to transcend national frontiers in the name of the universalization of the new world (epitomized by the cosmopolitan style of avant-garde art); the same constitution of groups in the forefront of change, either political activists or the artists of the avant-garde...[in short] modernism was the implementation of the revolutionary model in the sphere of art.
>
> (Lipovetsky 1983: 129–130)

In other words, if the Revolution killed the King who maintained the old hierarchical order, and removed God from the affairs of Man – 'from the law of God to the rights of the citizen', as Marcel Gauchet

(1989: 16) has said – then modernism simply explored the consequences of this new credo. In this sense, modernism was modernity's
advance guard (its *avant-garde*), exploring a human condition no longer
bound by the pre-ordained laws of a transcendent authority.
Modernism was ultimately part of the same body of belief as that
which inspired modernity, founded on the principles of freedom,
equality and emancipation.

In Lipovetsky's schema (or rather, that of Daniel Bell), postmodernism is simply the extension, or 'democratization', of the movement
towards individual expression and freedom first explored by cultural
modernism's avant-garde. It is the acceptance of permanent change, of
radical novelty, of the equalizing and relativizing of values, and of the
breakdown of the frontiers between art and the everyday.[6]
Consequently, it signifies the end of 'the shock of the new':

> [Postmodernism is] the moment at which the avant-garde no
> longer incites indignation, the search for the new has become the
> norm, and pleasure and the stimulation of the senses have become
> the dominant values of society. In this sense, postmodernism is the
> democratization of hedonism, the universalized consecration of
> the New, the triumph of 'anti-institutionalism' and the end of the
> divorce between the values of art and those of everyday life.
>
> (Lipovetsky 1983: 151)

Like Daniel Bell, Lipovetsky interprets postmodernism as the sign
of a more open, liberal, egalitarian and democratic society. On one
level, this seems to be incontrovertible. The modernist avant-garde
was a group of middle-class, bohemian and almost exclusively male
intellectuals whose position in the vanguard of cultural experimentation was symbolic of an elitist and hierarchical ordering of social and
cultural values. Most others (women, the working class, other minorities) were denied access to cultural practice and cultural recognition.
The democratization of culture today, and the relativization of cultural
values, has provided a space for a whole range of new voices and modes
of expression. The blurring of the distinction between high and
popular culture, and between works of the spirit and everyday life, is
part of the anti-authoritarian and anti-hierarchical thrust of modern
democratic societies which is empowering for that part of the population (the majority) who formerly occupied a subordinate position.
Today the hedonism and freedom of expression formerly practised by
the few is the prerogative of us all.

However, on another level there are a number of problems with

Lipovetsky's account of modernism and postmodernism. Not the least of these is the haste with which he confuses the rule of the liberal free market today with genuine pluralism and democracy. Lipovetsky's analysis implies the realization of an equality and democracy in contemporary society which might be every bit as illusory as the Utopian version of equality introduced in the era of modernity. Neo-liberal principles of democratization and egalitarianism might well mask new forms of disadvantage and inequality. As the sociologist Alain Ehrenberg (1991: 149) has pointed out, explicitly criticizing Lipovetsky's approach as typical of the woolly liberalism of a number of French intellectuals in the wake of 'the end of ideology', the appearance today of *homo democraticus* can be mistaken for what is, in effect, simply wider access to consumption (cf. also a similar critique of Lipovetsky's conflation of individualism and democracy by Castoriadis 1996: 99).[7]

Furthermore, Lipovetsky's discussion also employs a very general schema for the understanding of the modern era which paints that period with very broad brush strokes indeed. His tendency to find the same principles of equality and individualism underlying modernity and its cultural offshoot, modernism (that is, traversing the social and the cultural) is to collapse one into the other with little nuance. In the process, he effaces modernism's genuinely unsettling and challenging qualities as modernity's counter-culture. Crucial to the spirit of modernity was the creation of *separate* spheres of human activity (between, precisely, the real and the imaginary, the social and the cultural, the public and the private, men and women, civilization and barbarity, the nation and its others, and so on) whose binary logic many modernist works delighted in transgressing. It is certainly true to say that, in the modern period, culture was deeply informed by wider social processes; but it was also profoundly questioning of them as well.[8]

Where Lipovetsky is more interesting – and rejoins a number of other commentators on the contemporary period – is his description of postmodernism as the generalization, and hence 'banalization', of modernist techniques. The avant-garde has itself disappeared as its defining features – including hedonism, self-expression, the new and the spectacular – have become the common mode in society. The world of permanent revolution is our everyday reality, our senses are jumbled, we are dislocated in time and space, we do live each day without a safety net, we are split and fragmented, we do pursue the life of the senses in the here and now – indeed all the profoundly unsettling insights into the predicament of the human condition proclaimed by modernism are today our commonplace truths.

In other words, society has usurped the principles of the modernist avant-garde. But, as we noted in the previous chapter, we have arrived in this place not by reading Rimbaud and Surrealism but through the changes wrought by advanced technology and mass consumer society. Today technical developments and processes of consumption have entered a new accelerated phase which has reshaped the world. We are living through what Alain Touraine termed at the end of the 1960s a post-industrial age which has profoundly destabilized our concepts of time and space and our sense of identity. In an age of order, rational planning and new rational (cognitive) spacing of the social sphere, the modernist avant-garde shocked by its brash challenge to (and aestheticization of) the logic of these processes. But today, in an age of disorder, the end of rational planning and the fragmentation of rational social spacing, the cultural reproduction of these techniques looks more like the reflection of social processes than a challenge to them. As the American critic Fredric Jameson (1984) suggested in his seminal text on the relationship between contemporary culture and society, postmodernism could just be the cultural logic of late capitalism.

Although it is precisely the equivalence and conflation of culture and society which Finkielkraut, Fumaroli and others have critiqued, their desire to turn the clock back ignores the profound and irreversible shift in our societies which has taken place. Krishan Kumar puts the evolution from modernity to postmodernity in the following terms:

> Modernism was generally a cultural reaction to the main currents of modernity. In some of its forms it was a passionate rejection of them. The same cannot be said of the relation between post-modernism and post-industrial (or late-capitalist) society. All theorists, if they consider the relationship at all, see a convergence or complementarity between post-modern culture and post-industrial society. While therefore it may be proper to treat modernist culture as something distinct from modern society, in the sense that it represented a break or discontinuity within the general order of modernity, the same strategy cannot be applied to post-modernism. But the problem is even greater than this. For not only is it difficult to consider post-modernist culture apart from its social context; in most of the attempts to do so it is clear that much of the content of post-modernism is derived from the theory's particular understanding of contemporary society. Culture

and society are only apparently treated separately; in reality they are collapsed into each other.

(Kumar 1995: 113–114)

Kumar's argument suggests that the transition from industrial to post-industrial society has profoundly changed the relationship between culture and society. The cultural phenomenon of postmodernism simply cannot be extricated from the surrounding social and economic fabric of post-industrial society because the two are profoundly imbricated in a new way. Culture and society are simply indistinguishable today. This is not simply because of the commodification of culture but, as Kumar goes on to say, because culture itself is deeply implicated in the whole economic enterprise of late capitalism, to the extent that it has shifted from its former position as part of the superstructure to its present position as part of the economic base. Indeed, these terms, as Alberto Melucci observes, might no longer be appropriate for post-industrial societies:

> The spatial metaphors that characterized industrial culture (base vs. superstructure, centrality vs. marginality) are increasingly inadequate in describing the workings of centre-less, and by now head-less, complex societies. The decentralization of the loci of power and conflict makes it more and more difficult to identify 'central' processes and actors.
>
> (Melucci 1996: 47) (cf. Jameson 1984)

The imbrication of culture and society today is, of course, part of the larger picture of the transformation of contemporary post-industrial societies. The dichotomies, hierarchies, value judgements and truths inherited from the Enlightenment have been flattened, relativized and decentred, so that the former categories separating different spheres of human activity are no longer capable of containing the more complex interconnections of processes today. And no totalizing rational principles or grand narratives can pull these dislocated pieces back into shape. The realms of art and thought (*la pensée*) – indeed, knowledge itself – no longer occupy a transcendent realm over and above local beliefs but are today profoundly touched by wider developments (whether one likes it or not). Knowledge cannot be separated from the functionalist uses to which it is put for, as Jean-François Lyotard argued in his study of the postmodern condition, knowledge is no longer defined according to the old abstract criteria but is itself regulated, like any other product, by its exchange value (1979: 14) and by its position within the complex network of 'techno-science'. In his more recent *Le Postmoderne expliqué aux enfants* (1988a), Lyotard put it like this: 'We cannot deny the predominance today of techno-science, that is, the reduction of cognitive statements to the rule of the best possible performance, or (in other words) the predominance of the technical criterion' (1988a: 19). Knowledge has passed from the abstract world of the spirit to the everyday and purely pragmatic world of the performative, in the same way as culture in general. Given the nature of the information revolution in recent years, knowledge is not only a commodity but an integral part of the late capitalist *modus operandi*. Like culture, knowledge is not simply driven by the needs of capital; it is a fundamental part of the motor which drives it.[9]

Perhaps the most significant aspect of the conflation of culture and society today is the effect of technological mediations of reality which have loosened our grip on a sense of the real. At the heart of the reactionary search for a golden national age (epitomized by the writings of Finkielkraut and Fumaroli) is the very genuine sense of a loss of reality brought about by the blurring of the frontiers between representation and the real. Recent French debates on this issue are an important contribution to the analysis of the inheritance of modernism's obsession with a universe of form.

The 'democratization' of the image

What Walter Benjamin (1973) called 'the mechanical reproduction of reality' has entered new realms with recent advances in technology. Modernism challenged the reality principle of modern societies by undermining a sense of objective truth and highlighting the play of form and representation; postmodern culture – driven by more sophisticated developments in the mechanical reproduction of reality or, to use Paul Virilio's term, 'the art of the motor' (Virilio 1993) – appears to have abandoned the reality principle altogether and is immured in a virtual world of ceaseless simulacra. This feeling is at the heart of what Olivier Mongin (1994a: 174) has described as the contemporary 'questioning of the very conditions of possibility of experience'. We noted in Chapter 1 how the postmodern focus on textuality and representation has dramatically transformed our apprehension and comprehension of the Holocaust. But it is also interesting to note how the sense of 'malaise' derived from the problematization of experience is very often linked to the more general crisis of the republican nation-state, for the latter is never far from the surface of the debate.

A good case in point is the work of the writer and former political activist Régis Debray. Debray is a particularly acute observer of the transformation from modern to postmodern society (although he does not necessarily use those terms). This transformation is characterized by some of the by now familiar changes in recent times: from a belief in universal reason to a concern with individual liberty, from the pedagogy of the school to the entertainment of the television, from the political nature of the citizen to the market-led nature of the consumer. But for Debray the major framework for the contextualization of these changes is advances in the technological reproduction of reality. If modern society was founded on the word, then postmodern society is founded on the electronically transmitted image. In Debray's terms, we have passed from the era of the 'graphosphere' to that of the 'videosphere' (Debray 1993: 74–75).

For Debray this is a change of epistemological proportions. The ubiquitous nature of the image and the expansion of the 'mediatized market-place' (Debray 1993: 98) across all spheres of political, social and cultural life have transformed society from one concerned with meaning, explanation and interpretation to one concerned with expression, information and communication. The distances that formerly separated different spheres − between the state and the individual, between the word and the world, between here and there, and so on − have been abolished so that the *act* of communication is all that really matters (and not the *substance* of what is communicated), the *dissemination* of information (and not the information which is disseminated).[10] We have passed from a 'civilization of the symbol' to a 'civilization of the index' (Debray 1993: 31): the former consisted of codes of signification of the world while the latter abolishes the distinction between sign and referent 'to incorporate the public into the spectacle' (Debray 1993: 35). In the process, we have moved from a concept of culture founded on critical distance and analysis to one founded on proximity and effusion:

> In the world of the index, experience is more important than analysis. The first is physical, the second intellectual. Experience and first-person enunciation is immediate, live, 'hot'; analysis and impersonal statement are pre-recorded, removed from context, 'cold'. In the 'videosphere', the act of communication is more important than the content, and the act of enunciation counts for more than the statement enounced. What is fundamental is contact not discourse.
>
> (Debray 1993: 127)[11]

The age of the 'videosphere' has installed a new reality – '[the civilization of the index] has not simply modified our access to the real, it has become *another reality*' (Debray 1993: 31) – one which can be apprehended instantly and without recourse to interpretation, for there is now no longer any distinction between the medium and what is represented. Subject and object are fused, the illusion of direct apprehension made palpable, the boundaries between event and spectator, performer and audience, abolished through the instantaneous nature of the electronically produced message. Mongin (1993: 105) remarks on the 'perverse effect' of the 'communication society': 'On the one hand, it provides a present without history, a self-sufficient present, and on the other hand it establishes a direct relation between communicants at the expense of all mediation.'

In the political sphere, the distinctions between politicians and 'the people', and between political programmes and 'public opinion' are being progressively effaced. It is no longer a question of 'we will give you what's good for you' but 'we will give you what you want' because I am you and you are me. Martin Jacques has suggested that sport has become the clearest example of this process of identification which characterizes the new 'democracy': 'There is a continuum between star and punter; we are all enfranchised, it is a democratic activity. This makes the stars peculiarly accessible. They are people we can relate to and identify with' ('Worshipping the body at the altar of sport', *Observer*, 13 July 1997).[12] In his analyses of the links between sport, democracy and identity, Alain Ehrenberg would surely endorse this statement while underlining the fact that this identification of 'star and punter' is a potent indicator of the anxious quest for equality, excellence and individual value in societies traversed by inequalities and the breakdown of collective values (cf. Ehrenberg 1988). This form of identification accompanies the blurring of spectacle and life in the democratization of contemporary societies. In his book *Les Stars*, the sociologist Edgar Morin had already remarked on the confusion between the two as long ago as 1957. In the preface to the 1972 edition of this book, he states: 'the mythology of stars is situated in a mixed and confused zone between belief and entertainment.' Today that zone has become even more 'mixed and confused'.

This blurring of boundaries, the disappearance of reality into a world of simulations (which do not announce that they are images *of* the world but state simply 'we *are* the world'), underpinned by the advances in electronic mass media and information technology, clearly has much in common with Jean Baudrillard's analysis of the death of meaning, the destruction of the social and the ubiquitous nature of simulacra in contemporary society. Baudrillard's work has progressively moved towards a rejection of the Marxist distinction between economic structures and phenomenal forms (base and superstructure), and between regimes of truth and appearance. The commodification of the social order has destroyed the Enlightenment distinction between object and representation and created a depthless world of simulacra or, in Baudrillard's terms, 'hyperreality', whose function, as Steven Connor (1989: 57) observes, is to be 'more real than reality itself' (or 'realler than real', Kellner 1989: 82). This ceaseless world of commodified simulations, which is our lot in postmodern times, endlessly stimulates and seduces us but deprives us of any means to step outside its tyrannical rule (as the distinction between inside and outside no longer exists), and neutralizes all attempts at political contestation. Baudrillard's later work takes Jameson's theories on the dissolution of the distinction between socio-economic life and cultural forms to an extreme in which all boundaries (between, for example, reality and illusion, subject and object, theory and practice) have been collapsed into the smooth space of simulation. Georges Balandier offers a very similar analysis of the convergence of reality and illusion through advanced technology, and the corresponding disappearance of culture beneath the uniform rule of the image:

> Technical advances consume nature and the profusion of images swallows up culture. The configurations of today's world are constituted by this excess of images and the accompanying flow of words and sounds. They shape the world and transform it into a *hyper-world*. They sweep up everything in their movement, abolishing all links with a transcendent meaning and obscuring the fixed points of reality which orient our paths through life.
>
> (Balandier 1994: 137)

Debray employs a far more explicit *national* framework for the understanding of these developments. Audio-visual culture, which has replaced a word-based culture, is not simply the sign of the 'passivization' of the individual, forced to respond uncritically to the barrage of stimuli spewed out unremittingly day after day (cf. Finkielkraut's description of the 'zombie' in *La Défaite de la pensée*); it is also the sign of the passage from a *republican* to a *democratic* ethos, from 'republican distancing' to 'the ideal of democratic effusion' (Debray 1993: 34; see also Debray 1989). The former is associated directly with the French Enlightenment national tradition, the latter with the contemporary globalization (or, more accurately, Americanization) of post-industrial societies. Debray uses the antithesis between republic and democracy in the same way that Finkielkraut and Fumaroli use the antithesis between France and 'the Anglo-Saxon world'. Profoundly attached to the values of French republicanism, Debray therefore interprets the democratization of culture through the audio-visual media as antithetical to the French model of the nation-state: 'The arts which one could define as of national interest, in that they are coded by a language (theatre, literature, poetry), have given way to arts of world interest, in that they are not linguistically coded (music, dance, visual media in general)' (Debray 1993: 50).[13]

This national framing of the evolution from the word to the image is shared by a number of other French commentators. For example, Balandier (1992: 147) maintains, like Debray, that 'the process of democracy requires a pedagogy of the image. The image is as intrinsic an element in contemporary democracy as were reading and writing in the founding of the republican school and the Republic in general'. Paul Virilio sees this 'democratization' of the image in apocalyptic terms. In *L'Art du moteur* (1993) he suggests that the developments in technological mediations of reality have affected our perceptions of time and space in such profound ways that we are no longer able to appreciate the extent to which our notions of the real have been altered:

> Acceleration has effaced the distinction between here and there. All that is left is a mental confusion of near and far, present and future and real and unreal. What we have today is the mixing of history, of histories, and the hallucinating Utopia implanted by techniques of communication.
>
> (Virilio 1993: 55)

Paradoxically, the more sophisticated the technological mediation of reality, the less we can actually 'see'; the more images there are, the less skilled we become in using our imagination.[14] At the end of his book *Vie et Mort de l'image* (1992: 499), Debray outlines the frightening prospect that today's era of the dominance of visual culture (*le visuel*) – in which the world is instantly accessible and visible, as if unmediated – installs a new regime of truth: 'the Visible = the Real = the Truth'. All former civilizations believed that the image prevented seeing: we are the first civilization to reverse this formula. In the process, we are witnessing the death of the image. As Mongin (1994a: 219–220) says, 'an image without a world is the sign of the hegemony of the visual but also a sign of the death of the image for the distinction between inside and outside has been abolished'. Alain Ehrenberg, on the other hand, is more open to the new possibilities offered by the electronic transformation of reality. He wonders whether recent developments should be interpreted as a crisis in looking at the world or simply as a change to our habitual ways of looking (1995: 285; cf. the special section entitled 'Vices et vertus de l'image' in *Esprit* 1994). For Ehrenberg, virtual reality has the potential for opening up new spaces for imaginative interaction in the same way as certain drugs, although without the negative effects (1995: 290). Yet he is careful to avoid any unconditional celebration of cyberspace, for it reflects both the possibilities and the anxieties of individuals in an 'uncertain' age.

Paul Virilio believes that the germs of the above paradox – namely, that the era of *le visuel* is the era of the death of the image and the death of seeing – were there at the very beginning of the electronic revolution:

> From the beginning of the electronic revolution, the production of images destroyed a static organisation and, correspondingly, the restfulness of vision and the tranquillity of enlightened contemplation...and created a visual misinformation which would soon reduce the procedures of representation and communication to their simplest forms.
>
> (Virilio 1993: 97)

For Virilio, 'video-graphic tyranny' (1993: 102) is a new form of control far worse than state-run propaganda and misinformation. He believes that the dictatorship of the image heralds the demise of three-dimensional 'Man':

> Seeing the world presupposes a depth of field of vision. If the world is flattened and crushed it loses this depth and we lose our depth of action and reflection. We become two-dimensional. That is what the rule of the screen really means.
>
> (Virilio 1996: 103)

Tzvetan Todorov (1996: 179) adopts a similarly apocalyptic tone when he observes that 'the monotony of images transmitted by the media deprives us of our freedom and therefore even our identity'. Cornelius Castoriadis has also castigated the new 'democratization' of culture. He suggests that the result of 'consumer-telly' is a passivization of the individual and an obliteration of choice by a new mass conformism: 'I maintain that we are living through the most conformist phase of modern history' (1994: 48; cf. Le Goff 1996: 219). In his eyes, the 'arrogant' and 'stupid' theories of postmodernism merely give credence to what is, in effect, a realization of 'the most pessimistic prophecies that we have received, from Tocqueville and the "mediocrity" of the "democratic" individual, to Nietzsche and nihilism...up to Spengler, Heidegger and after' (Castoriadis 1994: 49). Virilio suggests that this immunization against experience by the technological virtualization of reality can only be countered by a return to writing and a recreation of the 'art of the eco' (Conley 1996).[15] Balandier also suggests that only the written word can provide the critical detachment from lived experience necessary for any genuine democratic life, for the simultaneity of the image encourages merely emotional affinity and is, by necessity, simplifying and impoverishing (Balandier 1994: 207).

However, Régis Debray is far more sceptical of turning back the clock. He is conscious of the irrevocable interpenetrations of culture and society discussed above, and hence the impossibility of rediscovering a 'pure' space of seeing, talking and writing which is untainted by the electronic information networks of our age. As he says, 'in reality, information and belief are interrelated' (1993: 69; see also Debray 1994: 70 and Mourier, ed., 1989). In his excellent introduction to the work of Régis Debray for an English-speaking audience, Keith Reader notes the difficulty in determining to what extent Debray 'is analytically accounting for the inevitable erosion of the imagination by the image or lodging a romantic protest against it'. I would suggest that Debray's response is usually a mixture of the two, 'the detached analyst and the concerned individual' (Reader 1995: 64; for a further discussion of Debray's recent work, see also the contributions in 'Identification d'un objet: la médiologie' in *Le Débat* 1995).

Whatever the reaction to current trends, one can detect common strands running through the writings of a number of the French commentators mentioned above: the breakdown in the distinctions between culture and everyday life and between the real and the image, and the decline of the written word and the republic in favour of the image and democracy, respectively, invariably run in tandem with an apocalyptic vision of the decline of the French 'model' of the nation. For some this is simply presented as a statement of fact. For others, it is part of a general critique of postmodern society and a nostalgic idealization of republican France, depicted as victim to the influence of foreign ideas and practices. For the latter, the ideas prevalent in the 1960s and those that informed structuralism and post-structuralism are the usual culprits for this departure from the rational humanism of the French republican tradition.

But even when this reactionary and nostalgic element is less visible, one can often detect a distaste for 'democratization' among French intellectuals. Democracy signifies the flattening and equivalence of the hierarchical distinctions which informed the republican model. It is a pick-and-mix and relativist multiculturalism which reduces real diversity to the same bland formula of market-led personal taste and individual desire, and in which it becomes impossible to distinguish or 'make sense of' anything at all. It is an individualistic interpellation of 'the people', a form of populism, which appeals to the base instincts of the masses; this is diametrically opposed to the republican moulding of *le peuple* into a homogeneous whole through an uplifting concept of culture and civilization.[16] Historically, it is therefore associated (as we have seen) with the German romantic tradition of the *Volk* and the anthropological definition of culture, as opposed to the French Enlightenment and classical tradition of *le peuple*, and receives all the opprobrium that the former tradition has attracted from a stream of French intellectuals over the decades.[17]

Yet it is also profoundly informed by the ambivalent reaction to American mass culture which has characterized the modernization of France from at least the 1950s. On the one hand, American-style economic practices and cultural forms were embraced enthusiastically by an administrative class and people respectively, keen to enter the modern world in the post-war reconstruction of the country. On the other hand, the brashness of the changes wrought (especially in the cities) and the associations made between new technology, mass culture and mass consumption were often viewed negatively as a new enslavement of France. The films of Jean-Luc Godard in the 1960s are a good example of this ambiguous response, for they frequently demonstrate both a fascination with and demonization of the Americanization of French culture, which is seen both as a force of liberation and democratization and as a neo-colonization of France (cf. Ross 1995). More recently, the transformation of museums of 'high culture' (the Louvre, the Musée d'Orsay) into cultural supermarkets, in which the trappings of commercialized mass culture are to the fore, is a further example of the tension between democratization and consumerism, the preservation of French national culture and enslavement to the norms of American mass culture (cf. Pugh 1997).

'Democratization' therefore has an ambivalent status, but in French intellectual life is often associated with a pejorative view of 'the popular' and 'the mass'. Olivier Mongin has remarked on this tendency in the following way:

The rejection of democracy is a very powerful force among French intellectuals. Whether they are conservatives or progressives, they have always seen the 'demos', the populace, either as the masses who have gone astray or as cattle with fascist tendencies. This contempt for the democrat and for the 'person in the street' remains very real at a time when the accusation of nationalism is used to discredit any opinion, by intellectuals for whom 'opinion' is usually seen as the most extreme form of ignorance and stupidity.

(Mongin 1994b: 63)

This pejorative conflation of democracy, popular culture and the masses, to which Mongin refers, has its equivalents in Britain but would be dismissed by many as simply a sign of an elitist and reactionary position. However, in France it would be wrong to dismiss it in the same way for, as Mongin points out, conservatives *and* radicals have shared this opinion. It is, to a large extent, the power of the republican Enlightenment tradition and its elites, the strength of the State and the relative 'poverty of civil society' (Minc 1995: 66; cf. Chapter 5) that explains how 'the popular', popular culture and democracy have often been conflated in this pejorative way.[18] It is therefore no surprise that what Jim McGuigan (1992) calls 'cultural populism' – which has significantly informed the British cultural studies tradition – does not have its direct equivalent in France, where ideas of popular culture have been fostered within a different overall context on culture in general (cf. Rigby 1991, Looseley 1995). This difference helps to explain why the anthropological and sociological definition of culture is often seen by French commentators as an 'Anglo-Saxon' (or German) invention.

However, 'national models' are always constructions which simplify the messy nature of reality. As we have seen, 'cultural populism' also has its advocates in France (see, for example, Lipovetsky 1987, Yonnet 1985), and there are as many problems with their 'uncritical populist drift' (McGuigan 1992: 5) as with the 'critical populist drift' outlined above. An uncritical celebration of the everyday pursuits of ordinary people (see, for example, in Britain the ethnographic work of Paul Willis) is frequently anti-intellectualist, has no mechanism for critiquing the 'nastier' aspects of everyday life (for example, popular racism), fails to view the interconnections between 'everyday life', popular culture and wider economic and social determinations (for example, the inseparability today of popular and advertising culture; cf. Pugh 1997: 167), and can simply reinforce a liberal free-market economic perspective by implicitly endorsing the rights of the consumer.

Caught between (republican) critique and (democratic) celebration, French commentators on contemporary culture (like those elsewhere) are uncertain of the definition of culture today, and its status and function. This uncertainty spreads to the role of intellectuals in defining and commenting on the nature of culture today. The final section in this chapter considers these wider aspects of recent cultural debates.

Culture, counter-culture and intellectuals

Even though the debate around postmodern culture in France often takes place within the partisan context of the republic versus democracy, and within a long French tradition of scepticism towards mass popular culture, we should not, for all that, underestimate the genuine fears and unease expressed by a diverse range of commentators on the nature of culture today. For the convergence of culture and society and the democratization of culture under the banner of a vigorous and (since the end of communism) triumphant phase of capitalism have put in question not only the distinctions between high, popular and mass culture and the values of the Enlightenment, but also the radical tradition of political, subversive or marginal counter-cultural forms whose very existence challenged the status quo. In Chapter 3 we touched on this issue in terms of the aestheticization of the social domain and the consequent conversion of the *flâneur* into the customer. I should like to pursue this question here, paying particular attention to the way in which these developments have affected concepts of culture and the intellectual.

If it is true, as Fredric Jameson (1984) has suggested, that eclectic postmodern culture is none other than the 'cultural logic' of late capitalism, then this would suggest that not only has the modernist avant-garde critique of modern society been blunted (as we suggested in the second section of this chapter) but that other non-elitist sub- and counter-cultures have also been absorbed into the mainstream, in which case cultural practices which were radical in the past have been transformed from industrial society's *bête noire* into the house style of post-industrial society. We need only think of the ways in which the modernist techniques of fragmentation, juxtaposition, montage and self-reflexivity – all of which unsettled views of reality and challenged a conventional sense of time, space and identity – are now employed liberally in advertising and pop videos to promote products for consumption. Do these techniques shock us any more, or have we been so over-exposed to 'the new' that they are now more likely to be received with a yawn than a frisson? Is it possible today to tell the difference between the techniques of advertising and those used in numerous films, in view of the fact that they not only resemble each other formally but are often made by the same people? Or would we agree with Adrian Searle ('Art and politics don't mix', *Guardian*, 25 February 1997) when he states, in relation to the photomontage technique of Peter Kennard, that 'we have seen too many such "subversive" images for them to be effective, and what was once a radical technique has become part of the mainstream media lexicon'? Lipovetsky (1987: 321) suggests that the built-in obsolescence of artistic experimentation today and the ceaseless coming and going of new artists have converted the artistic sphere into a 'theatre of frivolous revolution which shocks nobody'.

The debate around the *cinéma du look* or 'new new wave' film directors of the 1980s and 1990s, Jean-Jacques Beineix, Luc Besson and Léos Carax, highlights this point. Are films like *Diva* (1981), *Le Grand Bleu* (1988) and *Les Amants du Pont Neuf* (1990) simply 'spectacular publicity sequences' (Russell 1989/1990: 46) whose sole *raison d'être* is as a visual spectacle for the purpose of seduction (Frodon 1995: 575), 'the image for and of itself' (Hayward 1993: 247; see also Hayward 1987)? Has the cinema simply become the reflection of the consumer society of spectacle rather than its ideological critic (à la Godard)? Or does it still engage in defamiliarization and critique while trawling through the eclectic visual and aural vocabulary which constitutes contemporary cultures? David Russell (1989/1990: 47) situates Beineix at the crossroads of a number of convergences in contemporary culture: 'Just as [Beineix] is at the forefront of the postmodern dialogue between publicity and cinema, comic strips and narrative, opera and thriller, high and low art forms, so he is also part of the great European-American cinematic debate.' Yet the role he plays in this dialogue and debate remains controversial: is it simply as an agent of pick-and-mix postmodern eclecticism and pastiche, or is it as a serious commentator on the relationship between culture and society today?

The former response would suggest that the techniques of intertextuality, 'recycled materials' (Bassan 1989: 49), and the play of image and sound at the heart of postmodern culture herald the end of counter-cultures. If the ultimate sign of anti-conformism today is the democratization and repetition of techniques whose radical cutting-edge is long past its sell-by date, or, alternately, to display a Nike logo on your footwear (in imitation of the 'bad boys' and 'anti-heroes' of the world of sport) then counter-culture is indeed doomed. As Sami Naïr remarks (Morin and Naïr 1997: 226), 'today, even radical art fails to disturb the all-encompassing conformism. Commodification has swallowed up everything.'

The ideas expressed by Baudrillard, Debray and others on the implosion of meaning and the collapse of 'the real' into depthless surfaces and endless simulacra would tend to reinforce the notion of the end of counter-cultures. As we have seen, the subversive or transgressive nature of modernist techniques was linked to a tension between a concept of the real (very much still in place in the positivist and rationalist climate of the nineteenth century) and self-reflexive forms of representation. But if, today, we have lost a sense of the real and a sense of experience, if, that is, art has simply given up on notions of the 'real' and 'experience' to indulge in pure self-reflexivity and parody, then the tension in the modern era which produced modernism no longer exists and self-referentiality (having become the norm) is no longer challenging. As Michael Collins says in relation to ironic comedy on television:

> Irony has become to television what the installation has become to the art world. A concept that came up on the outside, and once kicked against the pricks, now lays the flagstones for a new orthodoxy...the trouble with an insurrection is that you can't keep it up.
>
> ('You must be joking', *Guardian*, 14 July 1997)

How can we be unsettled today if we are no longer able to tell the difference between reality and image? How can we be shocked if we have become anaesthetized against the real by the ceaseless bombardment of images? If everything exists (or appears to exist) on the same plane, the subversion of hierarchies becomes a contradiction in terms. Postmodernism would therefore be the depoliticization of culture. Despite his fairly uncritical celebration of postmodernism, Gilles Lipovetsky underlines this very point when he describes the 1960s (once again quoting the argument of Daniel Bell) as the moment at which the radical nature of modernism gives way to the depoliticized mass hedonism of postmodernism:

> The sixties were a beginning and an end. They signal the end of modernism, the final manifestation of the offensive launched against puritan and utilitarian values, the ultimate movement of cultural revolt (this time a mass movement). But they also signal

the beginning of a postmodern culture, that is, a culture which does not innovate and with no real daring, which is simply a democratization of the logic of hedonism and an extension of the process of privileging 'the basest tendencies rather than the most noble'.
(Lipovetsky 1983: 151–152; see also Lipovetsky 1987: 288–291)

This ambivalent epitaph to the 1960s is probably a more accurate reflection of the different tendencies which informed that decade than those descriptions which simply celebrate the movements of subversion of order and liberation through carnival. Margaret Atack (1997: 296) puts May 1968 firmly within the ambivalent hinterland between liberation and commodification, and between 'reality' and representation: 'Was May 1968 a great battle against the consumer society or did it show that in the society of spectacle, social protest itself was now appropriated as a consumer product?' (see also Jill Forbes on the nature of carnival in Forbes and Kelly 1995: 247). Atack suggests that the commodification of social relations through image-production is at the heart of a number of fictional critiques of the new mass culture of 1960s consumer society (Simone de Beauvoir's *Les Belles images*, 1966, or Georges Perec's *Les Choses*, 1965), as well as sociological critiques (Edgar Morin's *Les Stars*, 1957, and Guy Debord's *La Société du spectacle*, 1967).

Since the 1960s, the advance of the image-production of reality of consumer societies has continued apace. In the process, counter-cultures have become less and less distinguishable from the all-embracing market which dominates our lives. What Beauvoir saw as the task of demystifying the commodification of the image to reveal a reality full of jagged rather than smooth edges, and what the Situationists saw as the inherent contradictions of the 'society of spectacle' which opened up spaces of resistance to and subversion of capitalist society, Baudrillard has retheorized as the total appropriation of the real by the spectacle and, consequently, the end of all possibility of transgression and subversion. According to Baudrillard (1997: 183), the decline of *any* aesthetic principle today springs not from 'the extinction of art but from aesthetic saturation'; the democratization of creativity inherited from the 1960s (we are all creators) has led, paradoxically to the demise of creation itself. Sadie Plant's attempt to reinvigorate Baudrillard's jaded perspective by reviving the liberationist and optimistic potential of the vision of the Situationists, and her effort 'to reintroduce some sense of meaning, purpose and passion to a postmodern discourse of futile denial' (Plant 1992: 183) are admirable in principle but perhaps insufficient on their own as a critique of the 'dumbing down' of cultural radicalism today and the commodification of culture upon which it is premised. Even Castoriadis, an avowed opponent of the decline of the radical and critical tradition of culture and criticism (and the role of intellectuals), is pessimistic about current trends in the light of aggressive commodification and the effect of the media:

> The word 'revolutionary' – like the words 'creation' or 'imagination' – has become a publicity slogan. This is what a few years ago was termed 'recuperation'. Marginality has become something to be sought after and has moved to the centre; subversion has become an interesting curiosity which rounds off the harmony of the system. Contemporary society has a frightening capacity to smother all real divergence from the norm, either by silencing it or by transforming it into a phenomenon like all others, commodified like all others.
>
> (Castoriadis 1996: 86–87)

Castoriadis' analysis is a depressing assessment of current trends. It gives rise to a fundamental question raised by numerous other commentators on cultural and social developments: in an age of mass consumption, has the social function of culture simply given way to an aesthetic function, itself swallowed up by the insatiable appetite of commodity capitalism? If this is indeed the case, then we must agree that culture is no longer propelled by a concept of *le beau* or by a concept of critical engagement with and subversion of the status quo, but simply by the criteria of sensation, pleasure, entertainment and leisure, and driven ultimately by market forces. Seduction through spectacle has replaced striving for superior knowledge, contemplation in tranquillity or critical engagement through defamiliarization. As Steven Connor says (1989: 47) in relation to Jameson's theories of postmodernism and consumer society 'no means seem to be available to separate culture from everything else, and there is greatly reduced scope for claiming that within culture there may be ways of thwarting the inexorable rhythms of appropriation and alienation of consumer capitalism'.

If this is true then critical purchase on social norms has been abolished and its explanatory framework for the demystification of capitalism's modes of alienation recuperated as simply another form of representation. Cultural practitioners and critics have consequently been converted from crusaders whose mission is to unmask the hidden laws of alienating consumer society into tourists on a pre-packaged holiday. As Jean-Joseph Goux has remarked, salvation and liberation through art are simply no longer on the cards:

> For three-quarters of a century now, art itself has, more often than not, renounced...the task of idealist compensation assigned to it by Hegel. All it can do is recognize the very process which has rendered it less and less significant.
>
> (Goux 1994: 107–108)

François Hers and Bernard Latarjet describe how this might be a totally new phase in the history of art which signals dangers of all sorts:

> Despite its apparent fecundity, contemporary art has become more and more a self-referential practice. Cut off from any transcendent function, it has lost its role as a medium. Artists and those responsible for the dissemination of their works find it difficult to specify which essential needs of society are catered for by their practice.... Society itself has also become incapable of judging.... The current confusion could leave the way clear for the market to be the only social arbiter of what qualifies as art and what does not. This is hardly its role.
>
> (Hers and Latarjet 1990: 301)

The conclusion drawn by Hers and Latarjet, that the decision as to the function of art cannot simply be left to the market, is shared by a number of commentators of different persuasions, although their solutions (if offered at all) diverge. It is precisely the danger of the commodification of culture that has led Jean-François Lyotard, for example, to proclaim that cultural practice must, in the final analysis, resist all attempts at recuperation. His notion of 'the sublime' is that which is beyond naming and appropriation. For Lyotard, it is only by keeping alive the radical cutting edge of modernism – its problematization of language and representation – that we can pre-empt 'closure' and recuperation. Postmodern culture should therefore, ironically, be driven by the very spirit guiding modernism before it was colonized, anaesthetized and sanitized by capitalism: namely, the self-reflexive and open-ended search for forms which refuse representation but instead gesture obliquely towards the ineffable nature of 'the other' and the world. Julia Kristeva's description of the fleeting nature of 'the stranger' (his/her 'strangeness') gestures towards the same vision:

Let us not seek to fix the strangeness of the stranger or turn it into an object. Let us just touch it, skim it lightly, without giving it any definitive structure. Let us simply sketch the perpetual movement of some of its many different faces which pass before our eyes today.

(Kristeva 1988: 11)

However, this is an exercise fraught with difficulty, given that the processes of fragmentation, self-reflexivity and ceaseless reinvention – the very processes which Lyotard promotes as a means of problematizing closure, unity and totality – are those same processes exploited mercilessly by the new designers and the market. Indeed, some have suggested that Lyotard's emphasis on the absence of any privileged position from which to judge the plurality of language games and truth regimes in contemporary society provides the perfect rationale for the rule of unrestrained (and unethical) relativist liberalism (cf. Norris 1993).

Feminism presents perhaps the clearest example of this narrow line between subversion and recuperation, between marginality (or 'liminality') and the mainstream. The works of Hélène Cixous, Julia Kristeva and Luce Irigaray, for example, have all, in different ways, opened up radical spaces of contestation of the patriarchal dichotomies of modernity (Moi 1985), and might therefore be seen as exemplary of postmodern difference and the irrecuperable nature of 'the other'. However, if it is true that power is no longer located in centralized and (relatively) homogeneous institutions (for example, the state) but is dispersed in multiple local and global formations and on multiple micro and macro levels, then the distinction between the centre and the margins no longer holds in the same way today, and spaces of resistance and radical marginality become difficult places to inhabit for any length of time. The celebration and commodification of nomadism, difference and otherness that we discussed in relation to 'the Jew' in Chapter 1 and the *flâneur* in Chapter 3, and which can also be applied to 'woman' as other to 'male' rationality, can quickly nullify the subversive impact or 'radical openness' (hooks 1991: 149) of cultural difference, of *l'étrangeté*, and reappropriate it for the market, thereby obliterating the radical potential of feminist sexual politics.[19]

Philippe Sollers has suggested (with tongue in cheek) that – given that the opposition between the centre and the margins (or any opposition for that matter) has been abolished – 'the best way to be on the margins in a system which devours everything is to be at the centre....The subversive act par excellence is the avoidance of marginalization' (quoted in Mongin 1994a: 233).[20] This is not unlike

Baudrillard's notion that, according to Bauman's résumé (1992: 153), 'the bovine immobility of the masses is the best form of activity we have, and that their doing nothing is the most excellent form of resistance'. The (ironic?) suggestion that 'the apathy of the masses can be seen as a "strategic resistance"' (Kellner 1989: 89) is an indication of the profound cynicism which has marked approaches to political activity since the radical politics of the 1960s. These are the responses of intellectuals for whom the melting down of all that was solid (Berman 1982) and the disappearance of boundaries signifies the impossibility of old forms of subversion.

On the other hand, unreconstructed humanists like Alain Finkielkraut and Marc Fumaroli offer an equally problematic solution to the market logic of postmodern culture. They wish to cling on to the Enlightenment link between culture as a set of universal values to which humanity must aspire and the organic role of the intellectual in bringing this about. In *La Défaite de la pensée* (1987), Finkielkraut explicitly places his text in the context of Julien Benda's famous work on *La Trahison des clercs* (1977; first published 1927), in which Benda berates those intellectuals who have adopted partisan ideologies and abandoned the universalist principles of humanity (cf. also Finkielkraut 1996: 65–67). According to Finkielkraut, today's intellectuals have similarly 'sold out' the pursuit of reason, truth and justice and joined the pleasure-seeking masses by embracing market-driven cultural relativism. Fumaroli adopts a similar stance and believes that, instead of merely accepting the impoverishment of culture, intellectuals should play a role of 'reorientation and resistance' (Debray and Fumaroli 1993: 14). Both want to reinstate the Enlightenment link between learning and teaching (hence the centrality of the school in republican critiques of postmodern culture).[21] Theirs is an Arnoldian concept founded on the Enlightenment distinction between culture and anarchy which views postmodern culture, in George Steiner's terms, as 'a post-cultural condition' (cf. Bauman 1992: 34).

However, if Matthew Arnold could preach with the certainty and self-confidence that came with Western domination of the rest of the world (when Western culture *was* universal culture), today's imitators of Arnold sound more like the defensive guardians of a parochialism which, ironically, Arnold himself would have abhorred. Postmodern relativism has transformed old-style cultural crusaders into elitist and ethnocentric pedants. Furthermore, it has left their ideas on the crusading role of intellectuals as hopelessly outdated. Intellectuals today are no longer armed with the certainty of a transcendent version of truth which propelled them into the vanguard of modernity's crusade for freedom, justice and progress (cf. Silverman 1994). With the end of grand narratives, the demise of the heady ideologies of modernity, the decentring of the West, and the rise of mass audio-visual culture, the intellectual's voice (like the transcendent position of classical culture itself) has been relativized. Does the contemporary collapse of hierarchies signal the death of the intellectual, since the latter's existence as prophet and political and cultural crusader depended on a transcendent realm and the distinction between theory and practice which have now disappeared?

In Zygmunt Bauman's terms (1987), the passage from modernity to postmodernity has been accompanied by the transformation of the intellectual from legislator to interpreter. If, formerly, the intellectual acted as the legitimizing and proselytizing authority for the modern universalist ideals of freedom and progress, today the intellectual's task is a far more modest one of interpreting between different 'language communities'. They are now bound by the differentialist and pluralist ethos of the age and therefore speak, inevitably, from within a partic-ular tradition rather than proclaim universal truths (given that it is now understood that universalism was always only ever a particu-larism). In other words, the interpreter (unlike the legislator) implicitly recognizes the fact that knowledge is always 'situated'. At the same time that culture loosened its ties with the grand humanist project of social engineering, so many intellectuals have progressively dropped their view of culture as a social task to be accomplished in favour of the anthropological notion of culture as an attribute to be celebrated.

In an early issue of the journal *Le Débat*, Pierre Nora confirmed the changed status of the intellectual by suggesting that 'the reign of the superior thinker is coming to an end' (quoted in Peters 1993: 94). Lyotard's work has for long advocated this more modest role for intel-lectuals, in the context of the absence of any overall authority:

> It is probable now and for the foreseeable future [that] we, as philosophers, as much as we may be concerned by politics (and inevitably we are so concerned), are no longer in a position to say publicly: 'Here is what you must do.'... This is not to say that there are no longer any intellectuals, but today's intellectuals, philosophers in so far as they are concerned by politics and by questions of community, are no longer able to take up obvious and pellucid positions: they cannot speak in the name of an 'unques-tionable' universality.
>
> (cited in Smart 1993: 37)[22]

The proliferation, in recent years, of works on the intellectual (see, for example, Mongin 1994a, Rieffel 1993, Schiffer 1995, Sirinelli 1990, Spire 1996; see also the dossier entitled 'La Ve République des clercs' in *Le Débat* 1994) might itself be symptomatic of the demise of a tradition which was intricately connected to the abstract ideologies of the Enlightenment and their embodiment within the republican state (Macey 1995: 124). One tendency which clearly emerges from the current obsession with the intellectual is a revisionist one. Intellectual history is revisited in order to castigate the abstract ideological dogmatism and moral blindness of past gurus (see, for example, Lévy 1987 and Judt 1992), and hence to clear the way for a more 'sensible' return to the individual in the form of a neo-liberalism and celebration of Western democracy (as announced in the 'end of history' thesis proposed by Francis Fukuyama). As Castoriadis has observed,

> now that the totalitarian regimes have crumbled and Marxism-Leninism has been destroyed, the majority of Western intellectuals now pass their time glorifying the Western regimes as 'democratic', not ideal perhaps...but the best humanly possible, and suggesting at the same time that any criticism of this pseudo-democracy leads right back to the Gulag.
>
> (Castoriadis 1996: 85)

However, this revisionism should not necessarily be confused with the more general change in status and function of the intellectual outlined above. The postmodern condition does not inevitably (one hopes) lead to an unconditional neo-liberalism. It means, instead, a different way of talking to others and a different type of political engagement.

What, then, is the role of the intellectual in a postmodern age? Is the post-cultural and post-ideological age necessarily the post-intellectual age as well, or does it simply signify a different type of intellectual activity? This decentred figure can no longer occupy the moral high ground, can no longer speak with the voice of authority, can no longer 'legislate' in the same way as in the past. An absence of centre means an anxious quest rather than a confident and messianic proclamation. The postmodern intellectual is conscious of the 'end of grand narratives', conscious of the fragile and contingent nature of his or her voice, and conscious of the fact that it is one voice (itself ambivalent) jostling with others rather than speaking for them. The words which mobilized intellectuals in the past – involvement, responsibility, commitment, morality, and so on – may not be completely redundant today but may simply have taken on new meanings in a changed context. Today they find themselves in a deregulated and de-institutionalized age: that is, an age in which they can no longer be swallowed up by overarching grand narratives, mass social movements or a strong nationally oriented state, all of which, in their way, chan-nelled these terms – and channelled identity – into their own projects. Today, as Michael Walzer has said, 'morality is something we have to argue about' (quoted in Weeks 1993: 195). Jacques Derrida (1992) maintains that a recognition of our changed environment necessitates a redefinition of the intellectual:

> The complex game of new tele-technologies and the transforma-tions of public space demand new responsibilities. We can no longer talk in the same way as we did before. And if I am not being too ambitious here, I would like to call for the creation of a new type of intellectual, one who would be prepared to free him/herself from all the norms of institutionalized readings, discourses and modes of intervention.
>
> (Derrida 1992: 53)

The deregulation of the intellectual does not necessarily mean the death of the intellectual, as Lyotard points out above; simply the neces-sity to reconsider his or her function in a transformed landscape. Might we then agree with Georges Balandier when he talks of the fragmenta-tion of the intellectual milieu in the following way:

> Passions grow weaker with the loss of certainties, pluralism of ideas accompanies the 'compromise' with the market, and the 'logic of the spectacular' is the order of the day; but the space for intellectual activity is being reconfigured and the process of decline could well be reversed.
>
> ('A la recherche des intellectuels disparus', *Le Monde des Livres*, 22 October 1993, p. 31)

The intellectual adventure is being reshaped today according to the constraints of a postmodern cultural topography.

5 Citizens all?

The concept of citizenship which emerged from Enlightenment philosophy and the French Revolution was founded on an abstract humanism, on the separation between the particular and the universal and between the private and the public spheres, on the pedagogic function of the state and on the republican model of the nation. This Utopian dream of creating a uniform, egalitarian and neutral space, underpinned by rational order and elevated beyond the realm of individual belief, was pursued more rigorously in France than in any other country. Little surprise, then, that in France, living in the wake of modernity signifies (possibly above all else) a profound crisis in the modern concept of 'the community of citizens' (cf. Schnapper 1994). The hierarchically organized dichotomies on which that concept was founded have today been undermined: the public citizen has become increasingly confused with the private individual. And as the market appears to sweep all before it – exploiting that fragmentation of the uniform public sphere into different cultural identities – the very idea of the social and the public has been thrown into question. A general air of malaise thus pervades political and intellectual life. Yet there are also signs that France can rethink its Utopian version of citizenship in a way that is more appropriate to the pluralism of contemporary life.

Utopian citizenship

Like the Enlightenment project in general, the modern concept of citizenship which took shape in France in the nineteenth century was a Utopian dream of the creation of the ideal being. Detached from parochial origins, belonging to no gender, race or nation, and guided by a blind faith in the connection between reason and civilization, the new 'Man' (the 'Superman') became the image of humanity itself. Let us consider some of the contradictions that were effaced in this project to convert dream into reality – and which today have unravelled so dramatically.

A major feature of the construction of the abstract citizen was, as stated above, the separation of the universal from the particular, and the attempt to carve out a public space which would be governed by universalist principles. The subject was therefore divided into two figures: the citizen, who occupied the public or civic sphere, and the individual, who occupied the private and civilian sphere. The civic sphere refers to the subject who is part of a community of rights and is underscored by the principles of state intervention, egalitarianism and solidarity; the civilian sphere refers to the private subject and is underscored by the principles of liberalism, the market and inegalitarianism (Leca 1991a: 324–325). The policing of the frontier between the two spheres was achieved through a mixture of coercion and consent; laws enforced the divide (for example, the separation of Church and state in 1905) while the republican school became the primary locus for the inculcation of the hierarchy between the two spheres (an ideological training ground for the formation of future citizens; see, for example, Ozouf 1984).

What was resolutely effaced in this human rights version of citizenship (based on the egalitarian nature of the public sphere) were the material inequalities arising from modern capitalism, which traversed public *and* private spheres. As Eric Hobsbawm (1986) has pointed out, labour movements demonstrated the limitations of a 'human rights' approach to citizenship. We have since learnt that there is a profound gap between formal and substantive rights, the latter often having to be fought for outside the political-legal framework (as a way eventually of redefining that framework). In classical Marxism, the 'neutrality' and 'universality' of the public sphere – maintained through the apparatus of the state – merely masked the hegemony of bourgeois power and ideology. The dichotomies between civil society and the state, and (correspondingly) between private and public law (cf. Renaut 1993: 7–9), were therefore the result of an ideological 'trick' on the part of the dominant class to obscure social and economic inequality and relations of power. A more nuanced approach to the modern construction of citizenship is offered by the political scientist Jean Leca who suggests that this model not only benefited bourgeois individualism but also the solidarity of the welfare state:

> Citizenship is not only indispensable to bourgeois society to maintain the abstraction of an apparent universalism and to legitimize class domination under the guise of the State, as Marx maintained.

Citizenship is even more indispensable to the welfare state to sustain civil society through increasing social rights of individuals and organizing these within a concept of the needs of the community.

(Leca 1991b: 203)

Whatever one's view is on this, it is clear that the classical Marxist critique of the liberal version of citizenship did little to problematize the universalist project itself. On the contrary, socialism was a counter-culture which shared the modern conviction that science could explain the world ('For Marx, science ensured certainty', Edgar Morin in Morin and Naïr 1997: 11) and embraced unequivocally the proselytizing universalist aspirations of modernity; it simply posited a different view of the ineluctable onward march of history ('Marx believed in the profound rationality of History', Morin in Morin and Naïr 1997: 12). Though correct in unmasking the distinction between formal and substantive rights, the Marxist critique of liberalism believed that the solution to the problem necessarily lay in the provision of collective rights. The Left's response was therefore to exchange one universalism for another: that is, the abstract formal notion of rights in liberal-bourgeois culture for the collectivist notion of rights in socialist culture. This simply reinforced (rather than challenged) the binary opposition between the individual and the collectivity: an abstract individualism was opposed by an equally abstract version of 'the people'. Yet, as Stuart Hall and David Held point out (1989: 178–179), it is not always the case that 'the people' are necessarily and automatically the means towards greater rights and an extension of citizenship: we have only to consider the ambiguous results of the welfare state, the numerous infringements by the state on individual freedoms, the fact that 'the people' cannot always be relied on to be just to minorities, and so on, to realize the validity of this critique.

Both in Western democracies and under 'real existing socialism', modernity was characterized by the gap between the rhetoric of increased liberty and the entrapment of the individual within a labyrinthine bureaucratic and administrative apparatus. The point of convergence between two equally abstract concepts of citizenship – the first reifying the individual, the second the collectivity in the form of the proletariat – was clearly the role of the state. In republican France it was the state – more properly, the *national* state – which regulated the separation of the private from the public individual, the civilian from the citizen. The mission of the republican state was to carve out the uniform space of citizenship from the diversity of individual cultural experience, and to create a homogeneous nation from a land of regions (Weber 1976). This political-legal space would embody the Enlightenment precepts of freedom, justice and equality. This was the sphere in which the civilized face of the human condition would be realized in all its splendour.

However, the dream of a transcendent public sphere which allowed each individual to shed his or her private garb and become fully 'human' proved to be a false Utopia. Science, history and progress, on which the dream was founded, have turned out to be false Messiahs. The universality of 'Man' was little more than 'the brotherhood of men' (Anthias and Yuval-Davis 1993: 28), 'not universal but male' (Gaspard 1997: 165), humanity seen in terms of 'fraternity' (Ozouf 1989). According to Françoise Gaspard, the men of the Enlightenment 'followed the Rousseau of *Emile* who separates the sexes and the spheres and assigns to women the transmission of customs and to men the creation of laws' (1997: 161). Furthermore, the universality of 'Man' turned out to be the somewhat less-than-universal brotherhood of *French* men: the abstract and disembodied citizen of the modern world was, in reality, the transformation of the French male body into the blueprint for humanity. Citizenship was required to disavow both its gender and its nation; the mission of the state was to elevate this particular form of sectionalism to the heights of universal truth and to conflate national and natural law. The more recent emergence of new cultural and ethnic identities have, in the words of Hall and Held (1989: 187), presented 'new challenges to, and produce[d] new tensions within...the "universalising" thrust in the idea of citizenship'.

The conflation between national and natural law − France seen as the incarnation of humanity − was a fundamental feature of the revolutionary ethos. As Sieyès says in his famous 'Qu'est-ce que le tiers état?' of 1789, 'The national will...never needs anything but its own existence to be legal. It is the source of all legality' (cited in Todorov 1989: 255). This sentiment was echoed in Article 3 of the first Declaration of the Rights of Man and the Citizen, written in August 1789, which announced that 'the principle of all sovereignty resides essentially in the Nation' (cited in Todorov 1989: 255). Todorov (1989: 254) suggests that Sieyès only distinguishes between national and natural law to link them 'in an apparently unproblematic relationship'.

The same conflation between national and natural law, the nation and the universal, the citizen and 'Man' (cf. '"Droits de l'homme" et "droits du citoyen": la dialectique moderne de l'égalité et de la liberté' in Balibar 1992: 124–150) can also be seen in the thought of Rousseau and Michelet. For Michelet, France's laws were those of reason itself, for France was the home of universal thought. In the nineteenth century, citizenship and nationality became virtually indistinguishable, while both were conflated with universal human rights. As Rogers Brubaker (1992: 43) points out, '[a]s a democratic revolution, the French Revolution institutionalized political rights as citizenship rights, transposing them from the plane of the city-state to that of the nation-state, and transforming them from a privilege to a general right'. Alain Touraine (1994: 114) suggests that, over the last two centuries, it was the association between rights and national self-determination that created an unquestioned link between democratic and national aspirations. But, paradoxically, by making the nation (or rather the nation-state) the guarantor of the rights of 'the people', the Revolution created a unique machine for the suppression of a multitude of individual rights.

The modern construction of citizenship was therefore constituted by a cluster of discourses frequently pulling in different directions, yet whose problematic nature was obscured within an apparent coherence of purpose and design. This 'coherence' was especially maintained by the idealized, state-driven narrative of the French nation and (as we have seen in relation to concepts of culture) the opposition between France and Germany: the French model was based on the *jus soli*, individual assimilation, and a political-legal concept of the nation, in contrast to the German model which was based on the *jus sanguinis*, a predetermined and organic concept of the community, and hence an ethnocultural concept of the nation (cf. Schnapper 1994). Not that this description is entirely inaccurate. It is simply that, like all binary oppositions, it tends to present each term as a unified and coherent entity, whereas the inevitable interpenetration (or, as we have said previously, 'contamination') of processes denies any such unity and coherence of individual terms or absolute antithesis between them. As Brubaker says (1992: 2): 'To characterize French and German traditions of citizenship and nationhood in terms of such ready-made conceptual pairs as universalism and particularism, cosmopolitanism and ethnocentrism, Enlightenment rationalism and Romantic irrationalism, is to pass from characterization to caricature.' This is why the ritualistic republican invocation of Renan's famous dictum that the nation is 'a daily plebiscite' is so misleading: Renan's discourse in *Qu'est-ce qu'une nation?* is, as we have stated before, torn between 'Enlightenment rationalism and Romantic irrationalism', and between a 'political' and 'ethnocultural' perspective (Silverman 1992).

Rather than being a political-legal concept of citizenship *as opposed to* an ethnocultural concept, the French model should more properly be seen as a disavowal of its own ethnocultural particularism by projecting it on to Germany. This orthodoxy was established at the end of the nineteenth century with the triumph of the republican consensus on the nature of the citizen and the nation. The Dreyfus affair sealed this triumph. Henceforth, blood and soil definitions of the nation of the type propounded by Drumont, Barrès and Action Française (rooting the citizen deterministically within a community, a place, a culture and a nation) could be convincingly opposed by the message of egalitarianism and universalism, so that they appeared to be polar opposites. By associating ethnocultural or more overtly racist theories with the German tradition, republicans could more easily claim the neutral, progressive, rational, race-free, universalist and egalitarian tradition for the French.

The 'purity' of the French model of citizenship was therefore dependent on the assignment of positive and negative roles to France and Germany respectively. It was precisely this process of 'othering' – in which the subject's own difference is evacuated, disavowed and projected on to others – which underpinned the French Enlightenment project of which citizenship formed such a crucial part. As we have observed, the modern concepts of civilization and humanity only made sense in a system of classification which designated others as barbaric and sub-human who needed surveying, controlling, disciplining and assimilating. The purer the vision, the more the eye became attuned to all that did not conform, to all that was dirty, excessive and subversive, and which therefore had to be excised from view (or at least managed and tamed). In Chapter 2 we noted that herein lay the foundations for one of the major forms of modern racism. Other bodies were misshapen, ugly, exotic (perhaps) but definitely inferior measured against the abstract and strangely body-less citizen. They were termed 'subjects' instead of citizens (Balibar 1984), 'natives (*indigènes*)' instead of nationals, and were characterized by an excess of somatic traits. The dream of egalitarian citizenship was therefore also the nightmare of sub-human life; the latter was an inevitable by-product of the former. Like all repressed demons, it threatened, at every moment, to shatter the illusion on which the dream was built.

Today those 'demons' have emerged from that murky world of the margins to which they were consigned, as of course they had to. Universalism has turned out to be an illusion obscuring just another particularism – yet one which mobilized all the resources of a growing industrial/institutional/ideological complex in the attempt to convert this illusion into reality. The universal citizen was, in fact, the abstract product of bourgeois individualism and Western patriarchy. The model was founded on state-regulated antitheses which were eventually 'found out' (with the demise of the national state): between the public and the private, the political-legal and the socio-economic, the secular and the religious, the modern and the pre-modern, science and belief, centre and periphery, civilization and barbarity. (It is no surprise, then, that the classic texts of cultural modernism were constructed around the highly ambivalent frontiers separating these 'spheres'.) The 'space' of citizenship so constructed – purified of all forms of social division, converted into a pure, abstract, free-floating and ahistorical domain, the ultimate goal of humankind, as Sami Naïr says (1992) – is in the process of fragmenting. This is both a cause for celebration and a source of anxiety and danger.

The revenge of civil society

Postmodernity means learning the foremost lesson of modernism that, in Yeats' famous line from 'The Second Coming', 'things fall apart; the centre cannot hold'. The assault on the centre has come from numerous sources: the challenge to objectivity and truth has converted scientific and rational debate from grand narratives into local and situated discourses;[1] feminism has exposed the patriarchal assumptions of the modern order and shattered the division between the private and public spheres, between the personal and the political; anti-colonial and post-colonial struggles and consciousness have exposed the ethnocentric (and frequently racist) assumptions of assimilation; the advent of mass culture has exposed the class connotations of classical culture; globalization and advances in electronic communications have rendered problematic the links between state, nation and culture. The whole edifice on which modernity was built and which held in place that confident centre is today in the process of disintegration.

Perhaps the most dramatic example of this shaking of the 'centre' is the demise of the nation-state as the major context for the regulation of social, economic and political life and as the prime locus of imaginary identifications. As François Dubet and Michel Wieviorka observe in their introduction to a collection in honour of Alain Touraine:

> the era in which the nation constituted the imaginary and symbolic framework and within which economic modernization, cultural unification and the political treatment of social demands were organized seems to be fading, at least in many Western countries. The increasing difficulties that these countries face in

integrating these three registers – socio-economic, political and cultural – are evidence of a decline or crisis of modernity.

(Dubet and Wieviorka, eds, 1995: 13–14)

These developments have been felt across the developed world. Yet in France the crisis appears to be more acute than elsewhere. This is possibly due to the fact that the universalist and centralizing aspirations of the state and the consequent reification of the public sphere of citizenship were pursued with more zeal in France than other modern nation-states. The demise of the homogenizing nation-state has therefore unleashed pent-up forces which, formerly, had few outlets for self-expression. According to Sami Naïr (1992: 19), the crisis in France is perceived to be less the result of global processes than 'the revenge of civil society on a state which has always oppressed it'. The effect, according to Castoriadis (1996: 92), is that 'nobody knows today what it means to be a citizen'. What form has this 'revenge of civil society' taken in recent years and how has it affected questions of citizenship?

The clearest result of the developments of recent decades is the transformation of the citizen from abstract figure embodying humanity to everyday individual with warts and all. The revenge of civil society, in this sense, means the proud announcement of all those individual attributes, beliefs and passions which the modern mind considered ignoble and parochial, and which needed to be transcended – ethnic and religious affiliation, cultural identity, popular cultural forms, and so on. In other words, the particular has gained the upper hand over the universal. Naïr describes this development as a reversal of the hierarchy of the modern era:

> Now citizenship is driven by the predominance of the particular over the universal, the concrete over the abstract, the individual over the collective, the ethical over the ideological. While the major preoccupation of the republican concept was universality, the design of an abstract Utopia as the goal of every ordinary citizen, equality as the *sine qua non* of communal life, and the construction of a neutral public space, the new concept, more democratic, is centred on the individual subject, rejects the abstract project, prioritizes freedom over equality and opens up the public space to the clash of cultural particularisms.
>
> (Naïr 1992: 44–45)[2]

Naïr's analysis reveals, once again, how the decline of the modern concept of the citizen is seen in terms of the movement from a republican to a democratic model, and from a concern with equality to that of freedom.[3] Rights and duties are no longer enshrined in tablets of stone; they are what we make of them. We have rejected the formal, austere and uplifting ethos of modern humanist aspirations, guided by a profound belief in progress and the creation of a Utopian future. Today we are pleasure-seekers, content to pursue our desires in the present, following the rules of freedom, self-expression and self-gratification rather than the authoritarian moral codes proclaimed confidently by the republican fathers (Lipovetsky 1992).

In other words, this is the age of a new form of individualism and liberalism. No longer is the life project of the individual bound up with membership of (and sacrifice to) a particular class or nation; no longer does the state have the capacity (or even the desire) to mould individuals into citizens. In the republican model, the individual was simply part of the whole and therefore inevitably regulated by the rules which applied to the collectivity. As Alain Ehrenberg (1991: 283) says, this model was founded on 'the public effacement of the individual in the name of the collective with which he or she identified and which transcended him or her'. Today, on the other hand, the withering of the state and the celebration of the particular have led to 'the predominance of individual rights over collective obligations' (Lipovetsky 1992: 208). As we noted in Chapter 2, the individual is expected (or rather, required) to construct his/her own existence in a world bereft of institutional straitjackets and safety nets. The individual has been de-institutionalized and privatized, sold off like the rest of the family silver and left to fend for him/herself. We are all characters in search of an author; we have all been forced to learn the Sartreian lesson that existence precedes essence. The life project today is one of self-improvement and self-constitution. The impetus must come from within rather than be imposed from outside. This is the sign of contemporary democracies. As Debray says of the body today, 'the body as depicted in television advertising is no longer the disciplined body promoted by pre-war cinema; it is "in form", not in uniform' (Debray 1993: 40). Little wonder, as Ehrenberg (1991) has pointed out, that today's major role models come from the realms of business and sport, with their underlying principles of competition, ambition and personal performance as the general marks of success. But little wonder, too, that the self-reliance required today, in a world in which the individual has been privatized, runs in tandem with the general feelings of uncertainty and fear that deregulation has engendered (cf. Ehrenberg 1995, Mongin 1991) and the divorce between those who can swim with the new tide and those who cannot.

This is a new individualism which took off especially at the time of the modernization of France in the 1950s and 1960s and has since progressed along with the relentless commodification of the social sphere. Kristin Ross (1995: 11, 106) recalls that Cornelius Castoriadis, Henri Lefebvre and Edgar Morin all theorized the retreat in the 1960s from the social into an idealized version of the household and everyday life as a form of 'privatization' of the individual around consumption:

> With the decline or decomposition of identities based on work or social collectivities, what remains? For Lefebvre the answer lies in the qualitatively new way that everyday life, private or 'reprivatized' life, and family life...are intimately linked in this period around the identity of the home dweller, the *inhabitant*, and the practices associated with the sole remaining value, *the* private value par excellence, that of consumption.
>
> (Ross 1995: 107)

However, the new individualism is not the only outcome of the breakdown of the republic of citizens. As we saw in Chapter 2, new tribes grouping around new forms of communitarianism are the flip-side to the new individualism. As Sami Naïr says, 'the more pronounced individualism and communitarianism as a prop lead ultimately to the same result, which is the departure from the sphere of citizenship and exile from the collectivity' (1992: 214). The crisis of republican institutions and ideology has left a 'space' for the creation of new forms of collectivity (Wieviorka 1991), mobilizing not around the former codes of republican civic solidarity but around ethnic, religious and other cultural labels, used primarily as a sign of individual identity in a world which requires (ever more insistently) forms of identification. This new tribalism is every bit as 'postmodern' as the new individualism; neither should be confused with their counterparts of the modern era (Lipovetsky 1992: 158–159). The existence today of a new communitarianism (*néo-communautarisme*) alongside a new individualism (*néo-individualisme*) should therefore not be seen as a contradiction, since both are products of the fragmented political and social landscape of the contemporary era. As Ehrenberg (1991: 15) points out, 'they are the two faces of French society today.... Both are the result of the consensual nature of our society and of the crisis of the republican model of social integration through citizenship'.

'The revenge of civil society' means a redefinition of the political and social spheres along these two broad lines, and the emergence of new players in the game. The decline of the centralizing state, with its crusading mission to nationalize society, has therefore meant the disintegration of a whole politics constructed in direct proportion to the strength of the state and the homogeneity of the nation. As Laurent Cohen-Tanugi (1993: 96) has pointed out in relation to politics in the modern era, 'given that the nation was single and indivisible and the State was its incarnation, the aim of all political combat was the conquest of the State, which was the sole legitimate instrument capable of transforming society'. Today, however, 'it is no longer a question of transforming society, which was the aim of revolutionary politics, but of debating its concrete modes of organization within the framework of the principles of liberal democracy' (Cohen-Tanugi 1993: 25). Lyotard defines the same evolution, from an oppositional politics founded on the clash of grand ideological principles to a democracy of local skirmishes:

> The political warfare of the modern era was characterized by the clash of two legitimizing principles: God against the Republic, Race against universal Man, the Proletarian against the Citizen. Whether national or international, the conflict for legitimacy always took the form of a total civil war. Postmodern politics, on the other hand, is a question of strategic management, and the wars are simply police operations. These operations no longer set out to delegitimize the adversary but to oblige him to negotiate his integration into the system according to the rules.
>
> (Lyotard 1993: 172)

Marcel Gauchet (1990: 96) talks of the pluralist politics of postmodernity in terms of a 'negotiated juxtaposition'. It is therefore no longer a question of *transforming* society through a capture of the state apparatus, using the revolutionary rhetoric of old (Alain Touraine in Thibaud and Touraine 1993); all talk today is of *managing* change (Cohen-Tanugi 1993: 25) which, for a large part, emanates from sources other than the institutions of the state. The 'emancipatory' and centralized politics of old have given way to what Touraine defined in the 1970s as new social movements and what Anthony Giddens (1991: 209–232) has termed 'life-politics' or 'sub-politics', that is, the politicization since the 1960s of single issues such as questions of gender, sexuality, the regions, the environment, bio-technology, and so on. These issues are as much related to local and global factors as to specifically national state institutions. Social relations, as Scott Lash points out, 'are increasingly extra-institutional' (Beck *et al.* 1994: 214).

This decentred politics and release of civil society from its tutelage under an overbearing and unitary state has mixed consequences. Some argue that the new liberalism is the path towards a truly democratic and pluralist society. For example, Laurent Cohen-Tanugi (1993: 63) suggests that 'liberal democracy signifies in France today, more than ever before, *pluralist* democracy'. He argues that, unlike in other countries where a culture of liberalism and democracy went hand in hand, the construction in France of a uniform national culture established by means of a strongly interventionist state prevented this partnership and led to a weakening of civil society:

> The profound inability of French political culture, especially on the Left, to dissociate every public utility, every social form and every sense of virtue from the institutions of the state, and its inability to find a compromise between the law and the market, and between ethics and society, have put a block on thinking 'the political' in any other way than in relation to the State, to the consequent detriment of civil society and, in the final analysis, to democracy.
>
> (Cohen-Tanugi 1993: 99; see also Lipovetsky 1983)[4]

This form of neo-liberalism has a naïve (or perhaps cynical) faith in the ability of the market to bring democracy. It ignores the fact that the rise of a liberalized civil society and the decline of the state simply create new forms of power relations and inequalities, rather than removing them altogether. Yet even if one rejects Cohen-Tanugi's liberal thesis, it is difficult not to agree with his view that 'the revenge of civil society' is more dramatic in France than in other Western democracies. The national state apparatus of the Republic and its ideology (characterized by what Cohen-Tanugi calls 'grandpa's Republic, the authoritarianism of the nation-state and the protected economy', 1993: 22) were certainly more entrenched than in Britain and therefore have further to fall. The new liberalism – just as the new nationalism (or national populism) – seems much more brash, perhaps because there is a greater vacuum to fill. As in the former communist states, the strength of the backlash is perhaps in direct proportion to the power wielded by the state beforehand.[5]

However, the emergence of civil society into the political sphere is certainly not only welcomed by neo-liberals. The breakdown of the division between the private and the public and the personal and the political has led to the politicization of a whole range of issues which were formerly consigned to the private sphere, and hence a broadening of the concept of citizenship beyond its state-based definition and its historical link with the nation. Citizenship today is about recycling everyday household waste as well as codes of behaviour in the public sphere, domestic violence as well as public probity. The extension of politics to include any and every aspect of everyday life has democratized the political in the same way that culture has been forced out of its ivory tower.

The concern today about issues which were simply never on the political agenda in the past shows that the fragmentation of the republic of citizens into new individualisms and new tribalisms does not necessarily signify a decline of the political or the rise of a new amoralism. On the contrary, our obsession today with everything that touches on life and death (diet, cancer, abortion, Aids, euthanasia, and so on), and our awareness that our lives are inextricably bound up within a network of interlocking processes (local and global) are indications of the fact that today politics is everywhere. As Edgar Morin points out (Morin and Naïr 1997: 21), 'there has been a politicization of what is infra, extra and supra political'.

As regards morality, never before have so many issues been considered from an ethical point of view. The decline of state-controlled and prescriptive formulae as the solution to ethical problems means that everything is 'up for grabs' (although the problem is, of course, that left to our own devices we must make it up as we go along). Gilles Lipovetsky (1992: 15) maintains that 'the twilight era of duty' that we are living through today simply means that we are no longer willing to accept the sacrifices which accompanied 'the rhetoric of austere, all-embracing and manichean duty' of modernity. He detects two antagonistic logics underpinning new ethical concerns today:

> the first rejects the search for ultimate solutions, is aware of the complexity of social and individual situations, and adopts a pluralist, experimental and personalized approach; the second turns its back on social and individual realities in the name of a new ethical and juridical dogmatism.
>
> (Lipovetsky 1992: 16)

So if, as Lipovetsky suggests, we have rejected the duties that accompanied the disciplinary society of 'the age of morality' and have entered what he terms 'the postmoralist age of the new democracies', this in no way implies an end to morality as such, but simply an end to 'the ideology of disciplinary duty taken to the extreme, or in other words, the value of supreme self-sacrifice on the altar of the Family, History, the Party, the Fatherland, and Humanity' (Lipovetsky 1996:

28). According to Mongin (1996b: 61), it is precisely the abandonment of the moral framework (and certainties) of modernity that has led to a remoralization of diverse issues today: 'We have never spoken so much about ethics because we are worried about our responsibilities and about how we should put them into practice.' Lipovetsky's vision of contemporary society is of the co-existence of 'an irresponsible, I'm-alright-Jack individualism' alongside 'a responsible individualism linked to a certain number of ethical values' (1996: 26).

More generally, we have also seen how living in the wake of modernity (and especially 'after Auschwitz') means the search for a new ethics *vis-à-vis* 'the other' which aims neither to assimilate 'the other' to the same or expel 'the other' from the promised land (which are really two sides of the same coin). In this sense, postmodernity signals a rebirth in ethics starting from a position of *tabula rasa* (or at least with the benefit of hindsight), and the consequent construction of a new ethical (and practical rather than abstract) concept of citizenship.

However, we know too that the 'revenge of civil society' is accompanied by new dangers which the republic of citizens, for all its faults, held firmly in check. For example, the diversification and democratization of the political could be seen to herald the depoliticization of the social sphere, in the same way that, for some, the conflation of the cultural with everyday life means the end of culture. If politics can include anything and everything that affects our lives (from the local to the global), then the political is fragmented into a myriad pieces whose connections and totality we feel incapable of grasping and whose direction we feel powerless to alter. As Steven Connor points out:

> this expansion and decentring of politics...brings with it the possibility of a disastrous decompression of politics; if everything can be said to be political, then, for a politics of opposition, this can often be equivalent to saying that nothing is really or effectively political any more.
>
> (Connor 1989: 226)

This extension and diversification of the political could then be said to disempower individuals who, in the face of such a bewildering labyrinth of technical questions, are increasingly seeking refuge in narrow individualism or mythologized communitarianism.

Furthermore, if everything is political then life-style and cultural identity are as much a political statement as opposition to racist violence. Here we are back with Alain Finkielkraut's 'a pair of boots has the same value as Shakespeare' – the nightmare vision of a world in which all hierarchies have been flattened. From this perspective, any moral position is simply a non-starter, since ethics demands a code of conduct and a sense of values which pure relativism would deny. In Chapters 3 and 4 we discussed how this 'democratization' of culture has led to an expansion of the cultural or aesthetic realm across what was formerly designated as the social and political spheres. We also discussed the problematic link between this cultural turn and the production and consumption habits of late capitalism. Moreover, the flattening of time, achieved especially through advanced communications and information systems, has undermined former networks of solidarity for, as Jean Chesneaux (1996: 111) points out, 'it is precisely the sphere of citizenship – that is, the capacity to "think" the social collectively and actively – that is threatened by a time which is contracted into the immediate and the short term'.[6]

In other words, the shifting configurations of space/time, the victory of the particular over the universal, the demise of the transcendent realm of modern citizenship, the new celebration of the individual or 'new tribe' over the citizen, and the disappearance of the citizen behind the consumer, all are possible signs of the end of the social as a distinct space of meeting and solidarity beyond differences. These questions are at the heart of the current crisis of citizenship in France.

The end of the social?

At the time of the bicentenary celebration of the French Revolution, a drinks mat in Paris read: '1789: the subject becomes citizen. 1989: the consumer becomes citizen.' This raises, in succinct form, perhaps the most pressing question of all as to the state of citizenship today: is the 'revenge of civil society' simply the triumph of the market? Has the citizen (that social and public being) given way to the consumer (that individualistic and asocial being)? The fear of many commentators is that the loss of the power of the state to uphold the civic question and the principles of equality and solidarity, and to act as a check on the inequalities of the market-place, has left the path open to an aggressive neo-liberalism and a self-centred individualism. In other words – and to adopt the formula much used by French commentators – it is a question of 'the "disappearance" of the subject as citizen, along with the republican model on which the citizen was founded' in favour of 'the Americanization of the mode of social production' (Naïr in Morin and Naïr 1997: 211).

According to this scenario, the 'revenge of civil society' is, in reality, none other than the revenge of the Americanized liberal free market against the state, armed with the new ideological construction of freedom in the form of buying power.[7] Here the civic is either dropped completely (as in Margaret Thatcher's statement that there is no such thing as society, only individuals), or transformed from a space regulated by the natural entitlement to rights to one that is regulated simply by a variety of contractual arrangements and bargaining power. The social disintegrates into an unrestrained space of *competition* between individuals (cf. Ehrenberg 1991). As Chantal Mouffe (1993: 80) has pointed out, in the liberal conception 'it is the citizen which is sacrificed to the individual'. Jean Leca (1991b: 209) sees this state of affairs as marking the death-knoll for citizenship for 'without some sort of sense of community there is no citizenship, for a "political community" is not simply a collection of individuals'. Joël Roman also argues for a community of interest beyond the supposed autonomy of the individual:

> Citizenship can no longer be considered simply in terms of the autonomous citizen whose sovereign power consists in casting a vote at election time. Citizenship is rather more akin to a capacity for participation in social exchange, which is constitutive of both the stability of identity and of individual freedom.
>
> (Roman 1996: 40)

Cornelius Castoriadis, echoing the famous formula of Ernest Renan on the nation, expresses the same sentiment:

> Society is never simply a collection of individuals who come and go and are ultimately replaceable, living in a particular territory, speaking a certain language and practising 'externally' certain customs. On the contrary, these individuals 'belong' to this society *because* they participate in its social and imaginary meanings, its 'norms', 'values', 'myths', 'representations', 'projects', 'traditions', etc., and because they share (whether they know it or not) the will to be a part of this society and to perpetuate its existence.
>
> (Castoriadis 1996: 20) (see also p. 222)

The new forms of inequality which have arisen from the demise of the old social contract (cf. Fitoussi and Rosanvallon 1996) are not necessarily those of class exploitation but of social and economic exclusion on a number of different levels. This has led to what Alain

Touraine and his colleagues at the Ecole des Hautes Etudes en Sciences Sociales in Paris have termed the 'dualization' of society: that is, a division of society into those who can and those who cannot compete in the market. Touraine has suggested that the 'society of exclusion' corresponds to a post-industrial society in the way that exploitation and social conflict were the major features of industrial society:

> We have left a society of production and social conflicts and entered a society of consumption and communication. Consequently, our society is no longer one of conflicts but one of exclusion. Industrial society functioned on a 'high–low' axis; the society of communication functions on an 'inside–outside' axis.
>
> (quoted in Mongin 1992: 5–6)

Touraine describes this process in terms of a shift from a vertical to a horizontal paradigm, from a profoundly hierarchical structure to the so-called openness of our liberal democratic societies today. The oppositional nature of industrial society (capitalism/socialism) has given way to the simple 'in or out' formula of post-industrial society (given that there are no longer any alternatives on offer): 'it is no longer a question of *up or down* but *in or out*: those who are not *in* want desperately to be so, otherwise they find themselves in a social emptiness' (Touraine 1991: 166).

This is bleak indeed for the modern concept of the social which (in principle, it should be said) ironed out differences by bringing people together around the common project of equality and solidarity in the public sphere, or at least held out the possibility of improvement through the realization of an alternative political programme (socialism/communism). What we are witnessing today is the reduction of the social and the public sphere to the uniform rule of the market, and the decline of the ethical code of citizenship in favour of self-gratification and a carefree hedonism. We have noted how the state and the media have given up on the modern project of moulding individuals into citizens according to the criteria of national homogeneity and uplifting ideals of culture and morality; today it is simply a question of consumer demand and customer satisfaction. The horse is now following the cart, yet both are propelled by a media and advertising blitz on our senses. The private and the public have fused around the common denominators of sensation, spectacle, effusion and consumption. As Régis Debray says (1993: 60), 'the "in" State...has thrown in its lot with the cult of "civil society"'. And, in the process, the notion of social reality has receded as the real and the imaginary have merged through the ubiquitous presence of the image. Jean Baudrillard has noted how the proliferation of information through electronic circuits destroys genuine sociality and creates instead a 'simulated social' (Kellner 1989: 87) in which social interaction is transformed into the apathy and sluggishness of the masses (Baudrillard 1981). Georges Balandier (1992: 120) also believes that the corollary of the development of 'electronic societies' is the reduction of the political sphere to the demands of crude sensationalism. He suggests that this 'culture of the look and the spectacle' therefore constitutes 'a major perversion of the democratic process' (1994: 204). Given the changes that have taken place in recent years (many of which have already been discussed in previous chapters), the whole structure on which the republican concept of citizenship was based has simply disappeared – or at least been transformed.

Yet we have also seen the fierce rearguard action against these changes being fought in France – not only by cultural reactionaries and political extremists but by a whole range of commentators and activists who are fearful of the consequences of the demise of the republic of citizens, the end of the social and the triumph of the image over the word. Globalization (especially Americanization) and multiculturalism have been demonized as the culprits, allowing die-hard republicans to cling on to an idealized belief in the nation as the only hope of salvation (see Chapter 2). Diversification, difference and pluralism are commonly seen as harbingers of the fragmentation of the Republic and the breakdown of social cohesion, in that they promote individual liberty and cultural identity over and above the cause of social solidarity (and are anyway profoundly imbued with the ethos of liberal individualism and consumption). According to this vision, as we have already seen, the 'crisis' is interpreted as an invasion of the cultural into the political sphere, the particularist into the universal sphere, the differentialist into the assimilationist sphere (as if cultural particularism had been absent before), leading to a nightmare scenario of the Americanization of France (multiculturalism, the splintering of society into a juxtaposition of communities, affirmative action programmes for the advancement of minorities, and so on).

A deeper fear, habitually underplayed or simply not recognized, is the feminization of the 'masculine' public sphere of citizenship. The universalist tradition of the equality of citizens has been profoundly gendered according to the hierarchical organization of a masculine public sphere and feminine private sphere (Schnapper 1998: 459–466). Any challenge to the transcendent status of the public sphere (the sphere of republican citizenship) therefore carries with it a threat to masculine power. Given the profoundly entrenched nature of the republican concept of nation, citizenship and rights in France – which is accepted widely and often uncritically by commentators of both sexes and of all political persuasions (see, for example, Kristeva 1990) – it is no surprise that gender studies and women's studies, like ethnic studies, are virtually non-existent in the French academy, although (as we noted in the previous chapter) a particular strand of French feminism has had a profound effect on the academies in Britain and America. (For good overviews of feminism and the women's movement in France, see Duchen 1986 and 1987. See also the stimulating analyses of Colette Guillaumin in Guillaumin 1995.) As Françoise Gaspard (1997) has observed, the introduction of a gendered (and therefore differentialist) perspective into the 'non-partisan' (egalitarian) sphere constitutes a threat to the 'scientific' (and implicitly patriarchal) legitimacy of the republican universalist tradition.

A more general perception of the (Americanized) process of democratization and its threat to French republicanism is that it functions as a global anaesthetic which effaces the jagged edges of the world. By inducing the same reflex reactions to the imaginary as to the real, it undermines our ability to distinguish between the two (for what meaning is there beyond the phenomenal forms themselves?). We have consequently been converted from rational beings into zombies, at the mercy of fleeting images, sensations and experiences which we have become incapable of understanding or interpreting – or, more accurately, simply have no desire to understand, for 'understanding' has become secondary to 'feeling'.

The fears expressed above are part of a nightmare scenario in which the republic of citizens has given way, with catastrophic consequences, to a democracy of individuals, each one of whom is trapped within an impoverishing concept of cultural identity. Sunil Khilnani, writing in *Le Débat* (1990: 181–182), captures this pessimism when (as an outsider looking in) he finds no signs of a renewal of a 'citizenship of participation' in France but simply the dissolution of the values of citizenship into 'a narcissistic individualism'. It is precisely this fear of particularism and atomization which leads many to cling on desperately to a nostalgic belief in the universalism of old as the only cure for what is seen as the decline of civilization.

However, although the decline of the state and the 'revenge of civil society' might favour the forces of individualism within a liberal philosophy of the free market, this does not mean that there is not also another side to this debate. The problem of how to discuss questions of equality, citizenship and solidarity without recourse to the worn republican (and ethnocentric) rhetoric of national homogeneity, or the socialist rhetoric of the radical transformation of society through the appropriation of the state, or, on the other hand, the neo-liberal conflation of citizen and consumer, *is* being vigorously debated in France. The apocalyptic vision of many might simply be the inability to see beyond the classic dichotomies of modern sociological thought between universalism and particularism, the individual and society, and, in Louis Dumont's terms (1983), between 'holism' and 'individualism'. Contrary to Khilnani's bleak prognostications, there are numerous signs of a renewal of the concept of citizenship, not through a nostalgic recreation of the lost golden age of the Enlightenment but through a willingness to rethink the binary oppositions underpinning the construction of the abstract citizen of the modern era and confront the complex, plural and frequently ambiguous relationship between the individual and the world.[8]

For example, Alain Touraine (1992: 410–411) dismisses the sort of nostalgia expressed above as inappropriate in today's world, for 'modern men and women are no more citizens of the Enlightenment than they are God's creatures; they are responsible for themselves'. Touraine warns of the consequences of not heeding this warning:

> Do not let us give in to the temptation, born in the eighteenth century, of conflating 'Man' and the citizen. This was a grandiose project which produced the greatest catastrophes since it led to the destruction of all the barriers which could limit absolute power. Instead of confusing 'Man' and the citizen, democracy should explicitly recognize (in the same way as the Declaration of the Rights of Man and the Citizen) that popular sovereignty must respect natural rights, and even be founded on them.... The most advanced society is that which recognizes most explicitly the equal rights of rationalization *and* those of the subject, and understands the necessity to combine them.
>
> (1992: 401)

Touraine's redefinition of the nature of citizenship today (see Touraine 1992 and 1994) can be seen here as an attempt to forge a new relationship between what he terms 'rationalization (*la rationalisation*)' and the rights of the subject (*la subjectivation*): in other words, between the universal and the particular, between rational law and individual expression, and between social integration and individual freedom. Equal rights can no longer be considered in the abstract way in which they were conceived in the modern era, since this version of equality refused to recognize cultural difference and the multidimensional rights of the subject. On the other hand, cultural identity cannot be the sole base for the rule of law, as this would provide no common criteria for the establishment of social cohesion. Touraine also warns against the danger of subjects becoming mere consumers of policies and material goods at the mercy of 'public opinion'.[9] Touraine's recent work has been in the spirit of 'rethinking the subject', that is, viewing the subject between the poles of abstract law and individual needs and desires (see Dubet and Wieviorka, eds, 1995), in order to fashion a democracy appropriate to today's complex society.

Michel Wieviorka (1993c) pursues a similar course and also argues for an articulation between common rules and individual freedom which avoids the jungle mentality of the market-place. Chantal Mouffe has described the problem of harmonizing the general and the particular in the following way:

> How to conceptualise our identities as individuals and as citizens in a way that does not sacrifice one to the other? The question at stake is how to make our belonging to different communities of values, language and culture compatible with our common belonging to a political community whose rules we have to accept. As against conceptions that stress commonality at the expense of plurality and respect for difference, or that deny any form of commonality in the name of plurality and difference, what we need is to envisage a form of commonality that respects diversity and makes room for different forms of individuality.
>
> (Mouffe 1993: 80–81)[10]

Edgar Morin insists that the relationship between the general and the particular must be seen in the context of the local/global nexus. It has been the inability of the French political classes to think beyond the limited horizons of 'the compartmentalized thought of bureaucratic techno-science', on the one hand, and 'the more and more particularized thought founded on ethnicity or the nation', on the other hand, that has constrained all attempts to envisage the true complexity and ambiguity of today's problems (Morin and Naïr 1997: 24).[11] Furthermore, these problems must take into account the multidimensional needs of human beings rather than separating the rational from the emotional, for 'human needs are not only economic and technical but also affective and mythological' (Morin and Naïr 1997: 25). Only in this way can we hope to learn from the mistakes of the Enlightenment:

We must try to re-establish, in all its complexity, a being who cannot simply be reduced to relations of production or to economic relations, but who is, at one and the same time, biological, social, economic and mythological. We must not consider this being principally in terms of his/her prosaic activities – the technical, work, the search for material comforts – but also in terms of his/her poetic activities – festival and celebration (*fête*), play, dance, gaiety, love, ecstasy.

(Morin and Naïr 1997: 26; cf. Morin 1996 and Touraine 1992: 348)

Morin therefore adopts a modernist perspective on the interconnections between the technical world and the world of the psyche as a necessity for any understanding of the complexities of postmodern life (see also Morin and Naïr 1997: 140–143). As Kenneth Thompson points out in a discussion of what he terms 'constructive postmodernism', such attempts to reconsider what was discarded by rational and scientific thought of the modern era are not necessarily signs of a romantic or cultural conservatism as a reaction to postmodern developments:

They are efforts to articulate new identities, communities, and even Utopias, in the face of increasing ephemerality and social life that lacks foundation – a society of spectacles and fashions, fragmentation of work and class identities, destruction of local communities and natural resources.

(Thompson 1992: 249)

As Joël Roman observes (1996: 40), a new concept of citizenship in France depends on the capacity to break with the narrow legalistic and state-based version of rights and duties of the modern era (which was more tightly linked to the state than in other countries), and to construct a more 'lateral' version of citizenship which could incorporate the complex and multidimensional networks within which individuals find themselves today.

Etienne Balibar has consistently called for a new concept of citizenship (*la nouvelle citoyenneté*) which would be founded, first and foremost, on the dissociation of the link between 'the Rights of Man' and 'the Rights of the Citizen' established at the time of the Revolution, and a re-thinking of rights in a 'post-national' era (see, especially, the collected essays in Balibar 1992 and 1998). Balibar's starting-point is, invariably, contemporary forms of exclusion – the Front National's 'national preference (*la préférence nationale*)', the state's repressive measures towards illegal immigrants (*les clandestins*), the EU's creation of a citizenship of Europeans (*citoyenneté des Européens*) rather than a European citizenship (*citoyenneté européenne* or *citoyenneté en Europe*) (Balibar 1998: 69) – with a view to an imaginative reinvention of a democracy of inclusion. Balibar's unique contribution to this pressing task is to challenge the *historical* institutionalization of forms of exclusion (whether they are imposed through the state, the nation or the new global economy) as a prerequisite for rethinking democracy from the margins.

The social movements for a new citizenship which grew out of the anti-racist struggles of the 1980s are a good example of this more open, inclusive and pluralistic approach to rights and social participation. They have exposed the outdated, exclusive and frequently ethnocentric nature of the republican concept of citizenship (Silverman 1992: Chapters 4 and 5). Democracy can no longer be conceived in terms which bind citizenship rigidly to nationality (cf. Tassin 1994). As Dominique Schnapper points out (1998: 455), 'the link between nation and citizenship is not logical but historical'. The current conjuncture (post-colonial and arguably post-national) requires a reformulation of this link. Neither can democracy be conceived in terms which attempt to rationalize away pluralism, complexity and ambiguity. On the contrary, these are crucial to the very existence of democracy today. Abstract and rational blueprints for citizenship must now give way to a more pragmatic concern for the complex and ambiguous nature of rights. As Jean Chesneaux has remarked in relation to a democratic notion of time, 'contrary to all these pre-programmed and pre-conceived notions of time, democratic time is rich with diverse potential but also with ambiguities and possibly even dangers' (Chesneaux 1996: 115). However, despite the expressed desire (by numerous commentators and activists) to rethink citizenship in more pluralistic fashion, it should be reiterated that the moves for a redefinition of citizenship in France have emerged principally from debates around immigration, nationality and rights, and have by and large ignored what Nira Yuval-Davis has termed the 'gendered reading of citizenship' (Yuval-Davis 1997: 4; cf. Walby 1994).

Nevertheless, all those concerned with the reinvention of citizenship today share the general belief that individual subjectivity and social forms of collectivity need to be rearticulated in today's radically transformed landscape. The complexity, multidimensionality and ambiguity of identities and social life are at the core of this rethinking. Here we are once again confronted with the burning question of communication across differences. It is one thing to recognize the diversification of the world today; it is another to reinvent social life in the light of this knowledge. Jürgen Habermas believes that the tragic failure of the objectifying and instrumentalist rationality of modernity should not lead us to abandon rationality and modernity altogether (Habermas 1996), for it is the only means we have of preventing descent into total moral relativism, and our only chance of creating solidarities in the face of the destructive functionalism of capitalism (cf. Rose 1993). Habermas proposes a 'communicative rationality' as the counter-balance to 'instrumentalist rationality', for it alone can provide the necessary space for consensus beyond differences. It is also essential for the renewal of any left-wing project aimed at challenging the rule of the market.

Habermas's resistance to postmodern differentialism and relativism is championed in France by those who also believe that we abandon the Enlightenment project at our peril. The debate between Habermas and Lyotard during the 1980s polarized the rationalist and anti-rationalist positions. According to Lyotard's critique of Habermas's 'communicative rationality' (see, for example, Lyotard 1979 and 1988a), its endorsement of and faith in the legitimizing status of a transcendent reason (over and above 'local' language games) flies in the face of the postmodern reality of the end of meta-narratives. Habermas's view that truth and value can emerge from the communicative interaction between social actors is, in Lyotard's eyes, simply a restatement of Enlightenment emancipatory discourse, and consequently ignores the irrevocable heterogeneity and contingency of different discursive fields.

Habermas seems to place his faith in a rational public space which, as we have seen, might well have disappeared in recent years. What form of communication could there possibly be that was not already caught up in the complex network of 'situated' knowledges and mediatized representations, and was somehow beyond the social and economic determinations of contemporary democracy? Although he bemoans the demise of a transcendent rationality, Régis Debray at least recognizes that that pure space of reason is now a myth (if it ever existed at all), for what distinction can be made today between 'processes of communication' ('democratic discussion and argument') and 'technical processes' ('instrumentalist rationality')? Debray criticizes attempts to maintain the distinction between these two realms in the following way:

> It is as if public discussion of ends was not already subject to a whole array of technically determined means.... As if the exercise

of citizenship was not already conditioned by the nature of our 'networks of thought'. As if twentieth-century publicity had not already turned the eighteenth-century version on its head. Ahistorical and 'atechnical' (the two being mutually determining), the model of 'public space' now seems like a theoretical impasse that it would perhaps be better to abandon than attempt to renew.

(Debray 1993: 68)[12]

Lyotard's 'incredulity towards meta-narratives' and openness to *le différend* – which marks 'the incommensurability of all regimes of phrases, all genres of linking' (Readings 1991: 118) – might be a more appropriate response to the realities of postmodern life than Habermas's 'communicative rationality'. At the same time, Lyotard's position might not be as hopelessly nihilist and relativist as some critics have asserted (see, for example, Dews 1986 and Norris 1993). Refusing the 'closure' implied in totalizing discourses and rejecting the notion (inherited from modernity) of a pure public space of 'communicative rationality' does not necessarily lead to the abandonment of any sense of values or dialogue across differences; it simply recognizes the fact that values are always contingent rather than absolute, and that dialogue must be ongoing and open-ended if differences are to be respected. As we noted in relation to Maspero's journey through the suburbs of Paris (Chapter 3), encounters today cannot escape this reality. Dialogue across difference is tentative, relationships have to be negotiated, and the social must be sensitive to the ambivalence of 'the other'.

The contingency of values and the ephemeral nature of solidarities signify a new way of understanding social life today: no longer driven by the Utopian ideologies of modernity but dependent on forms of collective and associative action whose aims are more modest and less abstract. Lipovetsky (1987: 333) defines this mode of participation as 'in keeping with the basic desire for individual autonomy'. In this sense, collective action has not simply given way to egotistical individualism: it has accommodated itself to the demands for individual expression and freedom.

Despite the dangers that emerge from the decline of the republican concept of citizenship, there are also positive signs that a new sense of citizenship can be forged. New ideas share some of the premises outlined above: the need to go beyond the hackneyed oppositions of modernity and the cliché-ridden language (*langue de bois*) of the political class; the belief in the multidimensional nature of the relationship between the individual and society, and the interconnections between the different levels; the myopia of viewing the nation-state as the primary context for consideration of these questions (for individuals are members of a variety of 'communities') and the need to recontextualize them within the local/global network; and finally, the importance of reconstituting a concept of the social as a radical alternative to contemporary neo-liberalism which would reduce us all to atomized individuals.

The 'end of the social' is not at all a *fait accompli* in France. It is true that, like the demise of the classical concept of culture, the idea of the social which accompanied the modern separation of the public and private spheres has today disappeared. Furthermore, the overbearing nature of the national state and its profoundly entrenched narratives of republican legitimacy make it extremely difficult to step out from under their shadow now that the political, economic and social landscape is so different. Yet this is not to say that the social cannot be reinvented, along with a new version of citizenship appropriate to the pluralism of contemporary French society and the complexity of the modern world.

Conclusion
Millennium talk

In an essay on the tragic nature of the twentieth century entitled *L'Humanité perdue*, Alain Finkielkraut (1996) meditates on the ways in which the modern ideals of humanity and civilization – which scientific progress would make a reality – have been accompanied by the greatest inhumanity the world has ever known. 'Science and barbarity' (1996: 110) is a fitting paradox to define the age.

According to Finkielkraut, the dehumanization wrought by Nazism in a Germany at the forefront of scientific and cultural developments is only half the story of the paradox of the twentieth century. The other half has occurred since the Holocaust and has been ushered in by more recent scientific and cultural developments, especially those in information and communication. Finkielkraut suggests that, far from liberating humanity, these developments have forced humanity down another blind alley: the electronic revolution, which has provided us with the means to abolish distances, to communicate with others across differences and to be truly cosmopolitan, has in fact converted us all, quite simply, into brain-dead tourists in a global amusement park:

> 'Everyone a tourist, tourists for ever!' This is the ultimate outcome of the quest for emancipation and fraternity. Today the noble spirit of cosmopolitanism no longer signifies what Hannah Arendt... terms 'the desire to share the world with other people'; instead it signifies the globalization of the self. No longer is it that *expanded consciousness* so admirably defined by Kant as the ability to undertake a mental journey towards other points of view; instead it is the expansion of subjectivity and the inherent quality of 'global man' finally released from limbo.
>
> (Finkielkraut 1996: 156)

Finkielkraut's critique of today's bogus emancipation and cosmopolitanism, which simply masks a tourist's (or voyeur's) approach to others and the world, is echoed by a number of French commentators. Régis Debray also berates the crassness of those who confuse today's individualistic and hedonistic cosmopolitanism and humanitarianism (propelled by advanced technology) with genuine solidarity with others. Etienne Balibar (1998: 117–118) warns of the siren calls of liberation offered by this 'postmodern Utopia' and 'fascination for the possibilities of the new "virtual world"' which might simply be the seductive surface of contemporary globalized commodity capitalism. We have already noted how the lure of surfaces in the city and the stimulation of ceaseless differentiation are possibly a hollow gloss obscuring the accelerating commodification of social relations and the obliteration of a moral relationship with 'the other'. According to Finkielkraut, postmodern humanitarianism is none other than the betrayal of humanity by science for a second time this century, after the first disaster wrought by Nazi genocide. Finkielkraut (1996: 160) finishes his meditation by asking rhetorically what indeed has been the point of the twentieth century.

As with previous works (cf. especially 1987), Finkielkraut's reading of history is schematic and reductionist in the extreme and his perspective that of a die-hard Enlightenment humanist and republican universalist. Yet the link he makes between Nazi dehumanization and postmodern 'humanitarianism' is not without interest, whatever the dangers of making broad analogies of this sort (see, for example, the discussion on Nazism and deconstruction in Chapter 1). The point is that after the nightmare of totalitarian dictatorships earlier in the century, which obliterated a moral relationship to 'the other', we might be entering a new nightmare which will once again obliterate the moral dimension to relationships, not, this time, through state-planned genocide (although this has certainly not been eradicated in some parts of the world) but through the technological appropriation of 'reality' and superficial humanitarianism at the behest of advanced capitalism. If the former system (in its Nazi incarnation) used the category of 'race' to classify diverse communities (Jews, homosexuals, gypsies) as sub-species, the latter aestheticizes 'the other' for the purpose of sensual stimulation and self-gratification. This is what Gilles Lipovetsky (1987: 300) has called a 'neo-narcissistic age' in which 'the other' has become merely 'a means of being oneself'. And although Lipovetsky (1987: 327) believes that the new 'individualist logic' which predominates today is no longer premised on the eradication of 'the other', a bleaker view of contemporary processes would suggest instead that they may be leading (by other means) to the same effacement of the disturbing strangeness and difference of 'otherness' as that carried out under the banner of the heady ideologies of modernity. Indeed, as Tzvetan Todorov (1998: 13) suggests, the abolition of memory and the real produced by the over-abundance of information in contemporary societies may be a far more effective way of eradicating 'otherness' and plunging us into a new 'realm of barbarity' because it goes under the name of democracy rather than that of totalitarianism, and therefore receives our willing consent rather than provokes our resistance. In an explicit comparison between the Holocaust and today's 'real time' (which abolishes all distinctions between past, present and future), Jean Baudrillard (1997: 59) is certainly in no doubt that 'today's real time is our mode of extermination'.

In *L'Art du moteur*, Paul Virilio (1993: 171–172) compares Nazi eugenics and contemporary developments in bio-technology in a similar warning against the technological production of the human. Virilio's fear is that the human body is seen more and more in terms of a constantly accelerating machine (1993: 158). Using Marinetti's famous declaration in the Futurist Manifesto of 1910 – 'let us prepare for the next and inevitable identification of Man and machine' – he argues, 'eighty years later we have reached this state with the mass production of "ORGANOIDS" resulting from bio-technical research' (1993: 165). Once again the aims of each version of eugenics are different, in keeping with the demands of the age. Today it is no longer a question of the purification of the race (which was the motor behind Nazi eugenics) but rather the obsession with youth, the healthy body, the sporty body, the long-life body, which underpins the techno-logical intervention in the life-process:

> We do not simply want to *live better*...but to *live more forcefully*, to develop the nervous intensity of life by the ingestion of biotechno-logical products which will supplement other foods, and chemical products which provide greater or lesser degrees of stimulus. To be in really 'good health' in the future, will we have to be constantly doped up and artificially stimulated, like top sportsmen and women?
>
> (Virilio 1993: 157)

Virilio sees this manipulation of the body as part of the wider process of the technological 'virtualization' of the real which has become our habitual landscape today. His universe is akin to that of Jean-Luc Godard's brilliant dystopic portrayal of contemporary society in

Alphaville (1965) (which also equates totalitarian dehumanization with the scientific rationalization of the city).[1] Like Eddy Constantine's Lemmy Caution, whose mission is to destroy the logic of the computer-controlled city through riddles, humour, poetry and good old-fashioned love, Virilio seeks the density, ambiguity and strangeness of life beyond the two-dimensional recuperation of reality through technology. Virilio therefore views the technological appropriation of reality as a sign of the tragic demise of humanity. The prophecy of Laurence's father in Simone de Beauvoir's *Les Belles images* (1966: 40) expresses the same sentiment: 'Soon technology will seem to us like nature itself and we will live in a completely inhuman world.'

Both Finkielkraut and Virilio (though in very different ways) raise perhaps the single most fascinating question at the time of the new millennium: will advances in market-driven techno-science today, especially those in genetic engineering and the electronic transmission of information, betray humanity once again following the connections earlier in the twentieth century between science, eugenics and geno-cide? Or is there the possibility of a new 'ethical' humanity which, instead of detaching science from morality, responsibility and democ-racy, attempts to consider their complex and multifaceted interconnections? Finkielkraut and Virilio, like many of the other French commentators I have considered in this book, provide a pessimistic response to these questions. They tend to view contempo-rary developments through dark fin-de-siècle spectacles. Their version of humanity is the Enlightenment version. Contemporary develop-ments are judged by Enlightenment criteria, and found wanting.

This reaction to postmodernity is certainly not confined to France alone, as I have noted on numerous occasions. Yet it is indicative of a major French approach to the crisis of modernity. The republican tradition, an assimilationist model of the nation (whether real or imag-ined), a strong and centralized state, an abstract and universalist version of citizenship, a faith in the rationalization of social life, an elitist structure to maintain the hierarchical ordering of the public and private spheres: these are all powerful markers of 'a certain idea of France', and of human civilization in general, whose possible demise many bemoan. Contemporary 'democratization' is often equated with American imperialism and an impoverishment of values; difference and pluralism are deemed to be responsible for the fragmentation of society; hedonism and the gratification of the senses herald the end of rational 'Man'. The air therefore resounds largely to the despairing cries of those who conflate the death of the humanist subject with the death of humanity itself and whose only vision beyond modernity is nihilism, chaos and despair. 'What are we,' says Pierre Nora, responding to the accusation of the pessimism of French intellectuals, 'other than pedagogues of the tragic?' ('Quinze ans de "Débat"', *Le Monde des Livres*, 6 October 1995).

However, as I have also attempted to argue in this book, for those who know that the re-creation of modern ideals of humanity is no longer viable (let alone desirable after totalitarianism and the Holocaust), and that the sovereign and autonomous rational humanist subject must be consigned to history, a new realism can be detected which refuses to interpret the crisis of modernity either as unmitigated tragedy or as the unequivocal dawning of a new postmodern democracy. Edgar Morin, for example, acknowledges the shattered dreams of a modernity whose vision of progress was founded on the redemptive powers of science. He is also aware of the ethical dangers and potentially devastating effects today of a 'techno-scientific-bureaucracy' acting in the service of economic profit rather than the enhancement of life, which would constitute 'a new barbarism' (Morin and Kern 1993: 109). Yet for Morin (unlike Finkielkraut, Virilio and others) advances in techno-science do not necessarily, in themselves, lead to the destruction of civilized communication with others. It is rather these developments divorced from any moral dimension which poses a problem for humanity. The architect Paul Chemetov (1994) argues a similar case with regard to the city: solutions to problems can never be simply technical but must involve, instead, a consideration of the wider social, political and, especially, *ethical* dimensions. Morin's awareness of the absence of responsibility which accompanies 'techno-bureaucratic' over-specialization is a necessary starting-point for an alternative vision which, in Morin's words, would be 'a politics of civilization in which solidarity, conviviality, morality, ecology, and quality of life are no longer considered separately but conceived as a whole' ('Le discours absent', *Le Monde*, 22 April 1995; cf. Morin and Kern 1993).

We noted in the previous chapter that Morin's conception of a new 'politics of civilization' (Morin and Naïr 1997) is founded on a more holistic view of the complex networks of contemporary life, as opposed to those approaches which divorce science from ethics, or rational thought from the affective life of the individual. In his most recent work, Alain Touraine (1992 and 1994) also talks of bringing together mind and body, the abstract and the concrete ('rationalization' and 'subjectivization') in a way which breaks with the binary structures of Cartesian-inspired Enlightenment thought. Even Jean Baudrillard, not noted for his optimistic forecasts for humanity, reminds us that rethinking the binary structures of Western modernity might be the path towards a new form of civilization beyond Enlightenment humanism which, paradoxically, would signal a return to pre-Enlightenment modes of understanding humanity. He observes (1997: 174) that 'our modernity is defined by the humanist perspective of the Enlightenment, but what preceded us was much larger than this version of humanism and was not founded on its distinction between the human and the inhuman'. What Alain Minc has defined as a new state of uncertainty reminiscent of the Middle Ages (with increasing areas of human activity escaping the order and authority of the modern age and possibly signifying 'the return to the law of the jungle', Minc 1993: 68) is nevertheless the chance for a new way forward. As he observes, 'we must found our thought on the basis of what is uncertain with the same care that, previously, we founded our thought on the basis of what was probable' (Minc 1993: 11).

The ideas expressed above demonstrate that the crisis of modernity is perceived in France not only as tragedy but also, by some, as the chance for a reconsideration of the modern vision of humanity. Postmodern, post-colonial and post-national developments have opened up new spaces for the recreation of social life, and the hierarchical structures which held in place a single image of 'the human' have given way to a more pluralistic vision of humanity. For a growing number of French commentators it has become clear that the modern distinction between 'the human' and 'the inhuman' can no longer be maintained; as Baudrillard (1997: 55) has remarked, 'when one attempts to define humanity by excluding what is inhuman it becomes a derisory enterprise'. Forged in the white heat of modernity in the name of a new transcendent humanity, yet implicated eventually in the most inhuman acts the world has ever seen, the modern abstract notion of 'the human' (founded on the legitimacy of science and rational thought) is today being seriously rethought.

The fears of thinkers like Régis Debray, Alain Finkielkraut and Paul Virilio are real enough but present too bleak a picture of the French approach to postmodern developments. In the light of modern history, many now refuse to grant science, technical solutions and abstract concepts the legitimacy they once had. Instead, they are submitted to an intense ethical scrutiny so that advances in techno-science are constantly related to the wider questions of individual life and human solidarities. As I suggested in the introduction to this book, these new ethical concerns do not guarantee the safety of 'the other' under postmodern conditions. However, they do signal a passionate concern with redrawing the boundaries of humanity today and rethinking democracy beyond the traditional republican framework.

Whatever pathways are pursued in the new millennium for the redefinitions of humanity and democracy, it is unlikely that any single one will be elevated to the realm of universal principle and provide the foundations for a new Utopian model to be adopted elsewhere, as with the Enlightenment. Yet this would be no bad thing, since we now know that Utopias can end up as dystopias and that universal visions of humanity can breed monstrous inhumanity. Facing postmodernity in France means coming to terms with the shortcomings of the Enlightenment. And just as French ideas were at the heart of the Enlightenment project itself, so too are they now stimulating the reconstruction of 'the human' beyond the Enlightenment.

Notes

Introduction

1 Whether the contemporary scene is best defined as late modernity, accelerated modernity, reflexive modernization or postmodernity seems to me less important than the analysis of social and cultural change itself. Frequently proponents of these different definitions are distinguishable only through the definitions themselves, whereas the analyses often show much common ground. I propose not to get embroiled in a debate on definitions, which can be arcane and sterile. I am adopting 'postmodernity' throughout the text as an umbrella term to refer to the crisis in the structures of modernity and the new configurations of contemporary social and cultural life in France.

1 In the shadow of the Holocaust

1 Raphaëlle Rérolle and Nicolas Weill make a similar observation in *Le Monde des Livres* ('La parole contre l'extermination', 25 February 1994) when they note that, in the immediate post-war period, the archetypal concentration camp was Buchenwald rather than Auschwitz.

2 This retrospective 'cleansing' of France started as early as the trial of the Vichy leader, Marshall Pétain, in 1945. As Christian Delacampagne (1994: 124) points out, France was then depicted as a country where 'nobody (or almost nobody) had really been anti-Semitic'.

3 'The survivors arrived home at a time when the Cold War was beginning to transform perspectives and when, only a few months after Liberation, stories of martyrdom seemed to belong to another age' (Rérolle and Weill, 'La parole contre l'extermination', *Le Monde des Livres*).

4 Elsewhere Annette Wieviorka describes this context as comprising

> the attempt to unify the fate of all the deportees by making all the camps – Birkenau and Buchenwald, Dachau and Treblinka – one single mythical camp, opened in 1933 and liberated in 1945, in which everyone, Jews and non-Jews, experienced the same fate. *Nuit et brouillard* is emblematic of this vision.
>
> (A. Wieviorka 1992: 434)

5 Annette Wieviorka dates the use in France of the word 'Shoah' (which is the Hebrew for disaster) from the 1980s (1992: 436, note 3).

6 George Steiner has described the Holocaust as marking the tragic nature of our own times in the following terms:

> Using theological metaphors, and there is no need to apologize for them in an essay on culture, one may say that the holocaust marks a second Fall. We can interpret it as a voluntary exit from the Garden and a programmatic attempt to burn the Garden behind us....With the botched attempt to kill God and the very nearly successful attempt to kill those who had "invented" Him, civilization entered, precisely as Nietzsche had foretold, "on night and more night".
>
> (Steiner 1971: 42)

7 In *Le Différend*, Lyotard makes the distinction between *différend* (in which the heterogeneity and unfixed nature of the name is of prime importance) and *litige* (in which a solution is achieved and hence a closure of meaning). In this schema, the state of Israel is therefore a recuperation or naturalization of that which cannot or must not be recuperated:

> The *différend* attached to Nazi names, to *Hitler*, *Auschwitz* and *Eichmann*, cannot be transformed into *litige* and regulated by a verdict. The shades of those for whom not only life but the expression of the wrong done to them was refused by the Final Solution continue to roam indeterminately. In creating the state of Israel, the survivors transformed this wrong into a damage and the *différend* into litigation. In so doing, they put an end to the silence to which they had been condemned by beginning to speak in the common idiom of international law and conventional politics.
>
> (Lyotard 1983: 90)

For a discussion of Lyotard's description of the Holocaust as the major *différend*, see Mongin 1994a: 74.

8 For a similarly monolithic concept of 'the West', see, for example, Robert Young 1990. For a stimulating exposé and problematization of this approach, see Cheyette 1995.

9 A more nuanced presentation of the Hellenic and Hebraic traditions, which at once confounds the over-reductive antithesis underlying the above theories and replaces it with a troubling ambivalence, can perhaps be found in the figure of the 'Jewgreek', Leopold Blum, in James Joyce's *Ulysses*. Here the wandering Ulysses and the wandering Jew are fused rather than placed in opposition to each other (cf. Cheyette 1993).

10 The confusion between the allegorical use of 'jews' and the history of real Jews in Lyotard's *Heidegger et 'les juifs'* (see, for example, pp. 46 and 130) demonstrates the naïvety of Lyotard's own desire to distinguish between them. Why choose the term 'jew' in the first place if not because of the history of real Jews (cf. Boyarin and Boyarin 1993: 700)?

11 cf. the title of Derrida's essay on Lévinas mentioned previously, 'Violence et métaphysique' (Derrida 1967).

12 Tzvetan Todorov (1994: 124–125) believes that Blanchot's 'conversion' is compromised by the fact that his condemnation during the 1980s of the anti-Semitism of others (notably Paul Valéry's anti-Dreyfus engagement at the beginning of this century and Martin Heidegger's Nazism during the 1930s) contrasts markedly with his silence about his own adherence, between 1936 and 1938, to the beliefs of Action Française and his signed articles in the extreme right-wing journal *Combat* 'in which Jews were savaged and regularly associated with Bolshevism' (p. 124). For a critique of Blanchot's early anti-Semitism in *Combat*, see Mehlman 1983. See also Jean-Pierre Faye (Faye and Vilaine 1993: 36) who comments not only on Blanchot but on other French intellectuals who have attempted to marry the contradictory tendencies of Adorno's vision of writing after Auschwitz and Heideggerian philosophy. He recalls how Adorno himself could never understand the French fascination with Heidegger.

13 cf. Handelman:

> In his essay on 'Jabès and the question of the Book', Derrida traces the connection between the Jew and writing, defining Judaism precisely as "the birth and passion of writing...the love and endurance of the letter itself".... For the Jew – and the poet – the book becomes folded and bound to itself, infinitely self-reflective, its own subject and its own representation. The home of the Jew and the poet is the text; they are wanderers, born only of the book. But the freedom of the poet depends, in Derrida's interpretation, on the breaking of the tablets of the law (slaying Moses again).... Both the poet and the Jew must write and must comment, because both poetry and commentary are forms of exiled speech, but the poet need not be faithful nor bound to any original text.
>
> (Handelman 1982: 175–176)

14 cf. Mongin 1996a: 237: 'We have moved from a representation of the world facing the future to that of a timid approach to what will come to pass.'

15 Unlike Alain Resnais's *Nuit et brouillard*, which mixes archive footage with contemporary shots of the camps in an unsettling movement between past and present, Lanzmann's film avoids all use of documentary material, and therefore gestures towards an absent past (which cannot be represented) only through the tentative gropings of present-day witnesses and locations.

16 Elsewhere, Lyotard (1990: 114) similarly condenses European history into a fairly monolinear story by conflating 'Christian Europe', republicanism and liberalism in their effacing of 'the other'. Talking of 'the Jewish book', he says, 'this is what Europe – first Christian then republican and now liberal and permissive – refuses to know about or will simply never understand'. In this same article, Lyotard sweepingly equates Europe's anti-Semitism with the 'self-constitution' of the self characteristic of Europe's quest for totality.

17 See especially *Critical Inquiry* 1989. One of the contributors to this special issue, Jean-Marie Apostolidès, notes the following:

> What is indeed striking in deconstruction is that it escapes confrontation with historical development. That does not imply that it is linked to rightist thought (its technique can be used either for 'fascist' or 'liberal' purposes), but it implies that this method rarely confronts historicity, because history reveals the 'decidable', which sometimes means guilt.
>
> (Apostolidès 1989: 766)

18 Vergès was already renowned for equating French atrocities during the Algerian War with Nazi crimes during the Second World War (though here too he was merely appropriating arguments which originally started life on the anti-colonial Left during the Algerian War itself). Kritzman (1995a: 6) observes that 'Vergès's evocation of this "return of the repressed" ends up by becoming a grotesque form of manipulation, another example of the assassination of memory which entails a repetition of the pain of loss'.

19 Georges Bensoussan locates the same problem concerning the particularization or the generalization of the Shoah, but uses different examples to demonstrate this oscillation:

> The history of the genocide of the Jews is threatened by slippages in interpretation. For some, the event is absorbed into a general continuum in which all the disasters of Jewish history are subsumed within the commemoration of *Ticha Bé Av* or *9 Av*, the date of the destruction of the Second Temple....This is the crude religious discourse which denies the Shoah its radical uniqueness. For others, the event is seen *only* in terms of its absolute uniqueness, denying any interpretation which would place it within an historical and rational framework and thus clothing it in the single discourse of the 'unutterable' and 'indescribable'.
>
> (Bensoussan 1994: 95–96) (cf. Bédarida 1997: 218–219)

It is precisely this 'political minefield' that the British artist Rachel Whiteread stepped into when she was asked to design a memorial in Vienna to Austrian Jews killed in the Holocaust (see Lynn MacRitchie, 'The war over Rachel', *Guardian*, 5 November 1996).

20 Lyotard suggests precisely the opposite. It is representations of Auschwitz which are equivalent to the Nazi policy of effacing the traces of extermination, since the former (like the latter) are also ways of forgetting the crime (see Lyotard 1988b: 49–50). The polemic pitting representationalists against anti-representationalists was particularly bitter at the time of the opening of Steven Spielberg's film on the Holocaust, *Schindler's List*. Claude Lanzmann called Spielberg's fictionalization of the Holocaust a transgression of the forbidden (of the unrepresentability of Auschwitz) (*Le Monde*, 3 March 1994), while Pierre Billard retorted by calling Lanzmann, Raul Hilberg and others 'the new fundamentalists' (*Le Point*, 12 March 1994). For a fuller discussion, see Lehrer 1994.

21 Cornelius Castoriadis (1996: 89) highlights what he sees as the contradiction inherent in 'the deconstructionist mystification which condemns the

project of the Hellenic West' given that the 'sophists' who collapse Western versions of emancipation into extreme forms of totalitarianism are themselves 'not reticent about occasionally posing as the defenders of justice, democracy and human rights'.

22 The notion of the 'tragic' nature of the modern concept of history signified by the Holocaust unites a number of different thinkers, including Lyotard, Jürgen Habermas and George Steiner, although the conclusions they draw from this shared premise are very different. As regards Lyotard and Habermas, for example, if the former reads this tragedy in terms of the end of rationality and the end of modernity, the latter (as suggested above) sees it as the sign of the failure only of 'instrumentalist' rationality and consequently as a sign of the unaccomplished task of modernity to effect real freedom and emancipation.

2 New racisms

1 This ambivalence was mirrored in those who were at the receiving end of modern forms of 'othering'. As both Bauman (1991a) and Gilroy (1993) have shown, they were both inside and outside social structures at the same time.

2 Clearly this is not meant to imply that concepts of difference were employed for the first time after the Second World War. The Negritude movement before the war is a good example of the anti-colonial challenge to universalist hypocrisy through the adoption of differentialist criteria (see House 1997).

3 For an example of Benoist's approach, see Benoist 1986. The title, *Europe, tiers monde, même combat*, illustrates the way in which Benoist exploits an anti-Western, Third World discourse for his own ends. It is not difficult to see how his argument could simply be mistaken for a left-wing anti-imperialist defence of oppressed people through the proclamation of the 'right to difference'. For a detailed discussion of Lévi-Strauss's more recent proclamations on the subject, see Taguieff's chapter entitled ' "Racisme": usages et mésusages. A Partir de Lévi-Strauss', Taguieff 1995a: 9–20. For a brief survey of the ambiguous use of the concept of difference, see also Adler 1997.

4 cf. Renan's statements at the same time on the inequality of races. For example:

> It would be extending the pantheist concept of history to an absurd extreme to place all races on an equal footing and, according to the belief that human nature is always beautiful, to suggest that one can find in all the different races the same fullness and richness. I am therefore the first to recognize that the Semitic race, compared to the Indo-European race, is an inferior manifestation of human nature.
>
> (cited in Todorov 1989: 170)

5 This formula for the shift between modern and postmodern forms of racism runs counter to what Colette Guillaumin asserted in 1972 in an article entitled 'The specific characteristics of racist ideology' (translated in Guillaumin 1995).

6 Even if it is true that there are considerable differences between the Front National and the ideas of Benoist, especially concerning immigration (Adler 1995), nevertheless, on a more general level, they both exploit the logic of cultural differentialism.

7 For a concise version of Wieviorka's analysis, see Chapter 1, entitled 'La grande mutation', in Wieviorka 1992: 25–41 or his chapter entitled 'Culture, société et démocratie' in Wieviorka, ed., 1997: 11–60.

8 Surprisingly, given his habitual attention to the nature of the historical 'conjuncture' in the determination of social relations and processes, Etienne Balibar has equated the ideology of the Front National with fascism (see 'De la "préférence nationale" à l'invention de la politique' and 'Contre le fascisme et pour la révolte' in Balibar 1998: 89–132 and 133–144, respectively). Balibar suggests that the reduction of the plurality of levels of identification to one single identification, namely that of the nation (or, more specifically, 'the conflation of the family and the nation', p. 120), and the obsession with descendance and genealogy (p. 121) are precisely the characteristics which allow a comparison between fascism and the Front National. For my own part, the comparison obscures more than it reveals about the racialized nationalism of the Front National.

9 In France, Taguieff has been a victim of this confusion. His critiques of anti-racism and his fascination with Alain de Benoist have led some to suspect his involvement with the New Right (see Roger-Pol Droit in *Le Monde*, 13 July 1993). Following a call by a number of intellectuals for greater vigilance in dealings with (and hence giving legitimacy to) the New Right (reprinted in the same issue of *Le Monde*), this political correctness 'à la française' was in turn denounced by Taguieff and others who argue that new thinking around today's problems and the critique of old 'left-wing' ideas should not automatically be mistaken for colluding with the enemy (see 'Y a-t-il une affaire Taguieff?', *Globe Hebdo*, 21–27 July 1993; Michel Wieviorka, 'Qui est vraiment d'extrême droite?', *Globe Hebdo*, 28 July–3 August 1993; and 'Les dérapages de la vigilance', *Le Nouvel Observateur*, 12–18 August 1993).

10 For a critique of Yonnet, see the contributions by Lucien Karpik and Michel Wieviorka in 'Autour du malaise français', *Le Débat* 1993: 117–131. For a critique of Yonnet, and Béjin and Freund, see Todorov 1996: 123–129.

11 The opposition between universalism and difference is mirrored in the discourse on the city of integration (*à la française*) and segregation (*à l'américaine*).

3 City spaces

1 Rather more tendentiously, Ross argues (following Lefebvre, Castoriadis and Sartre) that the immobilization of time and history effected by the mobility of the automobile was echoed in the 1960s in the 'hygienic language of technique and efficiency' of both the technocratic young bureaucrat and the intellectuals of structuralism who provided the new managerial bourgeoisie with its 'ideological legitimation, its intellectual veneer' (Ross 1995: 176–177). In a fairly reductive reading of the

relationship between socio-economic developments and intellectual movements, she includes the Annales-school historians as also complicit in
legitimizing 'the ideology of capitalist modernization' and 'masking [its]
social contradictions' (ibid., p. 190):

> Just as modernization needed a new recounting of history that would
> dissolve beginning and end into a natural, quasi-immobile, 'spatial-
> ized' process, a kind of succession of immobilities, so it needed a
> system of signs that would establish a common intellectual currency,
> so to speak, between the various intellectual disciplines, a network of
> 'communication' by which to trace the buried structures common to
> all social life.
>
> (ibid., p. 191)

2 cf. the observation of the architect Paul Chemetov (1994: 65): 'Reflections
on the city necessitate more general reflections on how to found today
new concepts of life in the City, citizenship and the social contract.'
3 cf. Keith (1995):

> On the one hand the precariousness of the flâneur losing himself [sic]
> in the crowd always leads to an immersion in the street but also,
> through immersion in the crowd, to an identification with and
> fetishisation of the commodity. So that the flâneur, once confronted
> with the department store, finds that 'he roamed through
> the labyrinth of merchandise as he had once roamed through the
> labyrinth of the city' (in *Charles Baudelaire: A Lyric Poet in the Era of
> High Capitalism*). Making contradictory sense of oneself in the street
> is about locating the body in the possibly incommensurable matrices
> of economy and culture.
>
> (Keith 1995: 304)

4 cf. Michael Sheringham's observations (1995: 211) on the work of Marc
Augé: 'For Augé the crisis of identity is a crisis of alterity. We used to
know where the other was, now the other is everywhere: the dangers of
demonization and exclusion are acute.'
5 As a middle-class intellectual whose home is in the centre of Paris,
Maspero foregrounds his mobility in relation to the relative lack of
mobility of those he encounters. Similarly, by referring on numerous occasions to the problematic links between 'centre' and 'periphery' (according
to who is doing the speaking or the observing) he foregrounds the
different relationships to city spaces of these middle-class intellectuals *vis-
à-vis* those others (for the most part working-class and very often of
immigrant backgrounds), their different capacities for freedom and
choice.
6 cf. Olivier Mongin's trenchant critique of what he terms 'the democratic
Utopia' today:

> The only horizon of the democratic Utopia is the present. It makes
> the individual believe that he lives in a present which condenses all

history and a world which condenses all space. It devours time and space – those mainstays of all experience.

(Mongin 1994a: 15)

Like Maspero, Mongin (ibid., 25) seeks to reintegrate time and space and hence to oppose 'the tendency today [which] works instead to separate them and to privilege a time without space and a space in which historical time no longer has any real sense'.

4 Cultural debates

1 Régis Debray (1993: 117) defines *le culturel* as 'what happens to culture when it is televised'.
2 cf. Mongin:

> The space of the republican school has become fragmented into claims for ethnic identity and cultural individualism. It seems that the interpretation of culture has become culturalist, relativist and differentialist. This interpretation has now taken over from the republican conception which had the merit of unifying and hierar-chizing behaviour within the framework of state schooling.
>
> (Mongin 1994a: 190) (cf. Finkielkraut and Gauchet 1988)

3 I have discussed elsewhere (Silverman 1992) the problematic nature of this binary opposition between France and Germany, and especially the way in which Renan is habitually mobilized to support it, after his conversion in the 1870s from an ethnic nationalist position (emblematic of the 'German model') to one of republican universalism (emblematic of the 'French model').
4 Mongin demonstrates how the 'ethnological interpretation' of culture converts culture from an act of creation into an already acquired attribute of an individual or community:

> Pushing the ethnological interpretation of the 1970s to its extreme – that popular culture as well as high culture deserves respect – the approach to culture now favours the claims to difference made by marginal cultures and underlines the importance of the culture of the community of belonging.... This extension of the notion of culture progressively reinforces the idea that culture is both a given and an acquired trait in that it is either the individual's claim to identity or the desire to preserve the culture of the ethnic group or community of belonging.
>
> (Mongin 1994a: 189)

Hence, to formulate this development using the dichotomy between France and Germany employed by Finkielkraut and Fumaroli, the human project of the 'Enlightenment' version of culture gives way to the ethnic customs of the 'German' model. Dominic Wolton's critique of what he calls 'cultural television' (that is, thematic programming according to ethnic/cultural identity) in favour of 'a generalist television' also corresponds to a universalistic vision of culture (à la Lord Reith?) which will provide social cohesion and prevent ghettoization according to specialization (see Wolton 1990).

5 Danièle Sallenave's book *Le Don des morts* adopts a similar perspective with regard to the lost golden age of the book. Interestingly, Sallenave makes explicit the links between literature, the modern city and the age of Enlightenment which are today threatened by money and profit (and the image), and in which 'art itself risks becoming a simple commodity among others'. She muses nostalgically on 'the Utopia of city life, the life with books, and the life of the community of Man in a free space in which we will silently reawaken the life of the past' (1991: 19). For a critique of Fumaroli, see Roman 1991. For a critique of Finkielkraut, Fumaroli, and Sallenave, see Rigaud 1990: 395–402. For a *tour d'horizon* of these debates (including the position of Rigaud himself) in the context of developments in French cultural policy, see David Looseley's excellent book *The Politics of Fun* (1995).

6 Mike Featherstone also locates the breakdown of the division between art and everyday life as crucial to postmodernism:

> If we examine definitions of postmodernism we find an emphasis on the effacement of the boundary between art and everyday life, the collapse of the distinction between high art and mass/popular culture, a general stylistic promiscuity and playful mixing of codes.
>
> (Featherstone 1991: 65)

7 Ehrenberg is also targeting Laurent Cohen-Tanugi here, but one might easily put Paul Yonnet in the same category (see Cohen-Tanugi 1993 and Yonnet 1985).

8 It is useful here to think of Zygmunt Bauman's notion of the ambivalent status of modern counter-cultures which Paul Gilroy (1993) exploits in terms of the 'double consciousness' of black intellectuals in the modern period, both inside and outside the frontiers of modern society; or indeed of Etienne Balibar's notion of 'determined opposites'.

9 cf. Kumar 1995: 114: 'Knowledge in its postmodern form, is not simply a cultural extrusion of post-industrial society; it is an aspect precisely of the knowledge society.' See also Lyotard's definition of culture in *Le Différend* (1983: 259): 'The word culture already signifies the circulation of information rather than the work to be accomplished in order to be able to present what is not presentable.'

10 cf. Balandier:

> The media age is accompanied by the permanent power of images and therefore the constraint to found power on images. However, the continual flow of spectacular images reduces everything to one level and effaces the distance and separation without which the political sphere has no space of its own. What is secret (one of the weapons of those who govern) is therefore replaced with noise.
>
> (Balandier 1985: 11)

11 Gilles Lipovetsky locates the same process when he talks of:

expression at all costs, the primacy of the act of communication over the nature of what is communicated, indifference towards content, the playful absorption of meaning, communication with no goals and no public, the addresser who has become his/her own addressee. Hence this over-abundance of spectacles, exhibitions and interiors...and the need to express oneself whatever the 'message', the narcissistic pleasure derived from expression for no end other than expression itself (and the right to do this), but transmitted and amplified by a medium.

(Lipovetsky 1983: 23)

12 The bizarre phenomenon of the public reaction to the death of Princess Diana in August 1997 is a good example of this 'continuum of star and punter'. Régis Debray sees the adulation of Diana and the decline in the fortunes of the rest of the British monarchy in terms of the struggle between modern symbolic formality and postmodern 'fusional' informality ('sensory and tactile culture, humanitarian compassion, idolatry of the body and proximity'), leading eventually (although not quite on this occasion) to

the victory of the law of the heart over the law itself, of the horizontal over the vertical, of the Index over the Symbol, in which the sign is stuck to the object itself, like the photograph, rather than distanced from the object, like the word (to use Pierce's terms).

('Admirable Angleterre', *Le Monde*, 10 September 1997)

Jean-Pierre Le Goff's damning criticism of the 'society of spectacle' also seems particularly relevant to this phenomenon:

The spectacle and the cult of emotion and lived experience confuse the distinctions between the imaginary and the real, between what is tolerable and what is intolerable. The emotional impact counts for more than rational debate and the exchange of arguments. Words lose their sense for immediacy and feeling is all that really matters, which means that the situation is ripe for all sorts of manipulation.

(Le Goff 1996: 219)

See also Pierre Chambat and Alain Ehrenberg's discussion (1993) of television 'reality shows' which blur the distinction between private and public, spectator and star. (For a general discussion of 'reality shows', see Dauncey 1997.)

13 Debray's discussion of the transformation from the 'republican' school to today's 'democratic' school highlights the centrality of the republican ethos in the formation of *le peuple*, and the danger to the nation when the state embraces a democratic concept of *le peuple*:

People and School were the two historical faces of the republican Janus, since the concept of a Republic is first and foremost pedagogic.... To renounce the duty to teach leads to taking social facts as norms and replacing the 'general will' with collective psychology, which is what the demagogic state does, sometimes in the name of democracy.

(Debray 1993: 83)

14 Le Goff makes the same point in relation to information:

The over-abundance of information kills information, drowns every-thing in a sea of equivalence, renders the event unrecognizable and contributes to the death of meaning. Events and actors disappear under the weight of images and commentaries which resemble each other. The contours of the real lose their consistency in favour of a flow or magma of prefabricated images and sentences repeated ad infinitum, as in a state of hypnosis.

(Le Goff 1996: 218)

15 Elsewhere Virilio has said:

not to read is to cease to make mental images; it is to be a handi-capped voyeur....When one sees badly, one lives and walks badly....The crisis of mental images brings to a head an optical and ocular blindness in which it becomes impossible to recognize certain forms and leads to a loss of intuition. It is well known that intuition depends on a look which is attentive to the smallest details.

('Faire image', *Les Cahiers de Paris-VIII*, Saint-Denis, PUV, p. 242, cited in Mongin 1994a: 222)

16 In his critique of the 'democratic' nature of the image, Georges Balandier puts the opposition between republic and democracy in the following terms:

Genuine democracy requires the greatest possible loosening of those determinations which condition opinions, preferences and choices, while democracy in the hands of the media and the grand communi-cators is condemned to disappear beneath a populism whose authoritarian nature is hidden by the spectacle of images. In the past the Republic was fortified by its insistence on the cult of the textual and the law. Today the strength of democracy depends on the will to give to both of these a place and a space to flourish.

(Balandier 1994: 207) (cf. Debray 1989)

17 Zygmunt Bauman defines the way in which the Enlightenment project stigmatized popular culture and life-styles as follows:

Popular, locally administered ways of life were...constituted, from the perspective of universalistic ambitions, as retrograde and back-ward-looking, a residue of a different social order to be left behind; as imperfect, immature stages in an overall line of development toward a 'true' and universal way of life, exemplified by the hegemonic elite; as grounded in superstition or error, passion-ridden, infested with animal drives, and otherwise resisting the ennobling influence of the truly human – shortly to be dubbed 'enlightened' – order.

(Bauman 1992: 7–8)

18 See, for example, Alain Touraine who situates this approach to 'mass culture' within the wider context of the French Enlightenment and republican intellectual tradition:

> Those intellectuals who remain faithful to the heritage of the Enlightenment too often tend to condemn mass society and judge it crass. They denounce the impoverishment and dangers of mass cultural consumption and display their talent in criticizing this state of affairs rather than in proposing solutions.... This attitude is precisely that of the republican elite which has always wanted to conserve power within a narrow band of enlightened citizens, those who have particular skills, or even those considered to be qualified interpreters of the meaning and direction of history.
>
> (Touraine 1992: 418)

19 It has been argued (Adkins and Leonard 1996) that French feminism has been 'recuperated' in a different way: the popularization in America and Britain of the linguistic and psychoanalytical criticism of Cixous, Kristeva and Irigaray and its absorption into the Anglo-American post-structuralist critical tradition of the last two decades has tended to efface a different tradition of French feminism (as epitomized by the work of Christine Delphy, Colette Guillaumin and Monique Wittig and the women's studies journal, *Questions féministes*) which presents a far more materialist critical approach.

20 cf. Michael Collins ('You must be joking', *Guardian*, 14 July 1997): 'If figurative painting would now be the most radical move in an art world colonised by the installation, the most revolutionary route in a television racked by half-arsed attempts at irony is...to go straight.' See also, from a slightly different perspective, Gayatri Spivak:

> I find the demand on me to be marginal always amusing.... I am tired of dining out on being an exile because that has a long tradition and it is not one I want to identify myself with.... In a certain sense, I think there is nothing that is central. The centre is always consti-tuted in terms of its own marginality. However...certain peoples have always been asked to cathect the margins so that others can be defined as central...in that situation the only strategic thing to do is to absolutely present oneself at the center.
>
> (quoted in Soja and Hooper 1993: 203)

21 cf. Le Goff:

> The link between intellectuals and the people constitutes a crucial element in the construction of an education and a dynamic concept of citizenship to which we must all contribute. 'To instil the spirit of

critical awareness into the masses', 'to create a popular version of reason', to give everyone the opportunity to access our cultural heritage, to form elites from the people...these ideals of popular education can be reshaped today to form a new dynamism in the face of the intellectual confusion which predominates.

(Le Goff 1996: 227)

For a critique of Finkielkraut's position in relation to the school, see Peters 1993.
22 At a conference in Strasbourg in 1993 (Carrefour des littératures européennes de Strasbourg, reported as 'Le cri du monde' in *Le Monde des Livres*, 5 November 1993, pp. 27–30), Lyotard's perspective was shown to be in stark contrast to that of Pierre Bourdieu. Although Bourdieu agreed that 'we must be wary of...the figure of the intellectual as self-proclaimed bearer of the universal conscience', he nevertheless believed that the intellectual could still fulfil the role of 'functionary for humanity' (p. 29).

5 Citizens all?

1 As Lyotard has said (1979: 72), 'the principle of a universal metalanguage is replaced by that of a plurality of formal and axiomatic systems'.
2 Elsewhere, Naïr (1992: 46) puts this development more succinctly: 'Behind the social looms the ethnic, the cultural and the confessional.'
3 Naïr (Morin and Naïr 1997: 195–197) adopts the classic antithesis between French republicanism and 'Anglo-Saxon' democracy. In the context of a discussion of the future of Europe, he observes:

> if the fate of the republican idea inaugurated by the French Revolution is to suffer defeat at the hands of the Anglo-Saxon idea of individualist democracy, regulated solely by the principle of the market, then there is no reason whatsoever to defend that version of Europe.
>
> (p. 196; see also p. 210)

4 cf. Judt (1992: 154) who talks of 'the indigenous antiliberalism of the French republican intelligentsia'.
5 A good example of this backlash is the vigorous revisionism of intellectual history, which we noted in the previous chapter, in the wake of the disintegration of the former Cold War orthodoxies. The vicious attacks on what are depicted as the morally blind, hopelessly prescriptive, authoritarian nature of former gurus (far more ferocious than anything we see in Britain) are frequently the bearers (either explicitly or implicitly) of a neo-liberal democratic agenda and a renewed interest in liberal thinkers like de Tocqueville (see, for example, a number of the articles in the influential journal *Le Débat*).
6 Virilio expresses the same idea in the following way:

> Absolute speed is the opposite of democracy, which presupposes encountering others, discussion, taking time to reflect and sharing in

decision-making. If the consequence of continued acceleration is that we are left with no time to share, then democracy is truly impossible.

(1996: 97)

7 One thinks of John Major's 'Citizens' charter' in the UK. Was this a charter for citizens or consumers, and what was the distinction between the two?

8 Olivier Mongin (1994a: 277–296) traces the roots of this reformulation of the relationship between the individual and the world in terms of the penetration, over recent years, of American social and political theory into the French intellectual tradition.

9 Mongin makes a similar point when he says:

accepting the principle of democracy does not necessarily mean a dogmatic acceptance of the principles of liberalism or the rule of 'public opinion' but rather a concern for the future shape of the democratic adventure of equality after the failure of communist egalitarianism and in the face of resurgent nationalism.

(1994a: 25)

10 See also Weeks 1993: 206; Heller and Fehér 1988; Naïr 1992: 227.

11 Morin's position would here be diametrically opposed to that of Jean-Marie Guéhenno (1993: 12) for whom the decline of the nation signals the 'end of democracy': 'We must ask ourselves today whether it is possible to have democracy without a nation.'

12 Sami Naïr makes a similar point in relation to Habermas's notion of a public space of 'communicative rationality':

In reality, this approach simply displaces the problem of social transformation on to a space deemed to be open – that of democratic discussion – while forgetting that the real problem is precisely the already achieved fusion of the channels of finance, power and the perverted system of democracy itself.

(Morin and Naïr 1997: 223)

Conclusion

1 For a similar 'futuristic vision of the urban industrial world of capitalist development and authoritarian politics' (Westwood and Williams 1997: 3), see also Fritz Lang's *Metropolis* (1927) and Ridley Scott's *Bladerunner* (1981).

Bibliography

Adkins, L. and Leonard, D. (1996) 'Reconstructing French feminism: commodification, materialism and sex' in D. Leonard and L. Adkins (eds) *Sex in Question: French Materialist Feminism*, London: Taylor and Francis, 1–23.

Adler, F. H. (1995) 'Racism, "différence" and the Right in France', *Modern and Contemporary France*, NS3 (4), 439–451.

—— (1997) 'Différence, antiracisme et xénologique', *L'Homme et la Société*, 125, 59–67.

Anderson, B. (1983) *Imagined Communities*, London: Verso.

Anthias, F. and Yuval-Davis, N. (1993) *Racialized Boundaries: Race, Nation, Gender, Colour and Class and the Anti-Racist Struggle*, London: Routledge.

Apostolidès, J.-M. (1989) 'On Jacques Derrida's "Paul de Man's war"', *Critical Inquiry*, 15 (1988–1989), Summer, 765–766.

Aragon, L. (1975, first published 1926) *Le Paysan de Paris*, Paris: Gallimard/Folio.

Atack, M. (1997) 'Edgar Morin and the sociology of May 68', *French Cultural Studies*, viii, 295–307.

Augé, M. (1992) *Non-lieux: introduction à une anthropologie de la surmodernité*, Paris: Seuil.

—— (1996) 'Paris and the ethnography of the contemporary world', in M. Sheringham (ed.) *Parisian Fields*, London: Reaktion Books, 175–179.

Bailly, J.-C. (1992), *La Ville à l'oeuvre*, Paris: Jacques Bertoin.

—— (1994), 'La ville en proie à la communication', *Le Débat*, 'Le Nouveau Paris', 80, May–August, 269–280.

Balandier, G. (1985) *Le Détour: pouvoir et modernité*, Paris: Fayard.

—— (1992) *Le Pouvoir sur scènes*, Paris: Éditions Balland.

—— (1994) *Le Dédale: pour en finir avec le XXe siècle*, Paris: Fayard.

Balibar, E. (1984) 'Sujets ou citoyens?', *Les Temps Modernes*, nos. 452–453–454, 1726–1753.

—— (1991) 'Race, nation and class' in M. Silverman (ed.) *Race, Discourse and Power in France*, Aldershot: Avebury, 71–83.

—— (1992) *Les Frontières de la démocratie*, Paris: La Découverte.

—— (1998) *Droit de cité: culture et politique en démocratie*, Paris: Editions de l'Aube.

Balibar, E. and Wallerstein, I. (1988) *Race, nation, classe: les identités ambiguës*, Paris: La Découverte.

Barker, M. (1981) *The New Racism*, London: Junction Books.

Bassan, R. (1989) 'Trois néobaroques français: Beineix, Besson, Carax, de *Diva* au *Grand Bleu*', *La Revue du Cinéma*, 449, May, 45–53.

Baudrillard, J. (1981) *A l'ombre des majorités silencieuses, ou la fin du social*, Paris: Grasset.

—— (1991) 'L'Amérique, ou la pensée de l'espace' in *Citoyenneté et urbanité*, Paris: Editions Esprit.

—— (1997) *Le Paroxyste indifférent* (Entretiens avec Philippe Petit), Paris: Grasset.

Baudrillard, J. and Guillaume, M. (1994) *Figures de l'altérité*, Paris: Descartes et Cie.

Bauman, Z. (1987) *Legislators and Interpreters: On Modernity, Postmodernity, and the Intellectuals*, Cambridge: Polity.

—— (1988) *Modernity and the Holocaust*, Cambridge: Polity.

—— (1991a) *Modernity and Ambivalence*, Cambridge: Polity.

—— (1991b) *Postmodernity: Chance or Menace?*, CSCV Occasional Papers, no. 2, Lancaster: Lancaster University, Centre for the Study of Cultural Values.

—— (1992) *Intimations of Postmodernity*, London: Routledge.

—— (1993) *Postmodern Ethics*, Oxford: Blackwell.

—— (1996) 'From pilgrim to tourist – or a short history of identity' in S. Hall and P. du Gay (eds) *Questions of Cultural Identity*, London: Sage, 18–36.

Beauvoir, S. de (1966) *Les Belles images*, Paris: Gallimard/Folio.

Beck, U. (1992) *Risk Society: Towards a New Modernity*, London: Sage.

Beck, U., Giddens, A. and Lash, S. (1994) *Reflexive Modernization: Politics, Tradition and Aesthetics in the Modern Social Order*, Cambridge: Polity.

Bédarida, F. (1993) 'La mémoire contre l'histoire', *Esprit*, 193, July, 7–13.

—— (1997) 'La Shoah dans l'histoire: unicité, historicité, causalité', *Esprit*, 235, August–September, 217–228.

Béjin, A. and Freund, J. (eds) (1986) *Racismes, antiracismes*, Paris: Meridiens Klincksieck.

Bell, D. (1976) *Cultural Contradictions of Capitalism*, London: Heinemann.

Benda, J. (1977; first published 1927) *La Trahison des clercs*, Paris: Seuil.

Benjamin, W. (1973) 'The work of art in the age of mechanical reproduction' in W. Benjamin, *Illuminations*, Glasgow: Fontana, 219–254.

—— (1983) 'Paris, capital of the nineteenth century' in W. Benjamin, *Charles Baudelaire: A Lyric Poet in the Era of High Capitalism*, London: Verso, 155–176.

Bennington, G. (1998) 'Lyotard and "the Jews"' in B. Cheyette and L. Marcus (eds) *Modernity, Culture and 'the Jew'*, Cambridge: Polity, 188–196.

Bennington, G. and Derrida, J. (1990) *Jacques Derrida*, Chicago: University of Chicago Press.

Benoist, A. de (1986) *Europe, tiers monde, même combat*, Paris: Laffont.

Bensoussan, G. (1994) 'Histoire, mémoire et commémoration', *Le Débat*, 82, November–December, 90–97.

Berman, M. (1982) *All That is Solid Melts into Air*, New York: Simon and Schuster.

Bernal, M. (1987) *Black Athena: The Afroasiatic Roots of Classical Civilization*, vol 1: 'The Fabrication of Ancient Greece, 1785–1985', London: Free Association Books.

Bernstein, M. A. (1998) 'Homage to the extreme: the Shoah and the rhetoric of catastrophe', *Times Literary Supplement*, 4953 (6 March), 6–8.

Bertheleu, H. (1997) 'De l'unité républicaine à la fragmentation multiculturelle: le débat français en matière d'intégration', *L'Homme et la Société*, 125, 27–38.

Birnbaum, P. (1988) *Un Mythe politique: la 'République juive'*, Paris: Arthème Fayard.

Blanchot, M. (1980) *L'Écriture du désastre*, Paris: Gallimard.

Blatt, D. (1997) 'Immigrant politics in a republican nation' in A. G. Hargreaves and M. McKinney (eds) *Post-colonial Cultures in France*, London: Routledge, 40–55.

Body-Gendrot, S. (1993) 'Migration and the racialization of the postmodern city in France' in M. Cross and M. Keith (eds) *Racism, the City and the State*, London: Routledge, 77–92.

Bouretz, P. (1992) 'Histoire et utopie (Fukuyama/Hegel, Mosès/Rosenzweig)', *Esprit*, 181, May, 119–133.

Boyarin, D. and Boyarin, J. (1993) 'Diaspora: generation and the ground of Jewish identity', *Critical Inquiry*, 19, Summer, 693–726.

Bradbury, M. (1976) 'The cities of modernism' in M. Bradbury and J. McFarlane (eds), *Modernism 1890–1930*, London: Penguin, 96–104.

Breton, A. (1964, first published 1928) *Nadja*, Paris: Gallimard/Folio.

Brubaker, R. (1992) *Citizenship and Nationhood in France and Germany*, Cambridge, Mass.: Harvard University Press.

Bruckner, P. (1996) 'Enfants et victimes: le temps de l'innocence' in L. du Mesnil (ed.) *La Société en quête de valeurs: pour sortir de l'alternative entre scepticisme et dogmatisme*, Paris: Maxima, 41–51.

Cardinal, M. (1977) *Autrement dit*, Paris: Grasset.

Castoriadis, C. (1994) 'En mal de culture', *Esprit*, 205, October, 40–50.

—— (1996) *La Montée de l'insignifiance: les carrefours du labyrinthe IV*, Paris: Seuil.

Certeau, M. de (1990; first published 1980) *L'Invention du quotidien: 1. Arts de faire*, Paris: Gallimard/Folio.

—— (1993; first published 1974) *La Culture au pluriel*, Paris: Seuil.

Chambat, P. and Ehrenberg, A. (1993) 'Les *reality shows*, un nouvel âge télévisuel?', *Esprit*, 188, January, 5–12.

Chaumont, J.-M. (1994) 'Connaissance ou reconnaissance? Les enjeux du débat sur la singularité de la Shoah', *Le Débat*, 82, November–December, 69–89.

Chemetov, P. (1994) 'De la critique de la ville à la pensée de la Cité, *Le Débat*, 82, November–December, 64–67.

—— (1996) 'Le productivisme ne peut être le moteur de la ville' in *Les Grandes Entretiens du Monde: Tome 3 – Penser le malaise social, la ville, l'économie*, Paris: Le Monde Editions, 105–114.

Chesneaux, J. (1996) 'Tyrannie de l'éphémère et citoyenneté du temps' in L. du Mesnil (ed.) *La Société en quête de valeurs: pour sortir de l'alternative entre scepticisme et dogmatisme*, Paris: Maxima, 105–116.

Chevalier, L. (1978; first published 1958) *Classes laborieuses, classes dangereuses*, Paris: Librairie Générale Française.

Cheyette, B. (1993) *Constructions of 'the Jew' in English Literature and Society: Racial Representations 1875–1945*, Cambridge: Cambridge University Press.

—— (1995) 'Jews and Jewishness in the writings of George Eliot and Frantz Fanon', *Patterns of Prejudice*, 29 (4), 3–17.

—— (1996) 'Ineffable and usable: towards a diasporic British–Jewish writing', *Textual Practice*, 10 (2), 295–313.

Choay, F. (1990) 'La ville invivable', *Le Débat*, 60, May–August, 311–314.

—— (1992) *L'Allégorie du patrimoine*, Paris: Seuil.

Cohen-Tanugi, L. (1993; first published 1989) *La Métamorphose de la démocratie française: de l'État jacobin à l'État de droit*, Paris: Gallimard/Folio.

Conan, E. and Lindenberg, D. (1992) 'Que faire de Vichy?', *Esprit*, 181, May, 5–15.

Conley, V. A. (1996) 'Electronic Paris: from place of election to place of ejection', in M. Sheringham (ed.) *Parisian Fields*, London: Reaktion Books, 162–174.

Connor, S. (1989) *Postmodernist Culture: An Introduction to Theories of the Contemporary*, Oxford: Blackwell.

Critical Inquiry (1989), 15, Summer.

Dauncey, H. (1997) 'Les reality-shows en France: citoyenneté télévisée ou simple mauvais goût?' in P. Whyte and C. Lloyd (eds) *La Culture Populaire en France*, Durham: University of Durham, Durham French Colloquies, no. 6, 126–146.

Le Débat (1988) 51, September–October.

—— (1993) 75, May–August.

—— (1994) 79, March–April.

—— (1995) 85, May–August.

Debord, G. (1971; first published 1967) *La Société du spectacle*, Paris: Editions Champ Libre.

Debray, R. (1989) 'Etes-vous républicain ou démocrate?', *Le Nouvel Observateur*, 30 November–6 December, 115–121.

—— (1992) *Vie et mort de l'image: une histoire du regard en Occident*, Paris: Gallimard/Folio.

—— (1993) *L'État séducteur. Les révolutions médiologiques du pouvoir*, Paris: Gallimard.

—— (1994) *Manifestes médiologiques*, Paris: Gallimard.

Debray, R. and Fumaroli, M. (1993) 'Dictature de l'image?', *Le Débat*, 74, March–April.

Deguy, M. (1990) 'Une Oeuvre après Auschwitz' in *Au sujet de Shoah*, Paris: Editions Belin, 21–48.

Delacampagne, C. (1994) 'L'antisémitisme en France' in L. Poliakov (ed.) *Histoire de l'antisémitisme 1945–1993*, Paris: Seuil, 121–164.

Delannoi, G. (1994) 'Réflexions sur le nationalisme', *Esprit*, January, 198, 84–96.

Derrida, J. (1967) *L'Écriture et la différence*, Paris: Seuil/Points.

—— (1987) *De l'esprit: Heidegger et la question*, Paris: Galilée.

—— (1992) 'Marx, penseur du XXIe siècle', *Le Nouvel Observateur*, 1511, 21–27 October, 53.

Dews, P. (1986) 'Introduction' in P. Dews, (ed.) *Habermas: Autonomy and Solidarity*, London: Verso, 1–32.

Donald, J. (1992) 'Metropolis: the city as text' in R. Bocock and K. Thomson (eds) *Social and Cultural Forms of Modernity*, Milton Keynes: Open University/Polity Press, 417–470.

Donzelot, J. and Roman, J. (1991) 'Le déplacement de la question sociale' in J. Donzelot (ed.) *Face à l'exclusion: le modèle français*, Paris: Editions Esprit, 6–12.

Dubet, F. (1997) 'La laïcité dans les mutations de l'école' in M. Wieviorka (ed.) *Une Société fragmentée: le multiculturalisme en débat*, Paris: La Découverte/Poche, 85–112.

Dubet, F. and Lapeyronnie, D. (1992) *Les Quartiers d'exil*, Paris: Seuil.

Dubet, F. and Wieviorka, M. (eds) (1995) *Penser le sujet: autour d'Alain Touraine*, Paris: Fayard.

Duchen, C. (1986) *Feminism in France: From May '68 to Mitterrand*, London: Routledge and Kegan Paul.

—— (ed.) (1987) *French Connections: Voices From the Women's Movement in France*, London: Hutchinson.

Dumont, L. (1983) *Essais sur l'individualisme*, Paris: Seuil.

Ehrenberg, A. (1988) 'En quoi le spectacle sportif est-il politique?', *Le Débat*, 52, November–December, 191–192.

—— (1991) *Le Culte de la performance*, Paris: Calmann-Lévy/Pluriel.

—— (1995) *L'Individu incertain*, Paris: Calmann-Lévy/Pluriel.

Eslin, J.-C. (1990) 'Questions à Jean-François Lyotard', *Esprit*, 162, June, 117–118.

Esprit (1992) 'Que faire de Vichy?', 181, May.

—— (1994) 'Vices et vertus de l'image' (special section), 199, February.

Faye, J.-P. and Vilaine, A.-M. de (1993) *La Déraison antisémite et son langage: dialogue sur l'histoire et l'identité juive*, Arles: Actes Sud.

Featherstone, M. (1991) *Consumer Culture and Postmodernism*, London: Sage.

Felman, S. (1989) 'Paul de Man's silence', *Critical Inquiry*, 15 (1988–1989), Summer, 704–744.

—— (1990) 'A l'Age du témoignage: *Shoah* de Claude Lanzmann' in *Au sujet de Shoah*, Paris: Editions Belin, 55–145.

Finkielkraut, A. (1987) *La Défaite de la pensée*, Paris: Gallimard.

—— (1996) *L'Humanité perdue: essai sur le XXe siècle*, Paris: Seuil.

Finkielkraut, A. and Gauchet, M. (1988) 'Malaise dans la démocratie: l'école, la culture, l'individualisme', *Le Débat*, 51, September–October, 130–152.

Fitoussi, J.-P. and Rosanvallon, P. (1996) *Le Nouvel âge des inégalités*, Paris: Seuil.

Forbes, J. and Kelly, M. (eds) (1995) *French Cultural Studies: An Introduction*, Oxford: Oxford University Press.

Foucault, M. (1976) *Surveiller et punir: naissance de la prison*, Paris: Gallimard.

—— (1986) 'Of other spaces', *Diacritics*, Spring, 22–27.

Friedländer, S. (1987) 'Réflexions sur l'historisation du national-socialisme', *Vingtième Siècle*, 16, October–December.

—— (ed.) (1992) *Probing the Limits of Representation: Nazism and the 'Final Solution'*, Cambridge, Mass.: Harvard University Press.

Frodon, J.-M. (1995) *L'Age moderne du cinéma français*, Paris: Flammarion.

Fumaroli, M. (1992) *L'État culturel: essai sur une religion moderne*, Fallois/Livre de Poche.

Gaspard, F. (1997) 'La République et les femmes' in M. Wieviorka (ed.) *Une société fragmentée: le multiculturalisme en débat*, Paris: La Découverte/Poche, 152–170.

Gaspard, F. and Khosrokhavar, F. (1995) *Le Foulard et la République*, Paris: La Découverte.

Gauchet, M. (1989) *La Révolution des droits de l'homme*, Paris: Gallimard.

—— (1990) 'Pacification démocratique, désertion civique', *Le Débat*, 60, May–August, 87–98.

Genestier, P. (1994) 'La banlieue au risque de la métropolisation', *Le Débat*, 'Le Nouveau Paris', 80, May–August, 192–217.

Gibson, K. and Watson, S. (1995) 'Postmodern spaces, cities and politics: an introduction' in S. Watson and K. Gibson (eds) *Postmodern Cities and Spaces*, Oxford: Blackwell, 1–10.

Giddens, A. (1990) *The Consequences of Modernity*, Cambridge: Polity.

—— (1991) *Modernity and Self-identity. Self and Society in the Late Modern Age*, Cambridge: Polity.

Gilroy, P. (1987) *There Ain't No Black in the Union Jack*, London: Hutchinson.

—— (1992) 'The end of antiracism' in J. Donald and A. Rattansi (eds) *'Race', Culture and Difference*, London: Sage/Open University, 49–61.

—— (1993) *The Black Atlantic: Modernity and Double Consciousness*, London: Verso.

Girardet, R. (1972) *L'Idée coloniale en France de 1871 à 1962*, Paris: La Table Ronde.

Gobineau, A. de (1853–1855) *Essai sur l'inégalité des races humaines* in *Oeuvres* (introduced and annotated by J. Boissel), vol. 1, Paris: Gallimard, Bibliothèque de la Pléiade, 1983, 133–1174.

Goux, J.-J. (1994) 'L'Éclipse de l'art?', *Esprit*, 205, October, 104–116.

Graham, S. (1997) 'Imagining the real-time city: telecommunications, urban paradigms and the future of cities' in S. Westwood and J. Williams (eds) *Imagining Cities: Scripts, Signs, Memory*, London: Routledge.

Grosz, E. (1990) 'Judaism and exile: the ethics of otherness', *New Formations*, 12, Winter, 77–88.

Guéhenno, J.-M. (1993) *La Fin de la démocratie*, Paris: Flammarion.

Guillaumin, C. (1991) ' "Race" and discourse' in M. Silverman (ed.) *Race, Discourse and Power in France*, Aldershot: Avebury, 5–13.

—— (1995) *Racism, Sexism, Power and Ideology*, London: Routledge.

Habermas, J. (1996) 'Modernity, an unfinished project' in M. P. d'Entrèves and S. Benhabib (eds) *Habermas and the Unfinished Project of Modernity*, Cambridge: Polity Press, 38–55.

Hall, S. and Held, D. (1989) 'Citizens and citizenship' in S. Hall and M. Jacques (eds) *New Times: The Changing Face of Politics in the 1990s*, London: Lawrence and Wishart, 173–189.

Handelman, S. (1982) *Slayers of Moses: The Emergence of Rabbinic Interpretation in Modern Literary Theory*, New York: Albany.

Hargreaves, A. G. and McKinney, M. (eds) (1997) *Post-Colonial Cultures in France*, London: Routledge.

Hartman, G. H. (1995) 'The Voice of Vichy' in Lawrence D. Kritzman (ed.) *Auschwitz and After: Race, Culture and 'the Jewish Question' in France*, London: Routledge, 15–24.

Harvey, D. (1989) *The Condition of Postmodernity*, Oxford: Blackwell.

Hayward, S. (1987) 'France avance-détour-retour: French cinema of the 1980s' in J. Howorth and G. Ross (eds) *Contemporary France: A Review of Interdisciplinary Studies*, vol. 1, London: F. Pinter.

—— (1993) *French National Cinema*, London: Routledge.

Heller, A. and Fehér, F. (1988) *The Postmodern Political Condition*, Cambridge: Polity Press.

Hers, F. and Latarjet, B. (1990) 'Rendre l'art à sa fonction', *Le Débat*, 60, May–August, 300–302.

Hobsbawm, E. (1986) 'Labour and human rights' in J. Donald and S. Hall (eds) *Politics and Ideology*, Milton Keynes: Open University Press, 77–85.

hooks, b. (1991) *Yearning: Race, Gender and Cultural Politics*, London: Turnaround.

House, J. (1997) *Antiracism and Antiracist Discourse in France from 1900 to the Present Day*, unpublished Ph.D. thesis, University of Leeds.

Jameson, F. (1984) 'Postmodernism or the cultural logic of late capitalism', *New Left Review*, 146, 52–92.

Jonas, H. (1984) *The Imperative of Responsibility. In Search of an Ethics for the Technological Age*, Chicago: University of Chicago Press.

Judt, T. (1992) *Past Imperfect: French Intellectuals, 1944–1956*, Berkeley and Los Angeles: University of California Press.

Kedward, H. R. and Wood, N. (eds) (1995) *The Liberation of France: Image and Event*, Oxford: Berg.

Keith, M. (1995) 'Shouts of the street: identity and the spaces of authenticity', *Social Identities*, 1 (2), August, 297–315.

Keith, M. and Pile, S. (1993) 'The politics of place', Introduction to M. Keith and S. Pile (eds) *Place and the Politics of Identity*, London: Routledge, 1–21.

Kellner, D. (1989) *Jean Baudrillard: From Marxism to Postmodernism and Beyond*, Cambridge: Polity.

Khilnani, S. (1990) 'Un nouvel espace pour la pensée politique', *Le Débat*, January–February, 58, 181–192.

Klarsfeld, S. and Rousso, H. (1992) 'Histoire et justice: débat entre Serge Klarsfeld et Henry Rousso', *Esprit*, 181, May, 16–37.

Kofman, E. (1993) 'Cities: A decade of *la politique de la ville*', *Modern and Contemporary France*, Special issue: *Cities*, NS1 (4), 379–383.

Kofman, E. and Lebas, E. (1996) 'Lost in transposition – time, space and the city', Introduction to E. Kofman and E. Lebas (eds and trans) *Writings on Cities: Henri Lefebvre*, Oxford: Blackwell, 3–60.

Kristeva, J. (1988) *Étrangers à nous-mêmes*, Paris: Gallimard/Folio.

—— (1990) *Lettre ouverte à Harlem Désir*, Paris: Rivages.

Kritzman, L. D. (1995a) 'Introduction: in the shadows of Auschwitz: culture, memories and self-reflection' in Lawrence D. Kritzman (ed.) *Auschwitz and After: Race, Culture and 'the Jewish Question' in France*, London: Routledge, 1–11.

—— (1995b) 'Critical reflections: self-portraiture and the representation of Jewish identity in French' in Lawrence D. Kritzman (ed.) *Auschwitz and After: Race, Culture and 'the Jewish Question' in France*, London: Routledge, 98–118.

Kumar, K. (1995) *From Post-Industrial to Post-Modern Society: New Theories of the Contemporary World*, Oxford: Blackwell.

Kureishi, H. (1995) *The Black Album*, London: Faber and Faber.

Lacoue-Labarthe, P. (1988–1989) 'Neither an accident or a mistake', *Critical Inquiry*, 15, 481–484 (originally appeared in *Le Nouvel Observateur*, 22–28 January 1988).

Lacoue-Labarthe, P. and Nancy, J.-L. (1990) 'The Nazi myth', *Critical Inquiry*, 16 (2), 291–313.

Lapeyronnie, D. (1993) *L'Individu et les minorités: la France et la Grande-Bretagne face à leurs immigrés*, Paris: Presses Universitaires de France.

Leca, J. (1991a) 'La citoyenneté en question' in P.-A. Taguieff (ed.) *Face au racisme*, vol. 2 'Analyses, hypothèses, perspectives', Paris: La Découverte, 311–336.

—— (1991b) 'Individualisme et citoyenneté' in P. Birnbaum and J. Leca (eds) *Sur l'individualisme*, Paris: Presses de la Fondation Nationale des Sciences Politiques, 159–209.

Leclerc, A. (1974) *Parole de femme*, Paris: Grasset.

Lefebvre, H. (1968) *Le Droit à la ville*, Paris: Anthropos.

Le Goff, J.-P. (1996) 'Contre le nihilisme, reprendre l'initiative', *Esprit*, 218, January–February, 217–228.

Lehrer, N. (1994) 'Between obsession and amnesia', *The Jewish Quarterly*, Autumn, 155, 26–28.

Leiris, M. (1969, first published 1951) *Cinq études d'ethnologie*, Paris: Denoël.

Lévi-Strauss, C. (1952) *Race et histoire*, Paris: Gallimard/Folio.

—— (1955) *Tristes tropiques*, Paris: Plon.

—— (1983) *Le Regard éloigné*, Paris: Plon.

Lévy, B.-H. (1987) *Éloge des intellectuels*, Paris: Grasset.

Lipovetsky, G. (1983) *L'Ère du vide: essai sur l'individualisme contemporain*, Paris: Gallimard/Folio.

—— (1987) *L'Empire de l'éphémère: la mode et son destin dans les sociétés modernes*, Paris: Gallimard/Folio.

—— (1990) 'Virage culturel, persistance du moi', *Le Débat*, 60, May–August, 264–269.

—— (1991) 'Espace privé, espace public à l'âge post-moderne' in *Citoyenneté et urbanité*, Paris: Editions Esprit.

—— (1992) *Le Crépuscule du devoir: l'ethique indolore des nouveaux temps démocratiques*, Paris: Gallimard.

—— (1996) 'L'ère de l'après-devoir' in L. du Mesnil (ed.) *La Société en quête de valeurs: pour sortir de l'alternative entre scepticisme et dogmatisme*, Paris: Maxima, 23–30.

Looseley, D. L. (1995) *The Politics of Fun: Cultural Policy and Debate in Contemporary France*, Oxford: Berg.

Loyer, F. (1994) 'Paris, ville décor', in *Le Débat*, 'Le Nouveau Paris', 80, May–August, 38–52.

Lyotard, J.-F. (1979) *La Condition postmoderne*, Paris: Editions de Minuit.

—— (1983) *Le Différend*, Paris: Editions de Minuit.

—— (1988a) *Le Postmoderne expliqué aux enfants*, Paris: Galilée/Livre de Poche.

—— (1988b) *Heidegger et 'les juifs'*, Paris: Galilée.

—— (1990) 'L'Europe, les juifs et le livre', *Esprit*, 162, June, 113–116 (first published in *Libération*, 15 May 1990).

—— (1993) *Moralités postmodernes*, Paris: Galilée.

Macey, D. (1995) 'Death of the intellectual?', *Economy and Society*, 24 (1), 122–137.

McGuigan, J. (1992) *Cultural Populism*, London: Routledge

Maffesoli, M. (1986) 'Le polyculturalisme: petite apologie de la confusion' in A. Béjin and J. Freund (eds), *Racismes, antiracismes*, Paris: Meridiens Klincksieck, 91–117.

—— (1988) *Le Temps des tribus: le déclin de l'individualisme dans les sociétés de masse*, Paris: Meridiens Klincksieck/Livre de Poche.

Marks, E. (1995) 'Cendres juives: Jews writing in French "after Auschwitz"' in Lawrence D. Kritzman (ed.) *Auschwitz and After: Race, Culture and 'the Jewish Question' in France*, London: Routledge, 35–46.

—— (1996) *Marrano as Metaphor: The Jewish Presence in French Writing*, New York: Columbia University Press.

Maspero, F. (1990) *Les Passagers du Roissy-Express*, Paris: Seuil/Points.

Massey, D. and Jess, P. (eds) (1995), *A Place in the World? Places, Cultures and Globalization*, Oxford: Open University/Oxford University Press.

Mehlman, J. (1983) *Legacies of Antisemitism in France*, Minneapolis: University of Minnesota Press.

Melucci, A. (1996) 'Difference and otherness in a global society: individual experience and collective action' in S. Fridlizius and A. Peterson (eds) *Stranger or Guest? Racism and Nationalism in Contemporary Europe*, Stockholm: Almqvist & Wiksell International, 39–57.

Minc, A. (1993) *Le Nouveau moyen âge*, Paris: Gallimard/Folio.

—— (1995) 'Les élites, le peuple, l'opinion: entretien avec Marcel Gauchet', *Le Débat*, 85, May–August, 63–82.

Moi, T. (1985) *Sexual/Textual Politics: Feminist Literary Theory*, London: Methuen.

Mongin, O. (1988) 'Se souvenir de la Shoah: histoire et fiction, *Esprit*, 134, January, 85–98.

—— (1991) *La Peur du vide*, Paris: Seuil.

—— (1992) 'Le contrat social menacé?', *Esprit*, 182, June, 5–11.

—— (1993) 'Une mémoire sans histoire? Vers une autre relation à l'histoire', *Esprit*, 190, March–April, 102–113.

—— (1994a) *Face au scepticisme: les mutations du paysage intellectuel ou l'invention de l'intellectuel démocratique*, Paris: La Découverte.

—— (1994b) 'Reclassements et retournements: entretien avec Olivier Mongin', *Le Débat*, 79, March–April, 62–71.

—— (1995) *Vers la troisième ville*, Paris: Hachette.

—— (1996a) 'Insécurités sociales', *Esprit*, 218, January–February, 229–239.

—— (1996b) 'Le désenchantement démocratique' in L. du Mesnil (ed.) *La Société en quête de valeurs: pour sortir de l'alternative entre scepticisme et dogmatisme*, Paris: Maxima, 55–64.

Morin, E. (1972; first published 1957) *Les Stars*, Paris: Seuil.

—— (1996) 'Complexité et liberté' in L. du Mesnil (ed.) *La Société en quête de valeurs: pour sortir de l'alternative entre scepticisme et dogmatisme*, Paris: Maxima, 217–231.

Morin, E. and Kern, A. B. (1993) *Terre-Patrie*, Paris: Seuil.

Morin, E. and Naïr, S. (1997) *Une Politique de civilisation*, Paris: Arléa.

Mouffe, C. (1993) 'Liberal socialism and pluralism. Which citizenship?' in J. Squires (ed.) *Principled Positions. Postmodernism and the Rediscovery of Value*, London: Lawrence and Wishart, 69–84.

Mourier, M. (ed.) (1989) *Comment vivre avec l'image?*, Paris: Presses Universitaires de France.

Münster, A. (ed.) (1994) *La Pensée de Franz Rosenzweig*, Paris: Presses Universitaires de France.

Naïr, S. (1992) *Le Regard des vainqueurs. Les enjeux français de l'immigration*, Paris: Grasset.

Naïr, S. and Lucas, J. de (1996) *Le Déplacement du monde: immigration et thématiques identitaires*, Paris: Editions Kimé.

Nancy, J.-L. (1986) *La Communauté désoeuvrée*, Paris: Christian Bourgois.

Newman, C. (1984) 'The postmodern aura: the act of fiction in an age of inflation', *Salmagundi*, 63 (4), 3–199.

Nicolet, C. (1982) *L'Idée républicaine en France*, Paris: Gallimard.

Noiriel, G. (1988) *Le Creuset français: histoire de l'immigration XIXe–XXe siècles*, Paris: Seuil.

Nora, P. (1984) *Les Lieux de mémoire*, 1, 'La République', Paris: Gallimard.

Norindr, P. (1996) 'La plus grande France: French cultural identity and nation building under Mitterrand' in S. Ungar and T. Conley (eds) *Identity Papers: Contested Nationhood in Twentieth-Century France*, Minneapolis: University of Minnesota Press, 233–258.

Norris, C. (1993) 'Old themes for new times: postmodernism, theory and cultural politics' in J. Squires (ed.) *Principled Positions: Postmodernism and the Rediscovery of Value*, London: Lawrence and Wishart, 151–188.

Ozouf, M. (1984) *L'École de la France: essai sur la révolution, l'utopie et l'enseignement*, Paris: Gallimard.

—— (1988) 'Fraternité' in F. Furet and M. Ozouf (eds) *Dictionnaire critique de la Révolution française*, Paris: Flammarion, 731–741.

Paquot, T. (1990) *Homo urbanus: essai sur l'urbanisation du monde et des moeurs*, Paris: Editions du Félin.

Paxton, R. (1972) *Vichy France: Old Guard and New Order 1940–1944*, New York: Knopf.

Perec, G. (1965) *Les Choses: une histoire des anneés soixante*, Paris: Juilliard.

Peters, M. (1993) 'Against Finkielkraut's *La Défaite de la pensée*: culture, postmodernism and education', *French Cultural Studies*, 4, 91–106.

Plant, S. (1992) *The Most Radical Gesture: The Situationist International in a Postmodern Age*, London: Routledge.

Pollock, G. (1988) *Vision and Difference: Femininity, Feminism and the Histories of Art*, London: Routledge.

Pomian, K. (1990) 'Post – ou comment l'appeler?', *Le Débat*, 60, May–August, 261–263.

Prendergast, C. (1992) *Paris and the Nineteenth Century*, Oxford: Blackwell.

Pugh, A. C. (1997) 'Culture pop, ou culture pub? Essai d'herméneutique culturelle' in P. Whyte and C. Lloyd (eds) *La Culture Populaire en France*, Durham: University of Durham, Durham French Colloquies, no. 6, 147–169.

Rattansi, A. (1994) ' "Western" racisms, ethnicities and identities in a "post-modern" frame' in A. Rattansi and S. Westwood (eds), *Racism, Modernity and Identity: On the Western Front*, Cambridge: Polity Press, 15–86.

Reader, K. (1995) *Régis Debray: A Critical Introduction*, London: Pluto.

Readings, B. (1991) *Introducing Lyotard: Art and Politics*, London: Routledge.

Renaut, A. (1993) 'Genèse du couple état-société', *Projet*, 233, Spring, 7–16.

Ricoeur, P. (1985) *Temps et récit*, vol. 3, Paris: Seuil.

Rieffel, R. (1993) *La Tribu des clercs: les intellectuels sous la Ve République*, Paris: Calmann-Lévy.

Rifkin, A. (1993) *Street Noises: Parisian Pleasure 1900–1940*, Manchester: Manchester University Press.

Rigaud, J. (1990) *Libre culture*, Paris: Gallimard/Le Débat.

Rigby, B. (1991) *Popular Culture in Modern France. A Study of Cultural Discourse*, London: Routledge.

Rioux, J.-P. (1992) 'L'État culturel depuis la Libération', *Le Débat*, 70, May–August, 60–65.

Rolin, J. (1996) *Zones*, Paris: Gallimard.

Roman, J. (1991) 'Contre *L'État culturel* de Marc Fumaroli', *Esprit*, 175, October, 149–157.

—— (1995) 'Un multiculturalisme à la française?', *Esprit*, 212, June, 145–160.

—— (1996) 'Autonomie et vulnérabilité de l'individu moderne' in L. du Mesnil (ed.) *La Société en quête de valeurs: pour sortir de l'alternative entre scepticisme et dogmatisme*, Paris: Maxima, 31–40.

Roncayolo, M. (1994), 'Paris, capitale universelle', *Le Débat*, 'Le Nouveau Paris', 80, May–August, 36–37.

Rose, G. (1993) *Judaism and Modernity: Philosophical Essays*, Oxford: Blackwell.

Ross, K. (1995) *Fast Cars, Clean Bodies: Decolonization and the Reordering of French Culture*, Cambridge, Mass.: MIT Press.

Rousso, H. (1987) *Le Syndrome de Vichy de 1944 à nos jours*, Paris: Seuil.

Russell, D. (1989/90) 'Two or three things we know about Beineix', *Sight and Sound*, 59 (1), Winter, 42–47.

Sallenave, D. (1991) *Le Don des morts: sur la littérature*, Paris: Gallimard.

Sansot, P. (1996) *Poétique de la ville*, Paris: Armand Colin.

Sartre, J.-P. (1954; first published 1946) *Réflexions sur la question juive*, Paris: Gallimard/Folio.

Schiffer, S. D. (1995) *Les Intellos ou la dérive d'une caste*, Paris: L'Age d'Homme.

Schlegel, J.-L. (1990) 'Introduction: Juifs-chrétiens, éloge du franc-parleur', *Esprit*, 162, June, 76–80.

Schnapper, D. (1994) *La Communauté des citoyens: sur l'idée moderne de nation*, Paris: Gallimard.

—— (1998) *La Relation à l'autre: au coeur de la pensée sociologique*, Paris: Gallimard.

Schwarzmantel, J. (1998) *The Age of Ideology: Political Ideologies from the American Revolution to Postmodern Times*, Basingstoke: Macmillan.

Segalen, M. (1993) 'Identités culturelles et modèles d'appropriation de l'espace urbain' in J. Roman (ed.) *Ville, exclusion et citoyenneté* (Entretiens de la ville 2), Paris: Editions Esprit.

Sheringham, M. (1995) 'Marc Augé and the ethno-analysis of contemporary life', *Paragraph*, 18 (2), July, 210–222.

—— (1996) 'Introduction' in M. Sheringham (ed.) *Parisian Fields*, London: Reaktion Books, 1–7.

Sibony, D. (1988) *Écrits sur le racisme*, Paris: Christian Bourgois.

—— (1993) 'Institution et racisme' in M. Wieviorka (ed.) *Racisme et modernité*, Paris: La Découverte, 141–145.

—— (1997) *Le 'racisme' ou la haine identitaire*, Paris: Christian Bourgois.

Silverman, M. (1992) *Deconstructing the Nation: Immigration, Racism and Citizenship in Modern France*, London: Routledge.

—— (1994) 'The Dreyfus Affair: one hundred years on', *Patterns of Prejudice*, 28 (3–4), 29–37.

—— (1995a) 'Symbolic violence and new communities' in J. Windebank and R. Gunther (eds) *Violence and Conflict in the Politics and Society of Modern France*, Lampeter: Edwin Mellen Press, 161–173.

—— (1995b) 'Rights and difference: questions of citizenship in France' in A. G. Hargreaves and J. Leaman (eds) *Racism, Ethnicity and Politics in Contemporary Europe*, Aldershot: Edward Elgar, 253–263.

—— (1996a) 'Encounters in the City' in S. Fridlizius and A. Peterson (eds) *Stranger or Guest? Racism and Nationalism in Contemporary Europe*, Stockholm: Almqvist and Wiksell International/Göteborg: Sociologiska Institutionen, 95–107.

—— (1996b) 'The revenge of civil society: state, nation and society in France' in D. Cesarani and M. Fulbrook (eds) *Citizenship, Nationality and Migration in Europe*, London: Routledge, 146–158.

—— (1998a) 'Re-figuring "the Jew" in France' in B. Cheyette and L. Marcus (eds) *Modernity, Culture and 'the Jew'*, Cambridge: Polity, 197–208.

—— (1998b) 'Freedom of the city?' in C. J. Dolamore (ed.) *Making Connections*, Berne: Peter Lang.

Sirinelli, J.-F. (1990) *Intellectuels et passions françaises: manifestes et pétitions au XXe siècle*, Paris: Fayard.

Smart, B. (1993) *Postmodernity*, London: Routledge.

Soja, E. (1989) *Postmodern Geographies: The Reassertion of Space in Critical Social Theory*, London: Verso.

Soja, E. and Hooper, B. (1993) 'The spaces that difference makes: some notes on the geographical margins of the new cultural politics' in M. Keith and S. Pile (eds) *Place and the Politics of Identity*, London: Routledge, 183–205.

Spire, A. (1996) *Après les grands soirs: intellectuels et artistes face au politique*, Paris: Editions Autrement.

Steiner, G. (1971) *In Bluebeard's Castle: Some Notes Towards the Re-definition of Culture*, London: Faber and Faber.

Stern, D. (1989) 'Midrash and indeterminacy', *Critical Inquiry*, 15 (1988–1989), Summer, 132–161.

Sternhell, Z. (1983) *Ni droite, ni gauche*, Paris: Seuil.

Stoekl, A. (1995) 'Blanchot, violence and the disaster' in Lawrence D. Kritzman (ed.) *Auschwitz and After: Race, Culture and 'the Jewish Question' in France*, London: Routledge, 133–148.

Suleiman, S. R. (1995) 'The Jew in Jean-Paul Sartre's *Réflexions sur la question juive*: an exercise in historical reading' in Linda Nochlin and Tamar Garb (eds) *The Jew in the Text: Modernity and the Construction of Identity*, London: Thames and Hudson, 201–218.

Taguieff, P.-A. (1988a) *La Force du préjugé: essais sur le racisme et ses doubles*, Paris: La Découverte.

—— (1988b) 'Les métamorphoses du racisme', *Hommes et Migrations*, 1114, 114–28.

—— (1994) *Sur la nouvelle droite*, Paris: Descartes et Cie.

—— (1995a) *Les Fins de l'antiracisme*, Paris: Editions Michalon.

—— (1995b) 'L'identité nationale: un débat français', *Regards sur l'Actualité*, 209–210, March–April.

—— (1996) *La République menacée* (entretien avec Philippe Petit), Paris: Textuel.

Tassin, E. (1994) 'Identités nationales et citoyenneté politique', *Esprit*, 198, January, 97–111.

Tester, K. (1993) *The Life and Times of Post-Modernity*, London: Routledge.

Thibaud, P. and Touraine, A. (1993) 'Républicains ou démocrates?', *Projet* 'Citoyen en quel État?', 233, Spring, 26–34.

Thompson, K. (1992) 'Social pluralism and post-modernity' in S. Hall, D. Held and T. McGrew (eds) *Modernity and its Futures*, Cambridge: Open University/Polity, 221–271.

Todd, E. (1994) *Le Destin des immigrés: assimilation et ségrégation dans les démocraties occidentales*, Paris: Seuil.

Todorov, T. (1989) *Nous et les autres: la réflexion française sur la diversité humaine*, Paris: Seuil/Points.

—— (1994; first published 1991) *Face à l'extrême*, Paris: Seuil/Points.

—— (1995) 'Du culte de la différence à la sacralisation de la victime', *Esprit*, 212, June, 90–102.

—— (1996) *L'Homme dépaysé*, Paris: Seuil.

—— (1998) *Les Abus de la mémoire*, Paris: Arléa.

Touraine, A. (1991) 'Face à l'exclusion' in *Citoyenneté et urbanité*, Paris: Editions Esprit, 165–173.

—— (1992) *Critique de la modernité*, Paris: Fayard.

—— (1994) *Qu'est-ce que la démocratie?*, Paris: Fayard.

Urry, J. (1990) *The Tourist Gaze*, London: Sage.

Vidal-Naquet, P. (1990) 'L'Épreuve de l'historien: réflexions d'un généraliste' in *Au sujet de Shoah*, Paris: Editions Belin, 198–208.

Virilio, P. (1977) *Vitesse et politique*, Paris: Galilée.

—— (1989; first published 1980) *Esthétique de la disparition*, Paris: Galilée/Livre de Poche.

—— (1993) *L'Art du moteur*, Paris: Galilée.

—— (1995) *La Vitesse de libération*, Paris: Galilée.

—— (1996) 'Quand il n'y a plus de temps à partager, il n'y a plus de démocratie possible' in *Les Grandes Entretiens du Monde*: Vol. 3, 'Penser le malaise social, la ville, l'économie', Paris: Le Monde Editions.

Walby, S. (1994) 'Is citizenship gendered ?', *Sociology*, 28 (2), 379–395.

Weber, E. (1976) *Peasants into Frenchmen: The Modernization of Rural France 1870–1914*, Stanford, CA: Stanford University Press.

Weeks, J. (1993) 'Rediscovering values' in J. Squires (ed.) *Principled Positions: Postmodernism and the Rediscovery of Value*, London: Lawrence and Wishart, 189–211.

Westwood, S. and Williams, J. (1997) 'Imagining cities' in S. Westwood and J. Williams (eds) *Imagining Cities: Scripts, Signs, Memory*, London: Routledge.

Wieviorka, A. (1992) *Déportation et génocide: entre la mémoire et l'oubli*, Paris: Plon.

Wieviorka, M. (1991) *L'Espace du racisme*, Paris: Seuil (translated as *The Arena of Racism*, London: Sage, 1995).

—— (1992) *La France raciste*, Paris: Seuil.

—— (1993a) 'Introduction' in M. Wieviorka (ed.) *Racisme et modernité*, Paris: La Découverte, 7–20.

—— (1993b) 'Le sas et la nasse' in J. Roman (ed.) *Ville, exclusion et citoyenneté* (Entretiens de la ville 2), Paris: Editions Esprit.

—— (1993c) *La Démocratie à l'épreuve: nationalisme, populisme, ethnicité*, Paris: La Découverte.

—— (1994) 'Les paradoxes de l'antiracisme', *Esprit*, 205, October, 16–29.

—— (ed.) (1993) *Racisme et modernité*, Paris: La Découverte.

—— (ed.) (1997) *Une Société fragmentée: le multiculturalisme en débat*, Paris: La Découverte/Poche.

Wilson, E. (1992) *The Sphinx in the City: Urban Life, the Control of Disorder and Women*, Berkeley: University of California Press.

—— (1995) 'The invisible *flâneur*' in S. Watson and K. Gibson (eds) *Postmodern Cities and Spaces*, Oxford: Blackwell, 59–79.

Wolff, J. (1985) 'The invisible *flâneuse*: women and the literature of modernity', *Theory, Culture and Society*, 2 (3) (special issue on 'The Fate of Modernity'), 37–48.

Wolton, D. (1990) *Eloge du grand public: une théorie critique de la télévision*, Paris: Flammarion.

Yonnet, P. (1985) *Jeux, modes et masses: la société française et le moderne 1945–85*, Paris: Gallimard.

—— (1990) 'La machine Carpentras: Histoire et sociologie d'un syndrome d'épuration', *Le Débat*, 61, September–October, 18–34.

—— (1993) *Voyage au centre du malaise français*, Paris: Gallimard.

Young, R. (1990) *White Mythologies: Writing History and the West*, London: Routledge.

Yuval-Davis, N. (1997) 'Women, citizenship and difference', *Feminist Review*, 57, Autumn, 4–27.

Index